East Asian Popular Culture

Series Editors

Yasue Kuwahara
Department of Communication
Northern Kentucky University
Highland Heights, Kentucky USA

John A. Lent
Temple University, USA
School of Communication and Theater
Philadelphia, USA

Aims of the Series

This series focuses on the study of popular culture in East Asia (referring to China, Hong Kong, Japan, Mongolia, North Korea, South Korea, and Taiwan) in order to meet a growing interest in the subject among students as well as scholars of various disciplines. The series examines cultural production in East Asian countries, both individually and collectively, as its popularity extends beyond the region. It continues the scholarly discourse on the recent prominence of East Asian popular culture as well as the give and take between Eastern and Western cultures.

More information about this series at
http://www.springer.com/series/14958

S. Austin Lee • Alexis Pulos
Editors

Transnational Contexts of Development History, Sociality, and Society of Play

Video Games in East Asia

palgrave
macmillan

Editors
S. Austin Lee
Department of Communication
Northern Kentucky University
Highland Heights, Kentucky, USA

Alexis Pulos
Department of Communication
Northern Kentucky University
Highland Heights, Kentucky, USA

East Asian Popular Culture
ISBN 978-3-319-43819-1 ISBN 978-3-319-43820-7 (eBook)
DOI 10.1007/978-3-319-43820-7

Library of Congress Control Number: 2016957341

Cover design by Samantha Johnson

Printed on acid-free paper

This Palgrave Macmillan imprint is published by Springer Nature
The registered company is Springer International Publishing AG
The registered company address is: Gewerbestrasse 11, 6330 Cham, Switzerland

CONTENTS

About the Editors

S. Austin Lee holds a BA from Seoul National University and MA/PhD from Michigan State University. His areas of expertise include communication technology and intercultural communication. His scholarly work has been published in top academic journals, including *Journal of Applied Psychology*. He has also received a top paper award from the National Communication Association.

Alexis Pulos currently teaches games and culture, board game design, and video game analysis at Northern Kentucky University. He holds a PhD from the University of New Mexico where he studied rhetoric, new media, digital games, and film. His current work focuses on the ways player agency is structured through the design and social regulation of rule systems.

Contributor Bios

Arielle Goldberg earned her BA from the University of Cincinnati and her MA in Communication from Northern Kentucky University. She is published in the journal *Asian Communication Research* and earned the Top Student Paper award at the National Communication Association annual conference in 2015. Her research interests include communicatively constructed systems of power and expressions of gender in popular culture, family dyads, and organizations.

Bryan Hikari Hartzheim is an assistant professor of English and Liberal Arts at Reitaku University. He received his PhD in Cinema and Media Studies from the University of California, Los Angeles. His research areas of focus are in film and animation history, new media theory, and media industry studies. He is particularly interested in the creative industries of Japan, as he has worked in or observed the Japanese animation and gaming industries for over seven years. His work has appeared in *Mediascape* and various anthologies.

Mariko Koizumi is an associate professor, Faculty of Manga at Kyoto Seika University, Japan. She graduated from the University of Tokyo with a PhD in media environmental studies. She worked for Mitsubishi Corporation to develop a new Internet business model, as well as for University of California, San Diego, as a visiting scholar. Her research focuses on cultural economics. She authored books on media industries and lectured in several countries.

Claire Shinhea Lee is a PhD candidate at the Department of Radio-Television-Film at the University of Texas at Austin. Her research interests include new media and audiences and migrant studies. Her work has been published in *Asian Journal of Communication, International Journal of Communication*, and several book chapters. She also has job experiences in two different new media industries: *Naver* and *TU Media*.

Sara Liao is currently a doctoral candidate in media studies in the Department of Radio-Television-Film at the University of Texas at Austin. Her research focuses on new media, digital labor, gender studies, and globalization by using both ethnographic approach and discursive analysis of data collection and analysis. Her work has been published at peer-reviewed journals including *Games and Culture, Asian Journal of Communication*, and *Chinese Journal of Communication*.

Hogeun Seo is a PhD student in the Department of Radio-Television-Film at the University of Texas at Austin. He had worked for 9 years in four new media industries such as digital cable television, satellite mobile television, Internet protocol television (IPTV), and smartphones. He brings his industry experience to his research on game studies, media industry studies, and new media technology.

Akiko Shibuya is an associate professor of media studies at Soka University of America. She obtained her doctoral degree in sociology from Keio University, Tokyo. Her dissertation examined the effects of video game violence on children and parental mediation. She received her master's degree in journalism from the University of Missouri, Columbia and a bachelor's degree in philosophy from Tokyo Metropolitan University. Her research focuses on mass communication, media stereotypes, video games, social networking services, TV viewing, media use by children and adolescents, and parental mediation.

Akiyo Shoun is a doctoral candidate in social psychology at Ochanomizu University, Tokyo. Her research interests include the persuasive effects of narrative in the media, the influence of character identification in the media, and the effects of transportation into the narratives.

Mizuha Teramoto is a doctoral student in the Department of Humanities and Sciences at Ochanomizu University, Tokyo. She received a master's degree in management from Sophia University and a second master's degree in humanities from Ochanomizu University. Her research focuses on the intergroup anxiety and the attitudes toward outgroup members, particularly in online communication.

Hongsik Yu is a full professor in the School of Media and Communication at Chung-Ang University in Seoul, South Korea. His research interests include exemplars and frames in news and health communication messages, media entertainment and games, and virtual reality (VR).

LIST OF FIGURES

List of Tables

CHAPTER 1

Introduction: Histories and Industries of Gameplay

S. Austin Lee and Alexis Pulos

From the production of arcade video games in the 1970s to the development of E-sports in the early 2000s, East Asia has been a driving force in the global video game industry. In 2016, China, Japan, South Korea, and Taiwan have collectively generated more than 40% of the global games market revenues.[1] As of 2016, the global video game industry is a $101.6 billion industry,[2] while current global box office film sales are a $38.3 billion industry,[3] making video games one of the most profitable entertainment industries of the twenty-first century. While these numbers highlight the influence of the region on game sales, they do not cover the complexity of the video game industry. Current video game platforms offer more styles of games, game-playing demographics are more varied and wider than ever, "and games are now large, small, polished, experimental, two-dimensional, three-dimensional, text-based, gestural, genre-specific, or mashed up" (Consalvo 2016, 2). There is therefore no single context, industry, or community of games but a diverse multitude of game structures that have shaped the cultural milieu of video games in the region. Due to the intra-regional and transnational flow of content, East Asia is not

S. Austin Lee (✉) • A. Pulos
Department of Communication, Northern Kentucky University,
Highland Heights, KY, USA

only recognized as a historic global gaming center but is "marked by diverse consumption and production patterns of gaming, mobile and broadband technologies, subject to local cultural socio-economic nuances" (Hjorth and Chan 2009, 3). Moreover, in the historical and contemporary contexts of East Asia, video games have given rise to new forms of identity formation, social interaction, and virtual colonization that blur national boundaries and create transnational practices of interaction. From this multifaceted context and cultural flow of information across historical and regional boarders, East Asia is an automatic "must" when studying the global contexts of the video game industry.

Despite its importance in the global video game market, East Asia has not received sufficient scholarly attention. Since the beginning of the twenty-first century, the research into video games has increased in size to cover topics like game economies (McAllister 2004; Castranova 2005), player cultures (Turkle 2005; Flanagan 2009), gaming spaces (Wark 2007; McGonigal 2011), game rhetoric (Bogost 2007, 2008), and transnational relationships (Hjorth and Chan 2009; Jin 2010; Consalvo 2016). The rise in scholarship has given new credibility to the medium and spurred new interests in the field. However, much of the research listed here focuses on European and American contexts, and besides Hjorth and Chan's (2009) edited collection, there is no other collection that adds to the mapping of this region. Some notable work including Jin (2010) focuses on a specific nation rather than the transnational context. Thus, there remains a need to examine the multiple and intertwined issues in cultural transformation, glocalization, and transnationalism in the region of East Asia.

To address this necessity, the two books in the current *East Asian Culture Series* examine the development and prominence of East Asian video games within historical, industrial, cultural, and global contexts, highlighting: (1) the current state of video games in East Asia; (2) the developing production and consumption practices of East Asian game industries and players; (3) the ways video games function as a cultural medium in local and transnational contexts; and (4) the roles that video games have played in intercultural and international settings. Across the two books, these topics are addressed through a wide range of interdisciplinary work, written by scholars in diverse academic fields, to offer a comprehensive overview of the socio-economic, socio-material, and socio-cultural context of video games in the region.

The current volume consists of three interconnected socio-economic and socio-material contexts of the video game industry. Part I presents a history of the technological developments that have led to industry trends and transformations in the region. The provided history serves as a platform for the contemporary landscape of gaming technologies. Part II therefore examines the recent industry trends in social mobile games and the globally connected relationships that arise out of the developer and player interactions in this new gaming sphere. Through an investigation of the cultural impacts of games on players, and their communities, Part III builds on the cultural conversation started in Part II by discussing the social concerns over playing games. Through these chapters the reader is provided with an overview of the East Asian game industry that calls attention to the complex practices of and concerns over this transnational medium.

Part I

Part I works to compliment the previous literature on East Asian game history that has covered the development of game companies (Gorges and Yamazaki 2012), specific consoles (Parish 2016), the console wars (Harris 2015), the history of nationally sponsored gaming infrastructures (Jin 2010), and the rise of E-sports (Taylor 2012). To add to this conversation, Part I calls attention to the social history and technological material that has influenced the game industry. The second chapter written by Mariko Koizumi provides an overview of the historical development of the Japanese video game industry, focusing on how the unique industrial structure, business practices, and consumer preferences in Japan sparked the growth of video game industries. By tracing the development of console systems from the Famicom (released in North America as the Nintendo Entertainment System) to handheld gaming systems, the chapter works to first contextualize the influence and sales of gaming systems on Japanese markets. To complement the market analysis, Koizumi investigates the developing technologies that have given rise to online and mobile social games. By analyzing the sales and life of a product alongside the technological development, this chapter details the ways industry trends should be analyzed.

The third chapter written by Arielle Goldberg and her colleagues provides a closer look at a key player in the video game history: Nintendo. Nintendo boasts a 100+ year company history that consistently presents innovative new directions for game immersion and flow. Relying on tried-and-true, iconic intellectual properties, including Super Mario Brothers, the Legend of Zelda, and Pokémon, Nintendo focuses on delivering a remarkable gaming experience, in terms of the hardware with which people play. From plastic playing cards to the upcoming NX, Nintendo has a history of forcing its competitors to keep up in ways that go beyond sales numbers and graphics capabilities. The chapter provides an overview of Nintendo's impact on the technological landscape of video games, and video gaming culture, by popularizing portable games, pushing the innovation envelope in terms of player immersion, and finally combining those two approaches by immersing players in the game world outside of the gameplay experience. The chapter ends with a discussion of what's next for Nintendo, including the foray into mobile game development and augmented reality games like Pokémon Go.

Part II

Moving beyond the economic and technological history of the region, Part II focuses on the quickly developing mobile social game sector. Currently, East Asia dominates all other global regions with a generated mobile game revenue of 15 billion US dollars.[22] The explosion of mobile game revenues necessitates a closer investigation of the cultural impacts of mobile games on different "players," including economic practices, player communities, and developer practices. In chapter 4, Akiko Shibuya and her colleagues call attention to the emerging business model of mobile in-game purchases called *gacha*. *Gacha* is similar to a toy capsule vending machine that brings out random game items, in-game currencies, or rare valuable items. Players may use those items in the game or trade them for real money. Although *gacha* has become a major monetization technique for many Japanese free-to-play games, it is frequently criticized by the public, the media, and government agencies for its gambling nature. As a result of the controversy, as well as a government crackdown, major mobile game companies decided to restrict a specific form of *gacha* called *kompu gacha*, where players gamble to obtain especially rare and valuable items. However, many mobile game companies still rely on similar business models, and the mechanism of their monetization technique has not received scholarly investigations. The authors address this gap through a systematic analysis of *gacha* techniques, including the in-game purchases and special event features of mobile social games in Japan, and the player actions tied to these techniques.

While the first section of Part II focuses on the economic practices of mobile game companies, chapter 5 examines the social interactions that develop in and around mobile games. Inspired by Robert D. Putnam's influential work *Bowing Alone*, in the chapter titled *Bowling Online*,

Hogeun Seo and Claire Shinhea Lee discuss how mobile social games develop social capital and social networks among a population that are marginalized in the traditional video game sphere: high-school girls in South Korea. High-school girls in Korea have limited opportunities to socialize with their peers face-to-face. With the penetration of smartphones, however, they started to create their own digitalized peer culture. Social games on mobile platforms became an alternative space for South Korean high-school girls for communicating with one another, developing their peer relationships, and forming their own communities. In this chapter, the authors examine what makes Korean high-school girls actively participate in the mobile social game sphere and how their mobile social gaming relates to the concepts of strong/weak ties and bonding/bridging social capital.

Chapter 6 bridges the content of part II together through an analysis of player/producer practices related to Japanese mobile game design. When it comes to creative production today, Japan—with its multiple contents industries, concentrated urban centers, and frequent collaborative working environments in both the creative and technical fields—offers a unique perspective into the ways workers organize in a variety of complex production spaces. To understand these production spaces of mobile gaming, Bryan Hartzheim takes an ethnographic approach to examine, observe, and participate in the production spaces of the Japanese media mix, or its equivalent in the west, transmedia. Specifically, the author looks into collaborative global/local production among mobile game creators in Japan and the culture of international production in a single video game studio. He discusses how production processes have reorganized through mobile social gaming, how different cultures of players choose to react to active game designs, and how collective negotiations that occur in production spaces affect the realm of mobile games.

Part III

Part III discusses the social impacts of video games in East Asia through a focused analysis on the "dark side" of gaming. Digital games are frequently targets of controversial issues and are often inclined to present players with difficult moral and ethical dilemmas. Mortensen and Lindroth's (2015) edited collection calls attention to these "dark," or morally ambivalent, choices that players are frequently presented with, while Conway and deWinter (2015) detail how the games, and the players' choices, are often regulated by state agencies. However, the assumption of play as a dark practice frequently removes the voice of the players that are participating in these spaces. To address this concern, Sara Liao offers new insights into Hong Kong's net bar, also called Internet café, youth gaming culture, and lifestyle that has emerged as unique public gaming space in East Asian countries. The social discourse toward net-bar gaming is frequently negative and is often framed as a dark place where working-class youth gather and conduct delinquent behaviors, including violence, drug dealing, and adolescent sexual intercourse. Seldom are the youth given a voice to express their own ideas toward net bar and their gaming experience. The author reveals that the net-bar deviant label is strategically utilized to structure and sanction the identities and actions of net-bar goers. Because the net-bar culture is a daily activity, individuals use various negotiation strategies to resist, adapt, and appropriate the negative social designations that are often assigned to them. Through the youth's interpretation of the labels tagged to them, the chapter maps out the complex net-bar gaming identities and social meanings that are managed in these public game spaces.

While the first chapter of part III addresses the social concerns over gaming cultures, functioning to localize the historical impacts of gaming industries and serving as a bridge into the companion edition to this book, chapter 8 takes a diagnostic approach to understand gaming addiction and the study of it. Hongsik Yu discusses the issue of Internet gaming addiction, which has emerged as one of the fastest growing forms of addiction in East Asia. Especially in South Korea, the country that boasts the world's highest broadband penetration and the fastest Internet speed, Internet gaming addiction has become a major social issue. In this chapter, the author overviews the controversy over Internet gaming addiction and discusses diagnostic criteria for Internet gaming disorder. He conducts a large-scale survey on South Korean middle- and high-school students as well as young adults and develops a new research scale. This work contributes to research on new diagnostic criteria and reliable screening instruments for assessing Internet gaming disorder.

COMPANION EDITION

While the Asia Pacific region has dominated the global video game market, video games are a cultural artifact that is epitomized by the social functions that this medium offers. As more games are released, it is increasingly important to pay attention to the economic practices of this industry as well as the social practices that are imbued into and arise out of these games. In the companion edition to this book, *Transnational Contexts of Culture, Gender, Class and Colonialism in Play*, we move to address the growth of cultures in and around games, the construction of identity politics in game design, and the negotiation of transnational relationships across game spaces.

The first part of the companion edition highlights the transformation of player practices and gamer cultures from their localized contexts of play. Specifically, Mark Johnson covers the competitive systems built around high score games in a unique game genre called *danmaku*. Nobushige Hichibe and Ema Tanaka then investigate the development of independent game design communities. Anthony Fung and Boris Pun continue the discussion by taking a close look at the development of independent game design communities. The second part of the book focuses on the gender and class issues. Lucy Glasspool discusses the construction of Japanese gender stereotypes through fan-created texts on Japanese role-playing games. Fan Zhang and Erika Behrmann examine how mobile games simulate capitalistic realities by commodifying virtual goods, reinforcing production/consumption, and creating player hierarchies while minimizing meaningful relationships among players. The last part of the book deals with colonialism and transnationalism. Rachel Hutchinson discusses the representation of national identity from Japanese colonial period, particularly in the stereotypical ways demanded by the fighting game genre, and its implications in contemporary East Asia. By contrast, Holin Lin and Chuen-Tsai Sun describe Chinese World of Warcraft players' virtual migration to Taiwan, when the two nations' official relationship is marked by limited contact and political tension. With the topics listed above, the companion edition compliments the historical and sociopsychological approaches with a stronger emphasis on the critical-cultural analysis of East Asian video games.

Notes

1. "The Asian Games Market: Sizing Up Opportunities." *Newzoo*. 2016. https://newzoo.com/insights/trend-reports/asian-games-market-sizing-opportunities/
2. "Statistics and Facts About the Video Game Industry." *Statista*. 2016. http://www.statista.com/topics/868/video-games/

3. "Statistics and Facts About the Film Industry." *Statista*. 2016. http://www. statista.com/topics/964/film/
4. "The Global Games Market: Trends, Market Data and Opportunities." *Newzoo*. 2015. https://newzoo.com/wp-content/uploads/2011/06Newzoo_T11_ Beijing_FINAL_Public.pdf

BIBLIOGRAPHY

Bogost, Ian. 2007. *Persuasive games: The expressive power of video games*. Cambridge: MIT Press.
———. 2008. *Unit operations: An approach to videogame criticism*. Cambridge: MIT press.
Castranova, Edward. 2005. *Synthetic worlds: The business and culture of Online Games*. Chicago: University of Chicago Press.
Consalvo, Mia. 2016. *Atari to Zelda: Japan's videogames in global contexts*. Cambridge: MIT Press.
Conway, Steven, and Jennifer deWinter (ed). 2015. *Video game policy: Production, distribution, and consumption (Routledge advances in video game studies)*. New York: Routledge.
Flanagan, Marry. 2009. *Critical play: Radical game design*. Cambridge: MIT Press.
Gorges, Florent, and Isao Yamazaki. 2012. *The history of Nintendo 1889–1980 sc*. France: Pix'n Love Publishing.
Harris, Blake J. 2015. *Console wars: Sega, Nintendo, and the battle that defined a generation*. New York: HarperCollins.
Hjorth, Larissa, and Chan Dean (ed). 2009. *Gaming cultures and place in Asia-Pacific (Routledge studies in new media and cyberculture)*. New York: Routledge.
Jin, Dal Yong. 2010. *Korea's online gaming empire*. Cambridge: MIT Press.
McAllister, Ken S. 2004. *Game work: Language, power, and computer game culture*. Tuscaloosa: The University of Alabama Press.
McGonigal, Jane. 2011. *Reality is broken: Why games make us better and how they can change the world*. New York: Penguin Press.
Mortensen, Torill E., Jonas Linderoth, and Ashley M.L. Brown (ed). 2015. *The dark side of game play: Controversial issues in playful environments (Routledge advances in video game studies)*. New York: Routledge.
"The Asian Games Market: Sizing Up Opportunities." 2016. *Newzoo*. https://newzoo.com/insights/trend-reports/asian-games-market-sizing-opportunities/
"The Global Games Market: Trends, Market Data and Opportunities." 2015. *Newzoo*. https://newzoo.com/wp-content/uploads/2011/06/Newzoo_T11_ Beijing_FINAL_Public.pdf
Parish, Jeremy. 2016. *Game Boy World 1989/XL Color Edition: A History of Nintendo Game Boy, vol. I (Unofficial and Unauthorized) (volume 1)*. CreateSpace.

"Statistics and Facts About the Video Game Industry." 2016. *Statista*. http://www.statista.com/topics/868/video-games/

"Statistics and Facts About the Film Industry." 2016. *Statista*. http://www.statista.com/topics/964/film/

Taylor, T.L. 2012. *Raising the stakes: E-sports and the professionalization of computer gaming*. Cambridge: MIT Press.

Turkle, Sherry. 2005. *The second self: Computers and the human spirit*. Cambridge: MIT Press.

Wark, McKenzie. 2007. *Gamer theory*. Cambridge: Harvard-University Press.

PART I

History

CHAPTER 2

Japanese Video Game Industry: History of Its Growth and Current State

Mariko Koizumi

This chapter describes with quantitative data the current state of the Japanese video game industry (hereafter referred to as "VGI"), one of Japan's main industry sectors, and the history of its growth from birth up until the present. The VGI in Japan has developed along paths different from those taken by the same industry in the US in terms of key players, industrial structure, consumer preference, and so on. This explains why the Japanese VGI is unique.

The chapter is presented in the following sections: (1) snapshot of a globally dominant Japanese industry; (2) organization of VG (video game) types; (3) examination of the conditions and characteristics of the Japanese home VGI from the standpoint of how it developed and changes in scale of domestic market and exports; (4) clarification of these conditions and characteristics under the following topics: business strategies and methods of product development for Nintendo Co., Ltd. (hereafter referred to as Nintendo) and Sony Computer Entertainment (hereafter referred to as SCE), two hardware companies that sparked the growth of the Japanese home VGI, causes for SEGA's and NEC's market retreat, and Japanese software developers; (5) presentation of facts in regard to the growth of online games and online-game companies in Japan; and (6) summary and some examples for future prediction.

M. Koizumi (✉)
Faculty of Manga, Kyoto Seika University, Kyoto, Japan

© The Author(s) 2016
S.A. Lee, A. Pulos (eds.), *Transnational Contexts of Development History, Sociality, and Society of Play*, East Asian Popular Culture,
DOI 10.1007/978-3-319-43820-7_2

It is the author's hope that this chapter makes available to international readers research and facts laboriously compiled from many resources, especially Japanese, that until now have not been available either in Japanese or in English.

SNAPSHOT OF THE GLOBALLY DOMINANT JAPANESE VIDEO GAME INDUSTRY

Growth of the Japanese VGI was led by home VG console manufacturers. In 1983 growth of the console market was triggered by the release of Family Computer System (also known as the Famicom) by Nintendo and its sales success. This period coincided with the collapse of the US VG market. Figure 2.1 shows sales figures of the US home VG console market as well as those of Atari and Nintendo from 1979 to 1989.[1] These figures show that while Atari was driving the market in the earlier years, Nintendo, a Japanese company, became the main player around 1986. Over the subsequent thirty years, Japanese VG console manufacturers

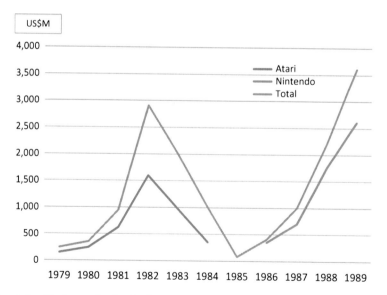

Fig. 2.1 Market scale, Atari sales, and Nintendo sales of video game consoles in the USA, 1979–1989

(*Source*: Data from Kobayashi 1990, 149.)

continued to play leading roles in the USA. Figure 2.2 shows US VG console/handheld market shares in 2014. We find the market dominated by three oligopolists: SCE, a subsidiary of Sony Corporation (hereafter referred to as Sony) at 36%, the US Microsoft Corporation (hereafter referred to as Microsoft) at 36%, and Nintendo at 28%. Going back to 1994, rivaling Nintendo, SCE entered the industry in Japan by releasing the console, PlayStation (PSX). By 1996, within only two years, SCE gained a larger market share in Japan than that of Nintendo. In 1997 the company went onto gain a 56.7% share of the Japanese market and also achieved global success (CESA 1998, 20). Subsequently Microsoft introduced the Xbox in 2002 to the Japanese market. As for Japanese market shares in 2014 of VG consoles/handhelds (unit: number of devices sold), the market was dominated by two oligopolists, Nintendo (48.4%) and SCE (49.8%), while Microsoft obtained a 1.6% share (CESA 2015, 58). The Xbox brand does not receive much attention in Japan.

Next, Table 2.1 shows Japan's position in global ranking of cumulative game software sales. Twelve software series of the top 20 were produced

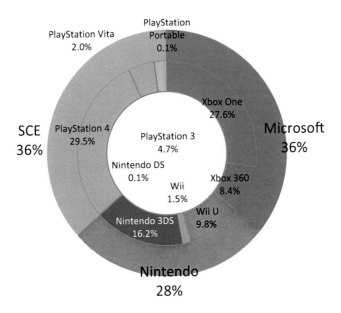

Fig. 2.2 Game console/handheld share by units in the USA, 2014 (*Source*: Data from CESA 2015, 139.)

by Japanese companies. The top two series gained far greater sales with figures above 100 million units (especially compared to sales of the series that ranked third or lower): Mario (Nintendo) with the highest sales at 193 million units, followed by Pokémon (Nintendo) at 155 million units.[2] As we see so far, Japanese VG products, hardware and software alike, have gained popularity worldwide.

Figure 2.3 shows market-scale rankings of home VG hardware and software by country and each country's market size. Japan ranked second

Table 2.1   Top 20 best-selling video game software franchise of all time

Rank	Franchise	Publisher with rights, 2008	Millions of units sold by 2007	Years of game's first appearance
1	Mario	Nintendo	193	1981 (as Jumpman in Donkey Kong) 1983 (Mario Bros.)
2	Pokémon	Nintendo	155	1996
3	Final Fantasy	Square Enix	68	1987
4	Madden NFL	Electronic Arts	56	1989
5	The Sims	Electronic Arts	54	1989 (SimCity) 2000 (The Sims)
6	Grand Theft Auto	Rockstar	50	1997
7	Donkey Kong	Nintendo	48	1981
8	The Legend of Zelda	Nintendo	47	1986
9	Sonic the Hedgehog	SEGA	44	1991
10	Grand Turismo	SCE	44	1998
11	Lineage	NCsoft	43	1998
12	Dragon Quest	Square Enix	41	1986
13	Crash Bandicoot	SCE/Vivendi	34	1996
14	Resident Evil	CAPCOM	31	1996
15	James Bond	Various	30	1983
16	Tomb Raider	Eidos Interactive	30	1996
17	Mega Man	CAPCOM	26	1987
18	Command and Conquer	Electronic Arts	25	1995
19	Street Fighter	CAPCOM	25	1987
20	Mortal Kombat	Midway	20	1992

Source: Adapted from Jenkins 2007, and Nichols 2014, 116

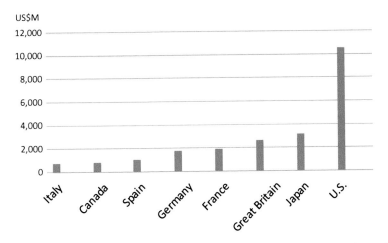

Fig. 2.3 Market scale of console/handheld game software and hardware by country, 2014
(*Source*: Data from CESA 2015, 58, 59, 138.)

place behind the USA. In the global VG market, the industry in Japan holds a significant position and has strong competitive advantage.

Organization of Video Game as Based on Device

Figure 2.4 is a diagram of VG types systematized here based on platform configurations to clarify terms often used with ambiguity. Covered in this chapter are games for which individuals own the platform, that is, VGs other than arcade games.

Arcade game machines were installed in Japan in recreational facilities such as VG arcades and shopping centers. The development of home VG consoles was based on these arcade game machines and was started in the mid-1960s by jukebox manufacturers. Well-known examples of early arcade games are Space Invaders (TAITO 1978) and PAC-MAN (NAMCO 1980).[3] Since the 1980s, development of home VG consoles followed that of arcade games, and the technologies for arcade games and consoles developed alongside each other. During the 1990s, differences in the levels of the two technologies regarding image quality and processing speed became insignificant due to advances in semiconductor and display technologies and increases in data memory size.

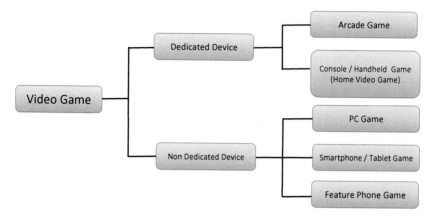

Fig. 2.4 Video game types
(*Source*: Created by the author)

Originally, home VG devices excluding non-dedicated devices were available only in the form of consoles such as the Famicom and the PSX that were connected to a television or other displays. "Console" refers to a floor-standing game machine in this chapter. Subsequently, with the advance in compact, high-performance electronic components, handheld hardware (called "handhelds") with a dedicated screen quickly became popular. The first commercially successful handheld was the Game Boy, released in 1989 by Nintendo. Then, the Nintendo DS (referred to as DS) and the PlayStation Portable (PSP), released in 2004, became popular products. Figures of the shipment of console/handheld devices in 2014 clearly show the unique characteristic of Japan, which is that in Japan handhelds are more popular than consoles: the number of handhelds shipped, 4.07 million units, and consoles shipped, 2.05 million units (CESA 2015, 58). Many software titles have been developed for home VG machines. The term "Home Video Game" includes consoles as well as handheld software/hardware and excludes non-dedicated-device game software in this chapter. Categories of these software products are extensive: role-playing games (RPGs) and massively multiplayer online role-playing games (MMORPGs) as well as action, shooting, real-time strategy, turn-based simulation, management/training simulation, adventure, sports, puzzle/quiz, racing, romantic-relationship simulation games, and so on. Game categories popular in Japan are action games and RPGs (less popular elsewhere), characterized by having a plot and distinctive characters (CESA 2014, 157; Industry Research Division, Mizuho Corporate Bank 2014, 116).

In Japan in the early stage of non-dedicated gaming, VGs played by using personal computers (PCs) were not popular, and the market did not grow (Industry Research Division, Mizuho Corporate Bank 2014, 117). In Japan playing VGs on PCs is relatively uncommon. However, with the popularization of feature phones starting in the late 1990s and the subsequent popularization of smartphones and tablets starting around 2010, playing games on these devices quickly became popular. Leveraging the features of the platforms and the varying preferences of the users, most of these games are simple and short. While the business model of dedicated devices is based on sales of hardware and software products, games for non-dedicated devices not only do not involve sales of hardware products but also offer software products for free and mainly either display ads or collect fees according to the conditions of how the game is played.

This section has described VG types. This chapter will cover games for consoles/handhelds and for non-dedicated devices such as smartphones. Based on extensive data, the following section describes changes in Japan's home VGI size from the 1990s and differences between the Japanese and foreign markets.

CHANGES IN THE SIZE OF JAPAN'S HOME VIDEO GAME INDUSTRY

Figure 2.5 shows the domestic market scale of home VGs including both hardware and software from 1990[4] to 2014. The term "market scale" refers to the sum of products sold based on consumer purchase price. The market steadily grew after 1990, reaching its peak in 1997 at $6.319 B.[5] It then shrank and recovered around 2006 but did not get back to the 1997's scale. The Famicom, the Super Famicom, and the PSX continued to be popular until 1997, but in subsequent years, people involved in the business began to be alarmed about the trend away from games (Matsumura 2011, 11).[6] Accordingly, the DS series and the Wii were developed as devices that could be handled easily in order to expand the gamer groups to middle-aged people and seniors, as well as females. These game systems gained popularity and the market recovered around 2006. The market has

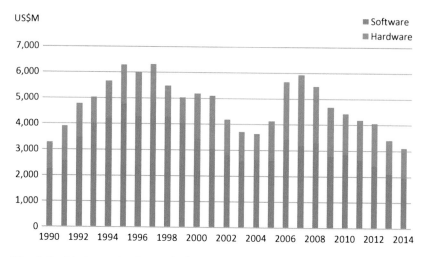

US$M

■ Software
■ Hardware

Fig. 2.5   Market scale of console/handheld games in Japan, 1990–2014 (*Source*: Data from Dentsu Institute for Human Studies 2001, 69; METI 2014, 103; CESA 2015, 58–59)

been shrinking since 2007; the market scale of 2014 was $3.111 B. As seen with the example of the DS series and the Wii, the size of the VG market often is accompanied by big changes in hardware products.[7]

Next, the VGI is examined by separately describing the value of goods shipped to wholesalers (total revenue of products shipped based on manufacturer's wholesale prices) for domestic sales and export sales. As shown in Figure 2.6, domestic sales in terms of the value of goods shipped continued to increase and reached their peak in 1997; then decreased, recovering between 2005 and 2007; and then decreased again.[8] The value of goods shipped in 2014 was $2.573 B. From 1996, sales of hardware products decreased yearly until 1999. In 2000 and 2001, hardware sales increased dramatically with the success of the PS2. Hardware sales decreased again in subsequent years until 2004, increased in 2007, and then decreased again. These sharp fluctuations elucidates that the VG business goes through cycles of good times and challenging times and thus is unstable, differentiating from other major industries. Periodically hardware makers incorporate cutting-edge technology to develop new consoles. One salient feature of the VGI is that degree and duration of popularity vary greatly depending on the console. The degree of the popularity of a console leads boom-and-bust cycles of the entire industry.[9] Software sales increased in 1996 and 1997, then decreased every year until 2003, and then continued to recover until

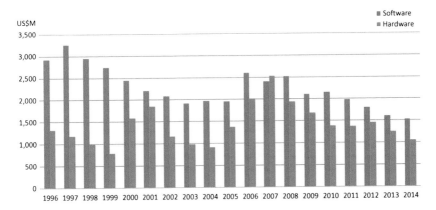

Fig. 2.6 Console/handheld revenue shipped by Japanese publishers/manufactures within Japan, 1996–2014
(*Source*: Data from CESA 1998, 27–28; CESA 2001, 38–39; CESA 2004, 73–75; CESA 2007, 103–105; CESA 2009, 139–141; CESA 2012, 119–121; CESA 2015, 73–75)

2006. The value of goods shipped for software sales in 2014 decreased to 52% of that of 1996. Software sales have similar cycle fluctuations but are not as sharp as those of hardware sales. Overall, software sales have been decreasing.

Figure 2.7 shows export sales in terms of the value of goods shipped to wholesalers. Though fluctuations are sharp, export sales have increased significantly from 1996 to 2014 as opposed to domestic sales. Between 2004 and 2007, both hardware and software sales increased dramatically by 5.4 and 2.4 times, respectively. Then, sales dropped rapidly until 2012. Generally sales of game systems reach their peaks after 1–4 years of release and decrease afterwards. PS3, DS Lite, and Wii were released in the same 2006, but the next-generation systems were not released until 2011. This is why sales dropped. This figure shows the Japanese VGI grew significantly as an export industry. However, similarly to domestic sales, fluctuations in the value of goods shipped are sharp and thus export sales also lack stability. Combining the sales of hardware and software products, the value of home VG exports in 2014 was $16.31 B; this figure accounted for 2.7% of the total value of Japan's exports in 2014 (calculated from Yanotsunetakinenkai 2015, 303). Combining domestic and export sales in terms of the value of goods shipped to wholesalers, the total value of hardware and software sales in 2013 was $15.59 B; the total production output of Japan's industrial products in the same year

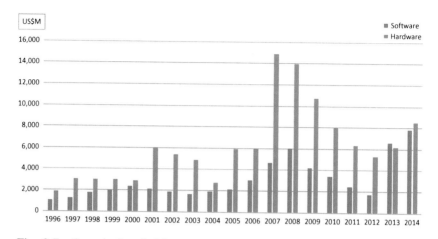

Fig. 2.7 Console/handheld revenue shipped overseas by Japanese companies, 1996–2014
(*Source*: Data from CESA 1998, 30–31; CESA 2001, 45–46; CESA 2004, 77–79; CESA 2007, 107–109; CESA 2009, 143–145; CESA 2012, 123–125; CESA 2015, 78–80)

was $883 B (Yanotsunetakinenkai 2015, 103). Accounting for 1.8% of this total output, the home VGI is definitely a large industry. The value of goods shipped for software products is higher than that for hardware products in domestic sales (Fig. 2.6); it is the opposite in export sales (Fig. 2.7). Figure 2.8 shows the export ratio of console/handheld software and hardware from Japan since 1996 to 2014. This industry relies on exports; particularly, the export ratio of hardware is high.

The unique characteristics of the domestic market can be illustrated by describing differences in popular VG systems. Table 2.2 shows the domestic and overseas shipped units of systems by model. First, as mentioned earlier, as of 2014, the Xbox had not gained popularity in Japan. Second, handhelds such as the PS Vita, the PSP, and the Nintendo 3DS were selling well. The ratios for these handheld models shipped domestically versus overseas were respectively 2.4, 5.3, and 4.1 times more. Third, the PS4 had not gained popularity in Japan but export sales were growing steadily. In November 2013, one million units were sold in North America within 24 hours after the release of the PS4. Worldwide, more than nine million units were sold within eight months of its release. In Japan, the PS4 was released in February 2014, and 0.32 million units were sold within the week after (METI 2014, 108). Since then, sales have been decreasing, and

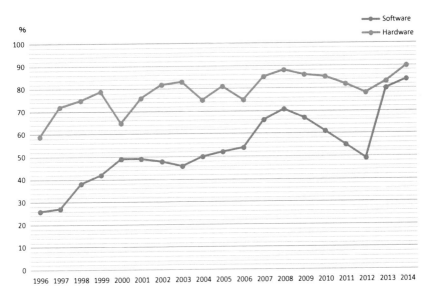

Fig. 2.8 Export ratio of console/handheld software and hardware from Japan, 1996–2014
(*Source*: Data from CESA 1998, 27, 28, 30, 31; CESA 2001, 38–39, 45–46; CESA 2004, 73, 75, 77, 79; CESA 2007, 103, 105, 107, 109; CESA 2009, 139, 141, 143, 145; CESA 2012, 119, 121, 123, 125; CESA 2015, 73, 75, 78, 80) (*Notes*: Software Data in 2011 and 2012 excludes overseas revenue shipped by overseas offices)

the number of units shipped in Japan has reached only 4.6% of that of units shipped overseas. This difference is due to the difference in image preferences between Japanese and Western consumers. The PS4 can display close to live-action images as its computing performance was improved by adopting supreme performance parts.[10] Utilizing this performance, many software products that take full advantage of 3DCG have been developed and have become popular in Western countries. On the other hand, Japanese users are not particularly interested in high-resolution images, preferring 2DCG over 3DCG. In 2013, all of the five software products with more than 100 million units' in sales in Japan were 2DCG (METI 2014, 109).

The information provided so far demonstrates that the home VGI is a large industry sector in Japan, and that the Japanese VGI relies on exports. Throughout the history of the Japanese home VGI, hardware companies have continued to develop new systems every few years by incorporating technological advancements. With the addition of popular software

Table 2.2 Share comparison between Japan and overseas by game-system type

Game-system type	Game-system model	Japan		Overseas	
		Total shipped units (K), 2012–2014	Share (%)	Total shipped units (K), 2012–2014	Share (%)
Console	PlayStation 4	887	24.9	19,485	72.8
	PlayStation 3	2378		24,950	
	PlayStation 2	30		970	
	Wii U	2300		6908	
	Wii	320		6140	
	Xbox 360	102		19,794	
	Xbox One	55		12,950	
	Total	6072		91,197	
Handheld	PlayStation Vita	2918	75.1	6376	27.2
	PlayStation Portable	1296		5561	
	Nintendo 3DS	14,044		21,334	
	Nintendo DS	16		750	
	Total	18,274		34,021	

Source: Data from CESA 2015, 72, 74

products, the market has fluctuated continuously. A small number of hardware companies have led the development of the VGI with the support provided by software companies.

In the next section we continue to focus on the home VGI by examining its history from birth up until the present and success factors including key players, their business strategies, and their track records.

Japan's Home Video Game Industry: Key Players in Hardware and Software

As described in section "Snapshot of the Globally Dominant Japanese Video Game Industry," the home VGI in Japan was formed and expanded by the release of the Famicom in 1983. Subsequently, one after another, SCE and other companies, including SEGA Enterprises, Ltd. (currently SEGA Games Co., Ltd., referred to as SEGA), and NEC Home Electronics Corporation (referred to as NEC) entered the VG system industry.

However, only Nintendo and SCE as the key players still survive the market. Atari, the company that drove the market of home VG consoles in the early years in the USA, originally developed arcade games. The home-game consoles it introduced to the world were developed based on arcade games. However, most of the above Japanese companies, including Nintendo, did not possess sufficient VG technology know-how or VG business experience.

Accordingly, the policies and actions of the companies that succeeded under these circumstances, that is, Nintendo and SCE, are discussed in sections "Nintendo's Development of Family Computer and Business Strategies," "SCE's Business Model for the PlayStation," and "Comparing Data Compiled for Nintendo and SCE, Which Reflects the Overall Japanese Market". Section "Video Game Console Manufacturers that Retreated from the Market" highlights the history of two minor players, SEGA and NEC, which no longer exist as console makers and whose effect on the Japanese domestic console market was short-lived (unlike the impact of SEGA on the US market). Section "Japanese Home Video Game Software Companies" covers software developers.

Nintendo's Development of Family Computer and Business Strategies

Nintendo was established in 1889 in Kyoto as a manufacturer of *hanafuda,* a Japanese card game featuring cards depicting flowers. *Ninten* means "leaving one's luck up to the gods." Adapting its business according to the times, the company later began to manufacture Western playing cards and later toys, eventually utilizing electronics; for example, the company developed a commercial entertainment system called The Laser Clay Shooting System, releasing it in 1973. Nintendo developed arcade games that were released in 1978 and gradually entered businesses close to home VG consoles. In 1980, Nintendo released the mobile game hardware Game & Watch. It fit into the hand, it had a liquid crystal display, and its software could not be replaced since it was installed on a ROM. The hardware could also be used as a clock and sold very well; including export sales, more than 40 million units were sold. Subsequently, the era of hardware/software combined devices changed to the era of consoles with exchangeable cassettes. The company policy upheld by the president of Nintendo at the time, the late Hiroshi Yamauchi, was "Nintendo completely devotes itself to entertainment" (Hatakeyama and Kubo 2000, 48). While having coherent management policies, Yamauchi was flexible in terms of product-development forms, always adapting to the times. The great grandson of Nintendo's founder, Yamauchi, assumed the post of company president in 1949 at age 22 and served as president for more than 50 years until 2002; Nintendo owes to Yamauchi its growth into a globally successful company. Yamauchi became interested in the VGs sold in the USA around 1980, a time when there were hardly any home VG consoles in Japan, and began developing consoles, ultimately releasing the Famicom.

Yamauchi analyzed that one of the reasons for the collapse of the US VG market was overproduction of poor-quality software products. Thus, he prevented the development of poor-quality software. His approach was to make profit with the software business; he opened up the development process and had other companies develop software but had those companies outsource software production to Nintendo. Furthermore, he aimed at gaining a greater market share by keeping hardware prices low and focused on selling software products in mass quantities. In order to maintain quality, Nintendo allowed only selected companies to develop software for its consoles and limited the number of software titles that could be sold yearly by one company to up to five titles (Maki 2011, 6). In addition to controlling quality, Nintendo also checked depictions concerning ethical issues such as violence and smoking. When a software development company signed a contract with Nintendo, the hardware specifications necessary for software development were disclosed to it. In most cases, hardware companies and software companies in Japan do not have capital ties (Yanagawa and Kuwayama 1999, 5).[11] The conditions set out by Nintendo for the contracting software company included the following: (1) the software company must acknowledge that the Famicom is an original creation of Nintendo, (2) the software company must obtain permission from Nintendo before selling software packages, (3) the software company must pay royalties for using Nintendo's logo and know-how and any other related fees, and (4) the number of software titles that can be released yearly is specified (Hirabayashi and Akao 1996, 59). ROM cartridges, expensive but fast reading, were used as the software storage medium; software companies had to outsource the production of this medium to Nintendo. They submitted the software master, made a proposal on the order quantity,[12] and paid the production outsource fee. The financial burden on software companies was heavy as they were required to pay 50% of the total amount of production order in advance and pay the remaining 50% upon delivery.[13] For this reason, well-resourced companies were selected for software development. It is assumed that 30% of the total outsourcing fee consisted of factory costs and the remaining 70% consisted of production outsourcing fees and royalties (Shintaku et al. 2003, 23). This is a much higher profit rate in comparison to that of general production orders in the manufacturing industry.[14] As described so far, Nintendo controlled the quality of software products, making profit from software production as well. We see then how one corporation, Nintendo, attempted to gain increasing market shares by control of both hardware and software development while controlling the conditions and terms of this development. In the years that followed, the company has had to change its policies concerning software companies with changing times and intensifying competition. Incidentally, Nintendo established a division for developing software of its own and has been creating original software titles.

One of the factors of the explosive popularization of the Famicom is the reasonable pricing of the hardware product based on the software strategy. Software exchangeable consoles were introduced to the market around 1981 in Japan, but the consoles with high-performance features did not become popular because of their high prices; the price range was between $250 and $500 (Yada 1996, 27). In comparison, the Famicom not only was much more inexpensive at $125 but also had supreme usability and attractive software titles. It is commonly understood that the factors for the success of the Famicom are (1) its high-performance hardware, (2) its low price, and (3) its excellent software products (Fujita 1999b, 76). Nintendo started exporting the Famicom as the NES (Nintendo Entertainment System) to the USA in 1985. Backed by the highly entertaining software *Super Mario Bros.*, as presented in Fig. 2.1, the NES sold enormously well in the USA, too (Matsumura 2011, 7). Worldwide, 1.23 million units were sold within one year of its release and sales continued to grow steadily; 2.11 million units were sold by December 1984, four million units by July 1985, and 10.75 million units were sold by August 1987. Cumulative sales up until the production termination in 2003 amounted to 61.91 million units (Uemura et al. 2013, 116).

Table 2.3 presents sales figures for Nintendo hardware and software products during the eight and a half years following the release of the Famicom. Overall, sales increased nearly ninefold. The total sales are nearly equally divided into sales of hardware and software products. While the rate of return has not been disclosed, it is assumed that Nintendo gained a large profit margin per title since the number of software titles was limited, and in general software products have small marginal costs. Although it did not sell as well as the Famicom, sales of the Game Boy, a handheld released in 1989, grew steadily too. It not only increased sales but significantly contributed to subsequent business projects as several handhelds released in the 2000s were based on it.

SCE's Business Model for the PlayStation

Nintendo's establishment of the home VG market with the Famicom, as well as the Super Famicom released in 1990 and the company's great success, led other companies to enter the market. One of them was SCE, which released the PSX, a 32-bit console, in December 1994. Sony got involved in the VGI through its development of a sound-source system for Nintendo's Super Famicom (Yanagawa and Kuwayama1999, 18). Rivaling Nintendo, which dominated the market, SCE added a high-performance image-processing feature to its product and adopted a software strategy differing from that of Nintendo. While Nintendo limited the number of software titles, SCE's approach was to create an extensive lineup of software products. For this reason, royalties and production outsourcing fees were lowered to increase the number of companies for its software development. Furthermore, the company covered the inventory risk by purchasing products from software companies and selling them to retailers. By this, SCE reduced the financial burden on software companies and supported sales activities. Moreover, the company created a software short-delivery-time system in which software production quantity could be adjusted flexibly and inventory could be controlled. SCE adopted the CD-ROM for the software storage medium as it can be manufactured in a few days. In contrast, it took two to three months to manufacture Famicom's mask ROM cartridge. Orders for the software for Nintendo consoles were received from the primary wholesalers two to six months before the planned release date, and the first production quantity was decided by predicting the demand based on the amount of these orders. This decision was made jointly by Nintendo, the software company, and wholesalers. Nintendo delivered the products to the software company two to three months after the order was placed, and then the software company sold them to wholesalers. Accordingly, sales preparation had to be started two to three months prior to the completion of software development. Furthermore, when the demand was greater than the sales amount predicted originally, additional software packages could not be supplied quickly. In contrast, with SCE's CD-ROM-based production, decisions on the production quantity did not have to be made until two weeks before the release date, and only the software company and SCE were involved in the decision-making process. Since the quantity was decided shortly before the release date, prediction

Table 2.3 Sales of Nintendo hardware and software from manufactures and publishers at family computer's peak in US$ M

Period	Hardware							Software							Total
	Family computer		Game boy		Super family computer		Total	Family computer		Game boy		Super family computer		Total	
	Japan	Overseas shipment	Japan	Overseas shipment	Japan	Overseas shipment		Japan	Overseas shipment	Japan	Overseas shipment	Japan	Overseas shipment		
1984/9–85/8	217	0	0	0	0	0	217	298	0	0	0	0	0	298	515
1985/9–86/8	382	83	0	0	0	0	466	460	39	0	0	0	0	499	965
1986/9–87/8	281	255	0	0	0	0	535	500	114	0	0	0	0	614	1150
1987/9–88/8	119	464	0	0	0	0	583	363	369	0	0	0	0	732	1314
1988/9–89/8	99	871	42	28	0	0	1041	289	581	26	8	0	0	905	1946
1989/9–90/3	63	482	78	114	0	0	737	211	592	76	40	0	1	920	1656
1990/4–91/3	98	782	175	374	172	2	1602	310	1136	176	200	128	215	1951	3553
1991/4–92/3	85	539	129	533	361	489	2135	238	472	174	307	482	887	1887	4022
1992/4–93/3	53	187	121	340	487	944	2132	131	206	133	231	942	724	2366	4498
Total	1398	3663	545	1387	1019	1433	9448	2798	3510	585	786	1552	940	10,171	19,619

Source: Data from Uemura et al. 2013, 52, 53

error was small and the financial burden was light. Moreover, since it is extremely difficult to predict demands for VG software, this type of production style can supply additional software packages quickly when the demand exceeds the predicted sales amount (Shintaku et al. 2003, 31–32).

In addition to the difference in adopted software storage mediums, the difference in the two companies' distribution networks due to the difference in their backgrounds also enabled SCE to materialize quick delivery VG software, demands for which predictions were difficult to foresee. While Nintendo was a well-established toy manufacturer and sold software products with its toy-distribution network, SCE organized a system for delivering products to retailers within a short period of time by utilizing the music software-distribution network of its parent company Sony Music Entertainment. The toy-distribution network requires time as it involves multiple stages of primary wholesalers, secondary wholesalers, and retailers. On the other hand, SCE simplified the network by functioning as a primary wholesaler, that is, purchasing the products from the software companies, and directly selling products to large retail stores and VG stores by utilizing the music software distribution network; SCE had a foundation to be involved in the distribution (Shintaku et al. 2003, 34–35).

As the reader can see above, the differences in market approach between Nintendo and SCE were derived largely from historical factors and corporate environment rather than competitive factors. As in the case of their distribution networks, Nintendo's approach derived from a toy-manufacturing background and that of SCE derived from a music-related background.

Figure 2.9 shows the current home VG software distribution structure. In general, software companies outsource the production of the medium to hardware companies (Institute for Information and Communications Policy, Ministry of Internal Affairs and Communications 2014, 87). As for sales, software companies either outsource sales activities to hardware companies or directly sell the products to wholesalers and retailers. Recently, software companies are increasingly selling products to consumers directly through the Internet. Some hardware companies sell software products to wholesalers, while others directly sell to retailers or directly sell to consumers through the Internet. Commonly, retailers purchase software products

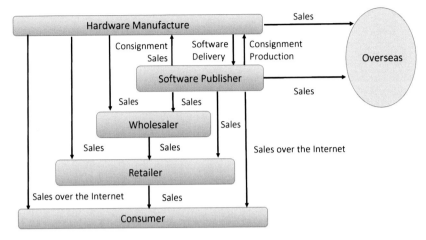

Fig. 2.9 Distribution structure of video game software in Japan (*Source*: Adapted from CESA 2012, 84.)

at approximately 75% of the retail price and usually the products are sold to consumers at approximately 90% of the original retail price due to competition with other stores and online shopping sites (Industry Research Division, Mizuho Corporate Bank 2014, 114).

As described so far, SCE succeeded by creating a generous system for software companies, adopting a storage medium that enables quick delivery, and utilizing existing distribution networks. Popular titles that were sold as software packages for Nintendo consoles such as Final Fantasy (Square) and Dragon Quest (Enix) began to be sold for the PSX. Taking advantage of Nintendo's distribution weak point, SCE managed to gain the largest share in the VG market that had been formed by Nintendo. SCE released the PSX in America and Europe in September 1995 and shipped ten million units by December 1996, 50 million units by December 1998, and 70 million units by December 1999. By December 2006, cumulative shipments of the PSX reached 102.49 million units (Sony Computer Entertainment Inc. 2015). Pitting against the PSX, Nintendo released the Nintendo 64 in 1996, but its market share remained small. One of the reasons for this was that the Nintendo 64 did not have an extensive lineup of attractive software titles. As of March 31, 1997, the number of domestic software companies was as follows: 177 Super Famicom software companies, 50 Nintendo 64 software companies, and 540 PSX software companies (Yanagawa and Kuwayama 1999, 33). In 2000, SCE released the PS2, a console succeeding the PSX, and maintained its position in the market; exceeding cumulative sales of the PSX (102 million units), the sales of the PS2 reached 155 million units worldwide. Leveraging the specialties of Sony, an AV equipment manufacturer, the PS2 was developed to be a high-performance console with enhanced image quality and sound quality. It was equipped with a DVD player, yet it was less expensive than a typical dedicated DVD player.[15]

Video Game Console Manufacturers that Retreated from the Market

Two noteworthy VG console manufacturers that succeeded for only a short time in Japan were SEGA and NEC. SEGA, a company that mainly manufactured and sold arcade game machines in the 1980s, released the console SEGA Mark III in 1985 and then the console MEGA DRIVE in 1988. Software for these consoles could be developed easily because of an adopted CPU feature. SEGA partially followed software strategies of Nintendo (Maeda 2014, 80), making for an extensive software lineup. The company started exporting consoles to North America in 1989 and shipped 3.58 million units domestically and 28 million units internationally (Maeda 2014, 81). SEGA showed its presence in the US market in which Nintendo held an overwhelmingly dominant position. SEGA possessed the know-how for developing software since it had been developing arcade games. The SATURN, which was released in 1994 in Japan, the same year in which the PSX was released, sold well, and by July 1996, its sales roughly equaled that of the PSX at 3.5 million units in Japan (Yada 1996, 51). Nevertheless, SEGA's VG business involved high costs and tumbled deep in the red around 1996 due to price competition with rival companies among other reasons; the company had no choice but to retreat. In order to recover from the failed VG business, the company released the Dreamcast in 1998 in Japan and the next year worldwide. This console was the world's first console with a built-in modem. However, the release was premature, and the product did not become popular; since at that time a fixed-rate system was not available for online connection, it was too costly to play with this console (Maeda 2014, 184). Sales of the Dreamcast did not increase for a number of reasons including failure to make software available at the time of hardware release due to delay in the development of the semiconductor for graphics (Maeda 2014, 186). The price of the console was reduced to increase sales, but this only resulted in the Dreamcast project going into the red. Production was terminated in 2001, and SEGA completely retreated from the VG console market.

NEC Home Electronics Corporation, a subsidiary of Japan's largest electronic manufacturer NEC Corporation, released the PC Engine in 1987. Its performance was much better than that of the Famicom and its size was compact. Similar to PCs, the PC Engine was a multipurpose game console to which peripheral devices such as CD-ROM drives, pen tablets, and printers could be connected. Its high performance was recognized, and the console gained a 24.7% market share in 1992 (Maeda 2014, 101); this was the next largest share following the share of Nintendo's Super Famicom. However, the PC Engine did not have the advantage over competing consoles due to NEC's weak planning for succeeding products and its limited lineup of software. Accordingly, its sales were terminated in 1997.

SEGA and NEC were both large companies; they possessed technological and financial strength as well as solid distribution networks, and their consoles were not inferior to those of their competitors in any way. Their console business, nevertheless, resulted in failure because of a lack of software strategy. While Nintendo and SCE took into consideration the mutual relationship between hardware and software products, the companies that retreated from the home VG console market focused on competing with high-quality hardware products, neglecting to give consideration to software development. The situation in Japan was that there were no (and still are no) uniform standards for software-hardware interface. Nintendo and SCE each had its own distinct software-hardware interface standards. Software developed for Nintendo consoles did not work on SCE and SEGA consoles and vice versa nor did it work on NEC consoles. The majority of software development in Japan was (and still is) provided by independent software developers even though Nintendo had a software development department. As for the software developers, they were attracted to developing software for the two biggest console makers in order to gain a better position in the software market. Thus, with weak software strategies, both SEGA and NEC were left in the Japanese market with a big disadvantage with high-quality consoles but over time with increasingly less software for these consoles. One more factor was the cost of their hardware products. In contrast, Nintendo's effective strategy was to increase market share by selling hardware products at low prices while making profit with software sales.

Comparing Data Compiled for Nintendo and SCE, Which Reflects the Overall Japanese Market

We saw above how Nintendo and SCE came to dominate the Japanese domestic market. This section provides data that resulted from their strategies and actions and clarifies their market positions both domestically and overseas between 1997 and 2014, positions which fluctuated. Focus on these two companies provides an overall picture of this market.

Table 2.4 shows Nintendo's and SCE's cumulative number of consoles/handhelds shipped by model worldwide. Nintendo shipped a total of approximately 680 million units, while SCE shipped a total of approximately 440 million units. Looking at the data by models, the best-selling consoles/handhelds were Nintendo's DS series and SCE's PS2; the number of units shipped for both models exceeds 150 million. Following, the Game Boy ranked third, the PSX ranked fourth, and the Wii ranked fifth. The original Famicom ranked ninth; the fact that the Famicom was shipped at such a significant amount in the early stage of home VGI shows the extent of the popularity of this console.

The number of VG consoles/handhelds shipped domestically by Nintendo and SCE from 1997 to 2014 is shown in Figure 2.10, and the number of consoles/handhelds domestically shipped for each model is shown in Table 2.5. Fluctuations in Fig. 2.10 are largely accounted for by the release of new consoles based on new technologies and concepts. The number of consoles/handhelds shipped by Nintendo, on average, is higher than that of SCE (Fig. 2.10). Looking at Table 2.5, the number of PSXs shipped has been decreasing since 1997 when 5.4 million units were shipped, and its product life practically ended with the release of the succeeding PS2 in 2000. While the number of PS2s shipped exceeds that of the PSX in total, the number of PS3s shipped is lower than that of the PSX and the PS2. While the number of PSXs shipped significantly decreased after the release of the PS2, sales of the PS2 have not decreased dramatically even after the release of the PS3.

Table 2.4 Worldwide Nintendo and SCE cumulative shipped units of game console/handheld, as of Dec. 31, 2014

Manufacturer	Game-system model	Released year	Units (10K)
Nintendo	Family Computer	1983	6191
	Super Family Computer	1990	4910
	Nintendo 64	1996	3293
	GameCube	2001	2174
	Wii	2006	10,144
	Wii U	2012	920
	Game Boy	1989	11,869
	Game Boy Advance	2001	8151
	Nintendo DS Series	2004	15,401
	Nintendo 3DS	2011	5041
	Total		68,094
SCE	PlayStation	1994	10,240
	PlayStation 2	2000	15,500
	PlayStation 3	2006	8000
	PlayStation 4	2014	1990
	PlayStation Portable	2004	7640
	PlayStation Vita	2011	976
	Total		44,346

Source: Data from CESA 2007, 189; CESA 2015, 178, 179

Meanwhile, prior to SCE with its handhelds, Nintendo achieved great results. As for the Game Boy released in 1989, in part due to the popularity of its software Pokémon released in 1996, the number of the Game Boys shipped was maintained until around 2000. The following year, the Game Boy Advance was released and nearly five million units shipped. The shipped units decreased in subsequent years, but the DS released in 2004, which presented a wide range of practical-use software themes including language learning, covered this drop. New user groups, for example, middle-aged people, seniors, and females, were acquired with the release of the DS. Furthermore, this handheld featured a touch screen and utilized Wi-Fi. In 2006, the Nintendo DS Lite with its bright screen and with new software availability sold extremely well. With the addition of the Wii console, Nintendo shipped the highest number of consoles/handhelds after 1997 in 2007. However, the number of consoles/handhelds shipped dropped sharply after 2008 because of a simultaneous decrease in shipped units for all main

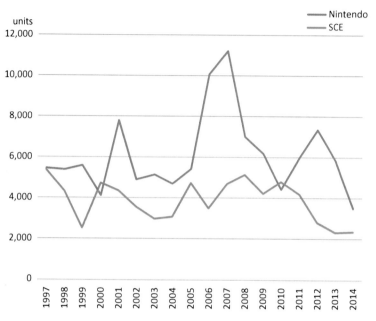

Fig. 2.10 Console/handheld units shipped by Nintendo and SCE within Japan, 1997–2014(*Source*: Data from CESA 1998, 27, 28; CESA 2001, 38–39; CESA 2004, 73, 75; CESA 2007, 103, 105; CESA 2009, 139, 141; CESA 2012, 119, 121; CESA 2015, 73, 75)

consoles/handhelds. It increased somewhat with the release of Nintendo 3DS in 2011, and the company maintained this level until 2014.

Indeed, 15 years after the release of the Game Boy, SCE released its first handheld PSP in 2004, and the number of PSPs shipped was maintained at a constant level until 2011. In addition to games, the PSP was the first handheld in which music and video were enabled by using them with AV equipment which utilizes its core competence, differentiating from Nintendo's handhelds. There was a significant difference in the number of handhelds shipped by the two companies. Combining the shipment of the PSP and the PS Vita, the number of handhelds shipped by SCE was 23 million units. On the other hand, combining the Game Boy, the Game Boy Advance, and the Nintendo DS Series, the number of handhelds shipped by Nintendo reached 101 million units. This success in selling

Table 2.5 Shipped units of game systems domestically in Japan, thousands of units, 1997–2014

	1997	1998	1999	2000	2001	2002	2003	2004	2005	2006	2007	2008	2009	2010	2011	2012	2013	2014	Total
PlayStation	5400	4314	2546	806	275	233	34	5	1										13,614
PlayStation 2				3920	4090	3343	2933	2592	2115	1254	758	460	200	90	70	30			21,855
PlayStation 3										614	885	1040	1780	1680	1550	1220	791	367	9927
PlayStation 4																		887	887
PlayStation Portable								496	2618	1634	3072	3650	2240	3020	2130	900	323	73	20,156
PlayStation Vita															440	670	1226	1022	3358
Game Boy	4016	4130	4472	3842	1509	243													18,212
Game Boy Advance					4988	3578	4048	2830	985	174	129	176	20						16,928
Super Family Computer	254	72																	326
Nintendo 64	1190	1185	1123	265	99														3862
GameCube					1199	1075	1096	420	190	40		20							4040
Nintendo DS								1450	4250	840						16			6556
Nintendo DS Lite										7890	7230	2350	540	190					18,200
Nintendo DSi												1660	3000	1040	190				5890

(*continued*)

Table 2.5 (continued)

	1997	1998	1999	2000	2001	2002	2003	2004	2005	2006	2007	2008	2009	2010	2011	2012	2013	2014	Total
Nintendo Dsi LL													700	1460	170				2330
Nintendo 3DS															4660	6234	4870	2940	18,704
Wii										1140	3850	2800	1930	1730	990	260	60		12,760
Wii U																830	920	550	2300
Xbox						400	80	40	20										540
Xbox 360									120	200	250	400	360	250	120	70	24	8	1802
Xbox One																	55	55	55
Total	10,860	9701	8141	8833	12,160	8872	8191	7833	10,299	13,786	16,174	12,556	10,770	9460	10,320	10,230	8214	5902	182,302

Source: Data from CESA 1998, 27, 28; CESA 2001, 38, 39; CESA 2004, 73, 75; CESA 2007, 103, 105; CESA 2009, 139, 141; CESA 2012, 119, 121; CESA 2015, 73, 75

handhelds accounts for why SCE was less successful than Nintendo in the overall domestic market.

Continuing onto examining the competition between Nintendo and SCE in foreign markets, while Nintendo enjoyed the bigger position in the domestic market, Figure 2.11 demonstrates that the two companies have competed with and balanced each other over the years in terms of the number of units exported. As mentioned in section "Organization of Video Game as Based on Device," handhelds are not as popular overseas as in Japan, and thus Nintendo, which has an advantage with handheld products, has less competitive advantages in foreign markets. As shown in Table 2.6, while the number of PSXs shipped in Japan decreased after 1997, the number of PSXs exported increased in 1998 and 1999. Though the PS2 was shipped in substantial quantities following its release in 2000, the number of PSXs shipped did not drop sharply, and the PSX was

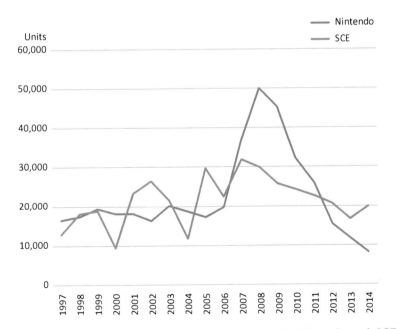

Fig. 2.11 Console/handheld units shipped overseas by Nintendo and SCE, 1997–2014

(*Source*: Data from CESA 1998, 30, 31; CESA 2001, 45–46; CESA 2004, 77, 79; CESA 2007, 107, 109; CESA 2009, 143, 145; CESA 2012, 123, 125; CESA 2015, 78, 80.)

Table 2.6 Shipped units of game systems excluding Japan, thousands of units, 1997–2014

	1997	1998	1999	2000	2001	2002	2003	2004	2005	2006	2007	2008	2009	2010	2011	2012	2013	2014	Total
PlayStation	12,900	18,056	18,738	7034	9193	5716	4142	2546	764										79,089
PlayStation 2				2438	14,248	20,791	17,438	9295	17,626	13,038	14,086	8440	6800	6810	4630	970			136,610
PlayStation 3										1090	9683	9660	10,620	12,720	12,550	13,380	8537	3033	81,273
PlayStation 4																	4972	14,513	19,485
PlayStation Portable									11,366	8387	8027	11,750	8360	4680	5470	3200	1939	422	63,601
PlayStation Vita															30	3130	1212	2034	6406
Game Boy	6100	8459	12,850	15,452	5199	830													48,890
Game Boy Advance					10,244	10,535	15,971	13,510	7525	4430	1745	549	15						64,524
Super Family Computer	1768	1569																	3337
Nintendo 64	8638	7296	6519	2683	1026	10													26,172
GameCube					1561	4826	4183	3680	2390	850	200	10							17,700
Nintendo DS								1390	7340	3010	537					440	310		13,027
Nintendo DS Lite										9440	21,416	27,420	12,900	3430	900				75,506
Nintendo DSi													11,770	6072	2828				20,670
Nintendo Dsi LL														7268	2372				9640
Nintendo 3DS															10,380	8574	8030	4730	31,714
Wii										2050	13,090	22,040	20,550	15,470	9330	4150	1460	530	88,670
Wii U																2228	1890	2790	6908
Xbox					1500	6100	5620	6160	2000	300									21,680
Xbox 360									1680	8400	7050	9900	10,640	10,750	15,880	9830	6976	2988	84,094
Xbox One																	3900	9050	12,950
Total	29,406	35,380	38,107	27,607	42,971	48,808	47,354	36,581	50,691	50,995	75,834	89,769	81,655	67,200	64,370	45,902	39,226	40,090	911,946

Source: Data from CESA 1998, 30, 31; CESA 2001 45, 46; CESA 2004, 77, 79; CESA 2007, 107, 109; CESA 2009, 143, 145; CESA 2012, 123, 125; CESA 2015, 78, 80

also shipped steadily until 2003. Although the number of PS2s shipped decreased by half in 2004, the number increased in 2005. With the addition of the PSP, the overall number of consoles/handhelds shipped by SCE increased. With no release of new models after 2007, the number of consoles/handhelds shipped began to decrease. The PS Vita was released in 2011, and more than three million units were shipped in 2012, but the number of PS Vitas shipped decreased in 2013. Released in 2013, the PS4 was shipped in significant quantities, more than 14.5 million units shipped in 2014. In contrast, with Nintendo's export of nearly 20 million units annually from 1997, the number of Nintendo's consoles/handhelds exported rivaled the number of PS series exported until 2003; Nintendo exported the Game Boy and its succeeding the Game Boy Advance as well as the Nintendo 64 and its substitute, the Nintendo GameCube. The number of Nintendo's consoles/handhelds exported decreased in 2004; it was increased by the number of DSs exported in 2005, but the number of PSPs shipped was higher. Then the number of Nintendo's consoles/handhelds exported grew higher than that of SCE in 2006 with the increase in the numbers of Nintendo DS Lites and Wiis shipped. However, the number of consoles/handhelds exported by Nintendo decreased in subsequent years, and it was lower than that of SCE's in 2012.

Two factors, the big market and the lengthy product life cycle account for the huge export sales of Nintendo and SCE. For example, while in the domestic market after 2000 with the release of the PS2 (Table 2.5) shipped units of PSX decreased dramatically, in the overseas market shipped units of PSX remained stable until 2003 with a decrease that was not dramatic (Table 2.6). Table 2.5 shows in Japan with the release of each successive new-generation console/handheld (with a few exceptions) a dramatic drop in the shipped units of the previous generation.

Japanese Home Video Game Software Companies

Until now this chapter has focused on hardware companies, which in Japan lead the industry. This section briefly introduces some current Japanese home VG software companies. While there are only two main hardware companies in the Japanese VGI, Nintendo and SCE, there are a number of software companies. The large software companies are Koei Tecmo Holdings Co., Ltd.; CAPCOM Co., Ltd.; Square Enix Holdings Co., Ltd.; Konami Corporation; SEGA Sammy Holdings Inc.; and BANDAI NAMCO Holdings Inc. The small- and medium-sized software companies include Nippon Ichi Software,

Table 2.7 Large software companies in Japan

Company name	Established	Sales (US$ M, fiscal year 2014)	Operating profit (US$ M, fiscal year 2014)	Features	Major software
Koie Tecmo Holdings	2010 with acquisition by Koei (established 1978) of TECMO (established 1967)	315	80	Sales of home video game software accounting for 65 % of the total sales (fiscal year 2014), known for its historical simulation games	Nobunaga's Ambition
CAPCOM	1979	536	88	Sales of game software accounting for 71 % of total sales (fiscal year 2014), known for combat sports game software	Street Fighter; Resident Evil; Rockman; Monster Hunter
Square Enix Holdings	2003 with the merger of Enix Co., Ltd. (established 1975) and Square Co., Ltd. (established 1986)	1399	137	Involvement also with publishing, successful management of online-game website	Dragon Quest; Final Fantasy
Konami Corporation	1973	1818	120	Wide business range (sports gyms, arcade game facilities, arcade game machines, and home video game software)	Metal Gear; Winning Eleven

(continued)

Table 2.7 (continued)

Company name	Established	Sales (US$ M, fiscal year 2014)	Operating profit (US$ M, fiscal year 2014)	Features	Major software
SEGA Sammy	2004 with acquisition by Sammy (established 1975) of SEGA. (established 1951)	2957	147	Former development of home video game consoles (SEGA), pachinko business	Sonic; Puyo Puyo
BANDAI NAMCO	2005 with the merger of BANDAI Co., Ltd. (established 1950) and NAMCO Limited. (established 1955)	4712	479	Manufacturing and sales of toys and operation of amusement facilities, copyright holder of prominent content such as Gundam	Tekken; Tales series

Source: Koei Tecmo Holdings Co., Ltd. 2015; CAPCOM Co., Ltd. 2015; Square Enix Co., Ltd. 2015; Konami Corporation 2015; SEGA Sammy Holdings Inc. 2015; BANDAI NAMCO Entertainment Inc. 2015; Nikkei Inc. 2015, 500, 1774

Inc.; Marvelous Inc.; Nihon Falcom Corporation; Broccoli Co., Ltd.; Level-5 Inc.; Spike Chunsoft Co., Ltd.; Mages. Inc.; and FromSoftware, Inc. Table 2.7 provides an overview of six large software companies.

Many of the large VG software companies had developed and sold arcade game machines in the 1960s and 1970s and, based on that know-how, entered the home VG software industry in the 1980s. Due to stagnation of the domestic market and increase in software development expenditures caused by the shift to high-performance VG consoles, many software companies were reorganized after 2000. Using the latest technology, game software development is highly advanced. Software companies are investing heavily in internal R&D and are enhancing the $1.7 M in production fees. The development of a PS2 action game requires two years, 1000 people per month, and $6–7 M in production fees. Developing a PS3 action game requires 2000 people per month and $12–13 M in production fees. As demonstrated by these examples, production fees rose sharply, and the development processes were prolonged as the models advanced (METI 2006, 14).

This section has focused on home VG consoles and the history of the VGI in Japan. Section "The Growth of Online Games and Online-Game Companies in Japan: The Internet Influence on the Video Game Industry" focuses on the rise of online games with the popularization of the Internet and provides details on the growth in Japan of the online-game market and online-game companies.

The Growth of Online Games and Online-Game Companies in Japan: The Internet Influence on the Video Game Industry

Over thirty years of technological innovations saw steep increases in production fees, as seen above, major changes in product development and big market fluctuations. One innovation, online games via the Internet, had a major influence on the Japanese VGI. Utilization of the Internet brought about dramatic changes. Starting around 2000, a new type of VG, the online game, came into widespread use. The market scale of online games exceeded that of home VGs (both hardware/software) in Japan in 2012. In 2014, while market scale of conventional types remained $3.112 M, the online-game market scale reached $5.527 M in Japan, 64% of the total VG market. Online games are often played on non-dedicated devices and significantly differ from VGs for dedicated game devices in several ways: content, business forms, and businesses involved.

The term "online game" used in this chapter is based on the definition provided by the Japan Online Game Association (established 2004): "A game played by multiple players through the Internet." Because various online-game types have emerged along with the diversification of game-playing environments, online games have been organized accordingly in this chapter: As shown in Figure 2.12, online games have been grouped by platforms (console/handheld, PC, smartphone/tablet, and feature phone); those connected with Social Networking Services (SNS) are grouped as social games.

Before the development of online games, VGs utilizing communication functions were developed. For example, ASCII released F-16 Fighting Falcon for MSX PC in Japan in 1985, which had a function for one-to-one fighting, although this particular way of playing did not become popular

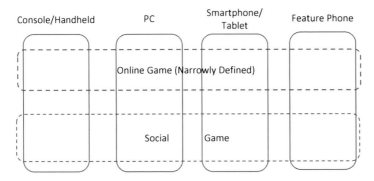

Fig. 2.12 Online-game types (broadly defined)
(*Source*: Adapted from METI 2014, 112.)

at the time; eventually SEGA adopted this software for its console. The Game Boy allowed for game data exchange via mutually connecting VG devices with communication cables. Interesting to note, in Japan in 1988, Nintendo had started a stock market trading service through the Famicom communication function (Tanaka 2008).

Later, in Japan, online games, that is, games specifically played by connecting to the Internet, became popular gradually. Among the first online-game software used in Japan but actually developed in the USA and imported to Japan were the following titles: Diablo (Blizzard Entertainment) and Ultima Online (Electronic Arts), which arrived in Japan shortly after their release in the USA in 1996 and 1997, respectively. In order to play these games, on top of purchasing the software package at a store, consumers were required to pay monthly fees. Though these games were received by some fans enthusiastically, they did not become popular in Japan because the communication environment had not been established. Figure 2.13 shows the penetration rate of the Internet and communication devices in Japan. Around 2000 the Internet penetration rate was only about 30%. Subsequently, online games for PCs that had become popular in Korea, for example, Lineage, Ragnarok Online, and MapleStory, were imported into Japan. Acquisition of new users was easier with the business form of these games as free software could be downloaded after which users paid monthly fees. The item-fees billing service started in Korea in 2003 was later introduced to Japan; this is the main billing method used today. (Item-fees billing refers to a billing method in which playing the game is free, but fees are required to obtain tools and abilities that give advantages

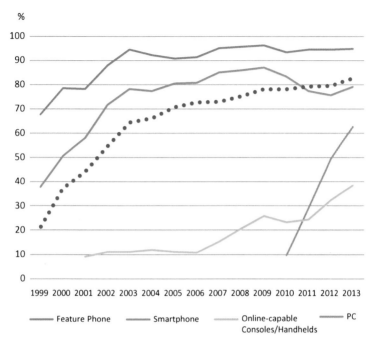

Fig. 2.13 Penetration rate of Internet and communication device usage in Japan, 1999–2013(*Source*: Data from Ministry of Internal Affairs and Communications 2003, 195; 2005, 28; 2014a, 337–338.)

to users.) Japan's online-game market was mainly formed by importing Korean games for PCs.

Before, in Japan, games had been played mainly with home VG consoles rather than with PCs. An example is the online game Final Fantasy XI for the PS2 by Square released in 2002. Around 2005, online games became popular rapidly: as Fig. 2.13 shows, the Internet penetration rate reached as high as 70% around 2005. Eventually, however, a social issue arose: the problem of minors receiving enormous bills for purchasing items. This problem became so serious that the Consumer Affairs Agency had to create regulations for online-game-related purchases.

Figure 2.14 shows the online-game market scale from 2005 to 2012. The market scale grew to $1.184 M The market scale grew in 2012, a size 1.7 times that of 2005. In comparison to the home VG software market

Fig. 2.14 Market scale of online games in Japan, 2005–2012 (*Source*: Data from METI 2013, 125) (*Note*: "Service sales" refers to subscription fees and in-game purchases)

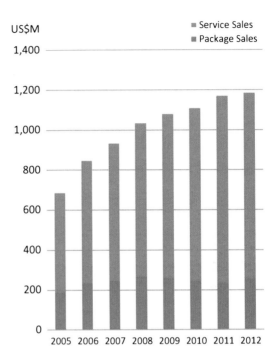

scale shown in Fig. 2.5, the scale of the online market was 26% that of the home VG software market in 2005, increasing to 48% in 2012. As for its business model, online games are sold more often in the form of services rather than as packages at stores. Online-game-services sales forms are diversifying; a software product may be downloaded for a fee or for free, but services for playing it require fees. In other cases, profit is made from advertising revenues with downloading and playing free.

Figure 2.15 shows the number of online-game software titles by billing methods from 2005 to 2012 increased. The number of online games using the billing method in which users download software for free and then are charged for items used gradually increased; by 2012, 238 titles out of the 354 titles of software used for online games were paid for with this billing method (accounting for 67% of the total billing methods). The second most used billing method is the one in which users download the software for a fee and then do not have to pay for any service. Players that pay for playing games spend, on average, about $50 monthly. The

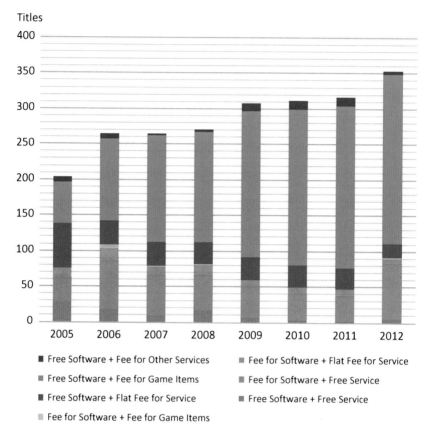

Fig. 2.15 Online-game software titles by billing methods in Japan (*Source*: Data from METI 2013, 121.)

20s–40s age groups have high conversion rates. Among them, 20–30% of the people pay fees to play games (METI 2014, 116).

As Fig. 2.13 presents, smartphones came into widespread use rapidly around 2010, and subsequently the smartphone online-game market came into existence. The ratio of hardware types used for online games (2013) is shown in Figure 2.16. Smartphones and tablets were used the most and account for 65% of the total. The next most used hardware type is the feature phone (19%).

Fig. 2.16 Online-game platform share by sales in Japan, 2013 (*Source*: Data from METI 2014, 116.)

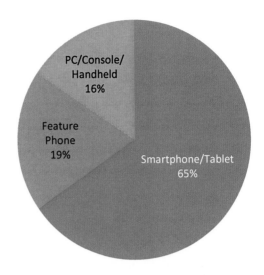

PC/Console/Handheld 16%

Feature Phone 19%

Smartphone/Tablet 65%

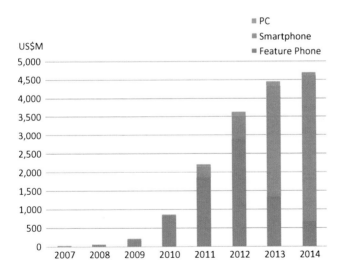

Fig. 2.17 Social game market scale by non-dedicated gaming devices in Japan, 2007–2014 (*Source*: Data from CESA 2015, 157)

Among the different types of online games, social games, defined here as online games played through a SNS site, started to grow popular in Japan around 2007. As Figure 2.17 shows, the popularity of social games rose rapidly from 2010, and in 2014 sales of social games reached $4.685 M surpassing the sales of domestic software products ($1.963 M). Originally, feature phones were the main platform for social games. However, in 2013 smartphones rapidly became more popular than feature phones as the platform for social games. Characteristic of Japan is that social games are almost always played on mobile platforms and hardly played on PCs as Fig. 2.17 shows. The Internet connection service for feature phones started in Japan early (1999); thus, Japanese people were used to using the Internet with mobile terminals. Figure 2.18 presents the business structure of social games. The typical setup in Japan is illustrated on the left. The software developer supplies software to Social Networking Services (SNS), which in turn supply this software to the consumer; the consumer pays for this software through his telecom company, which in turn pays the SNS. This is in contrast to the setup commonly found in other countries illustrated on the right of Fig. 2.18. Convenient for game companies, communication carriers in Japan provide an excellent service for collecting various fees; they bill communication fees together with fees for online games.

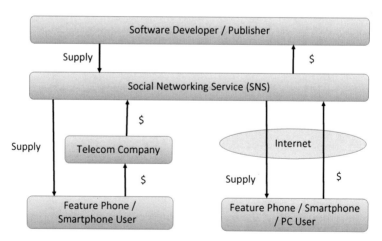

Fig. 2.18 Business structure of social games in Japan (*Source*: Adapted from CESA 2012, 86)

No research is available as to the reason social games became rapidly popular in Japan from 2010 till 2014. However, as Fig. 2.13 illustrates, this same period coincided with the rapid diffusion of the smartphone. In 2012 was a 77.7% social media utilization ratio among smartphone users which rose in 2014 to 91.6% as many people came to use social media (Ministry of Internal Affairs and Communications 2014b, 80). Social media was the environment in which social games were played; however, for 2010 no data exists as to the percentage of social media users in Japan's population. For 2012 the ratio was 41.4% of the population, and by 2014 it had increased to 62.3% (Ministry of Internal Affairs and Communications 2014b, 79). We can assume one reason is that with the popularization of social media came the need to satisfy

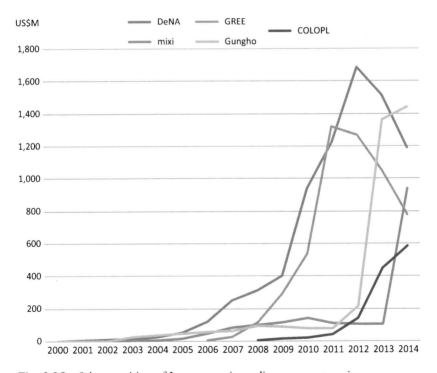

Fig. 2.19 Sales transition of Japanese major online-game enterprises (*Source*: Data from Nikkei Inc. 2005, 252, 457; 2009, 171, 263, 519, 541; 2012, 161, 243, 485, 515; 2015, 165, 244, 498, 513, 541)

the demands of the social game players. As a reference, in Japan the market scale of movie-downloading services via the Internet for 2007 was $40 M; for 2010, $63 M; and for 2013, $150 M. Along with the rapid growth of social games from 2007 on the Internet was a period of growth for the use of moving images (Dentsu Institute for Human Studies 2015, 87).

Figure 2.19 shows the sales of large Japanese online-game software companies from 2000 to 2014. Among these companies, those involved in social games were DeNA Co., Ltd. (referred to as DeNA), mixi, Inc. (mixi), and GREE, Inc. (GREE). These companies were not involved in home VG software but operated online shopping and SNS sites. They were start-ups that began growing rapidly around 2009. The largest of all, DeNA, was established in 1999 as a company for operating online-auction and shopping sites. This company grew substantially by entering the VGI targeting feature phones. The history of mixi in 1997 when university students started a website for online recruitment. The company started an SNS site for PCs in 2002 and grew with advertisement revenues and membership fees for video distribution. In 2009 mixi was the first company succeeding in Japan to adopt social games for an SNS site. In 2004 GREE was established to operate an SNS site for PCs. However, mixi was much more successful, and thus GREE changed its SNS site into a website for feature phones. In 2007, the company started offering free-to-play social games that involved fees for obtaining items. This was a great success. Item fees can be readily billed in Japan since feature-phone carriers have an established system for collecting fees (Fig. 2.18); online-game software companies have been making profit not only from advertising revenues but also from item fees. As mixi provides mainly the SNS platform to other software companies, Japan's social game market has been driven by the Japanese companies DeNA and GREE.

There are many differences between social games and home VGs. First of all, social games require much lower development fees. While, on average, under one million dollars are required to develop a social game, more than a few million dollars are required to develop a home VG in Japan since, for example, it uses high-resolution computer graphics that create images like live-action images. Furthermore, the software of social games can be modified after the title is released. Business risks are insignificant with social games as companies can respond to the needs of players quickly and in detail, for example, change the game's degree of difficulty by researching player trends in real time. Moreover, since software bugs can be fixed promptly, the financial burden of quality assurance is dramatically lightened. With home VGs, once a software bug occurs, the company must bear the cost of collecting the products; a lot of time and effort is put into quality control prior to the release of a home VG. The product life of a home VG is short; its sales drop within a few weeks of its release (Shintaku et al. 2003, 145–152). In contrast, users of social games often gradually increase after the release of these games since the network of co-players expands during the process of their enjoying a game together (Ikeo 2013, 55). Furthermore, obviously, there is no need to purchase a new platform to play social games. For this reason, there are few obstacles for starting to play social games, especially since they can be played for free. Similarly, in terms of development fees and development capabilities, there are only a few obstacles that stand in the way of software companies intending to enter this industry; this is the reason for the emergence of start-ups.

In addition to social games, another online-game genre that has been increasing in popularity since 2012 is the native app. Native app games are processed directly by the device. These games are commonly referred to as smartphone games. Unlike social games, smartphone games do not involve SNS sites and are sold by online stores such as iTunes Store and Google Play. As of December 2013, Japan ranks second to the USA in the global iOS market and ranks at the top in the global Android market (Industry Research Division, Mizuho Corporate Bank 2014, 121). Japanese start-up companies driving the market are GungHo Online Entertainment, Inc. (referred to as GungHo), known for Puzzle & Dragons, and COLOPL, Inc. (COLOPL). Driving the market are the following large companies that also handle home VG software: Konami Digital Entertainment Co., Ltd.; BANDAI NAMCO Entertainment, Inc.; SEGA; and Square Enix. Though GungHo was established in 1998 as an online-auction company, the company terminated its auction business in 2002 and began to engage in the online-game business. Blessed by popular titles, GungHo has grown steadily since then. Established in 2008, COLOPL started out as a provider of location information service for feature phones. The company, which entered the online-game industry in 2011, became successful, and now online-game business is its main source of income. Fig. 2.19 shows the sales of Japan's two large smartphone game companies (GungHo and COLOPL) from 2000 to 2014.

It is often stated one factor for the popularization of online games for non-dedicated devices is the stagnation of home VGs (e.g., Saeki and Nishi 2013, 49; Yasuyama 2014, 3). There is no research data on the number of online-game players that switched from playing home VGs; detailed examination is required to make a judgment on whether or not the number of players that switched is large. There is the difference in the age groups of the players. The age group with the highest home VG console/handheld use rate is the group of users 14 years old and under. Within this group, while the console/handheld use rate is 11%, the non-dedicated device use rate is 1.1% (gameage R&I Co., Ltd. 2013). GungHo's decision to start distributing its extremely popular smartphone game Puzzle & Dragons for the Nintendo 3DS in 2013 was based on the company's conclusion that there would be no mutual encroachment of customers since players and playing conditions differ between home VG consoles/handhelds and smartphones (Saeki and Nishi 2013, 52).

As described so far, while VGs have always been an interactive entertainment, the Internet enabled simultaneous playing of a VG by multiple players. By this, players have developed strong networks and VGs have become even more interactive. The Internet has also enabled close communications between players and companies. Furthermore, significant changes were brought about to the VGI with the popularization of the Internet; a few new communication devices were developed, and it became possible to play VGs with these new platforms. With the appearance of online games in Japan, the Japanese game industry dramatically changed. While the market scale of the home VG remained largely unchanged, the market scale of the online Japanese game grew by leaps and bounds. The online game was neither an extension of the home VG nor were its companies, billing methods, or assembly players the same. An understanding of online games in Japan helps us better grasp the status quo of and predict the direction of the Japanese VGI.

The Past, Present, and Future of the Video Game Industry in Japan

This chapter has shown, as clearly seen in the example of online games in section "The Growth of Online Games and Online-Game Companies in Japan: The Internet Influence on the Video Game Industry," how many changes in the Japanese VGI have been since the release of the Famicom in 1983 until now. With the participation in the industry of new companies and the introduction of new technologies, it is anticipated that the Japanese VGI will continue to see changes. In order to best predict the future of the industry, it is important to know both past and present as well as general characteristics of the VGI not limited to Japan. Lastly in order to better predict the future of the VGI, this section briefly summarizes the description of the Japanese VGI presented in this chapter.

In addition, as a hint of what is to come, this section introduces some extremely new examples in terms of the influence of technology on the industry and business adaptations.

As we have seen in sections "Changes in the Size of Japan's Home Video Game Industry" and "Japan's Home Video Game Industry: Key Players in Hardware and Software," the home VGI in Japan grew significantly after its emergence and developed into an industry with a strong competitive advantage in the global market; as of 2014 the percentage of exports from Japan accounted for more than 80% of total sales. Nevertheless, sales have been decreasing since 2007. At this point, it is not possible to judge whether this decrease corresponds to the downward movement of cycle fluctuations or is a result of the end in growth. Meanwhile as we have seen in section "The Growth of Online Games and Online-Game Companies in Japan: The Internet Influence on the Video Game Industry," online

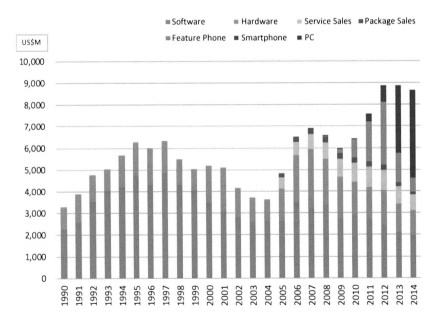

Fig. 2.20 Market scale of home video games and online games in Japan, 1990–2014
(*Source*: Data from Dentsu Institute for Human Studies 2001, 69; METI 2013, 125; 2014, 103; CESA 2015 58, 59, 157) (Note: Service sales means subscription fees and in-game purchases)

games started to grow rapidly from around 2005. Though the market was formed by importing foreign games, similarly to the growth of home VGs, Japanese companies are currently exporting online games.

In order to present a picture of the overall VGI, the market scale of home VGs and online games combined is shown in Figure 2.20. Overall, when the two are combined, it can be argued that even after 2007 the industry was growing domestically. Alongside the changes that have occurred in people's lifestyles and advancements in technology, games have also changed. The VGI not only creates jobs and contributes to economic growth, it also provides entertainment to a great number of people; VGs have diffused to the extent that one in two households owns a home VG

Table 2.8   Top 25 companies by game revenues, 2014

Rank	Company name	Annual revenues (US$ M)
1	Tencent	7211
2	Sony	6040
3	Microsoft	5023
4	Electronic Arts	4453
5	Activision Blizzard	4409
6	Apple	3199
7	Google	2623
8	King.com	2260
9	Nintendo	2092
10	Ubisoft	1806
11	NetEase	1586
12	GungHo Entertainment	1447
13	Nexon	1446
14	Disney	1280
15	DeNA	998
16	Take-Two Interactive	978
17	Facebook	974
18	Square Enix	949
19	GREE	883
20	Konami	841
21	NCSOFT	769
22	ChangYou	755
23	SEGA	735
24	Zynga	692
25	BANDAI NAMCO	681

Source: Data from Newzoo 2015

device, 13% of Japanese citizens play VGs daily, and more than 40% of Japanese citizens have experienced playing VGs (CESA 2015, 102–103).

Table 2.8 presents the companies with globally high game revenues (Dec. 2014). The top companies include companies that mainly engage in VG businesses such as Square Enix and SEGA, but also include many companies engaged in other business sectors that had connections with game businesses and then entered the industry. SCE rivaled Nintendo by leveraging AV technology, Sony's specialty, and has built a solid position in the home VGI. Microsoft established its game business based on its wide range of personal-computer technology. Other companies include computer companies like Apple, which as of 2014 was in sixth place for annual game revenues, and Internet-related companies like Google, which followed Apple in annual game revenues. These companies possess technologies differing from those held by companies that specialize in VGs developed prior to the diffusion of the Internet and have strong technical development capabilities. Using their own core technologies, these companies can get involved in VGs from a viewpoint differing from that of conventional VG companies. As in the case of online games, since these companies from other business sectors have entered the VGI, it is expected VGs based on new concepts will continue to be developed.

The number of original software products being released is decreasing due to risk avoidance and decrease in development fees. Comparisons of the top 100 software products in terms of sales in Japan from 1996 to 2004 show that game series increased yearly; in 2004, 90% of the top 100 software products were series. Original titles decreased, and there were few software products that were attractive at a groundbreaking level (Koyama 2006, 1).

The late Hiroshi Yamauchi, former CEO of Nintendo, made the following comment: "Our company is creating products that are not essential for life. A special know-how is required for succeeding with non-essential products" (Nomura 2003, 120). Essential goods can be sold as long as a certain price and quality are ensured. Unless customers find something special about a VG, they will not purchase this non-essential commodity. Nobody wants to purchase cheap unattractive VGs. Looking on Nintendo's history until now, the company has a pattern of introducing new products that have adapted to new times; they are not a modified version of past products. In 2015 Nintendo took some unusual steps: the company formed tie-ups with DeNA (its first attempt to establish connection with an outside online-game company) and Universal Parks & Resorts, the managing company of Universal Studios.

In order to materialize the long-term development of the VGI, it is expected that companies will utilize the anticipated developments in scientific technologies, that new companies of other business sectors will enter the industry, and that new VG types may well appear which change our current thoughts about entertainment products. While this chapter mainly dealt with the quantitative changes in the Japanese VGI, the qualitative changes are also interesting themes for academic discussions. The information and data for this chapter has just been gathered. It is hoped this research will facilitate further research so that stories behind the movements in the markets eventually become discernible. From the information, there is one clear story that appears, however. That is, the Japanese VGI has had its own unique formation. It is the author's hope that the material presented in this chapter be used by other researchers to make geographical comparisons while extracting common characteristics to further research the VGI.

Notes

1. Some research exists (e.g., Fujita 1998) regarding reasons for the video game crisis at that time. Nintendo determined one big reason was overproduction of poor-quality software products. (See detail section "Nintendo's Development of Family Computer and Business Strategies.")
2. Approximately 275 million units, as of the end of March 2015 (The Pokémon Company 2015).
3. Details of the arcade game business around the 1970s are provided in (Fujita 1999a).
4. For Figs. 2.5, 2.6, 2.7, 2.8, 2.10, 2.11, 2.14, 2.15, 2.17, 2.19, and 2.20, and Tables 2.5 and 2.6, the earliest year is the year from which data became widely available.
5. In this chapter, the exchange rate is assumed as $1 = 120 yen at any point in time.
6. At the time, the late Satoru Iwata, previous president of Nintendo, made the following comment: "The outcomes we achieved by putting in efforts to create even more outstanding games were not recognized. People who had no time or energy for video games had lost all interest and quietly left the scene. The more I researched, the more I felt that this was a serious situation" (Inoue 2009, 45). This period of decline in the video game

market in Japan became widely known as the *geimu banare* (literally: "departure from games") phenomenon.

7. For specifics regarding the number of consoles/handhelds shipped from 1997 to 2014, refer to Table 2.5 in section "Comparing Data Compiled for Nintendo and SCE, Which Reflects the Overall Japanese Market."
8. Statistical data have been analyzed and organized in detail since the establishment of the Computer Entertainment Supplier's Association (CESA) in 1996.
9. Many other factors influence boom-and-bust cycles such as the availability of critical raw materials like coltan, a mineral "vital for electrical capacitors" (Dyer-Witheford and De Peuter 2009, 222).
10. Specifically, x86-64 Jaguar 8-core CPU and 8GB GDDR5 memory.
11. In Japan, it is usual to have capital ties among business-related companies in many industries. For example, all major automobile companies have capital ties with their parts providers. Toyota and Nissan own 20–30% capital of their own parts providers (Nikkei Inc. 2015).
12. Nintendo originally specified the minimum number of production quantity as 10,000 units and later changed this number to 5000 (Maki 2011, 6).
13. As for software units for Super Famicom, between 20 and 25 dollars per unit had to be paid in advance. To order 0.1 million units, a company had to pay approx. 2.5 million dollars (Furuhata 1995, 70).
14. The average gross profit percentage of large manufacturers in Japan is 18%. This rate is about 10 % lower than that of American manufacturers (The Cabinet Office 2013, 171).
15. Then, while the average price of a DVD player was around $450, the price of PSX at the time of its release was $330.

BIBLIOGRAPHY

BANDAI NAMCO Entertainment Inc. 2015. Kaisya gaiyou [Corporate profile]. http://bandainamcoent.co.jp/corporate/overview/index.php. Accessed 1 July 2015.

CAPCOM Co., Ltd. 2015. Kaisya syokai [Company introduction]. http://www.capcom.co.jp/ir/company/info.html. Accessed 1 July 2015.

Computer Entertainment Supplier's Association (CESA). 1998–2015. *CESA game hakusho [CESA Games White paper]*,Tokyo: CESA.

Dentsu Institute for Human Studies. 2001. *Jyouhou media hakusyo [Information media trends in Japan]*, Tokyo: Dentsu, Inc.

———. 2015. *Jyouhou media hakusyo [Information media trends in Japan]*, Tokyo: Dentsu, Inc.

Dyer-Witheford, Nick, and Greig De Peuter. 2009. *Games of empire: Global capitalism and video games*. Minneapolis: University of Minnesota Press.

Fujita, Naoki. 1998. Beikoku ni okeru video sangyou no keisei to kyugeki na hou-kai Gendai video game sangyou no keiseikatei (1) [The formation and rapid collapse of the video game industry in America – The formation process of the present-day video game industry (1)]. Kyoto: Kyoto University Economic Society. *Keizai-ronso: The Economic Review* 162 (5/6): 54–71.

———. 1999a. Famicom toujyou mae no nihon video game sangyou Gendai video game sangyou no keiseikatei (2) [The Japanese video game industry prior to the release of Famicom – The formation process of the present-day video game industry (2)]. Kyoto: Kyoto University Economic Society. *Keizai-ronso: The Economic Review* 163 (3): 59–76.

———. 1999b. Famicom kaihatsu to video game sangyou keiseikatei no soug-outeki kousatsu [A comprehensive examination of the development of Famicom and the process of the video game industry formation]. Kyoto: Kyoto University Economic Society. *Keizai-ronso: The Economic Review* 163 (5/6): 69–86.

Furuhata, Junpei. 1995. Gyakusyu suru Sony soft ni fuanmo Kokunai gameki busi-ness saizensen [Sony fights back, software doubts – The front line of the domes-tic video game system business]. *NIKKEI BUSINESS*, July 17: 68–71.

———. 2002. Nintendo shinsyacho keiei mo game mo wakaru rironnha [The new Nintendo president is a theorist who understands management and video game development]. *NIKKEI BUSINESS*, June 3: 16.

Furuhata, Junpei, and Naoki Kobayashi. 1994. SEGA Nintendo ittkiuchi [A head-to-head battle between SEGA and Nintendo]. *NIKKEI BUSINESS*, November 21: 42–50.

gameage R&I Co., Ltd. 2013. JOGA online game sijyou chousa report 2013 hap-pyoukai [Report session: JOGA online games market research report 2013]. 4Gamer.net. http://www.4gamer.net/games/999/G999901/20130723092/. Accessed 1 April 2015.

GREE vs DeNA [GREE vs DeNA]. 2012. *TRENDY*. Tokyo: Nikkei Business Publications, Inc. May: 40–44.

Hatakeyama, Kenji, and Masakazu Kubo. 2000. *Pokemon story [Pokémon story]*. Tokyo: Nikkei Business Publications, Inc.

Hirabayashi, Hisakazu, and Koichi Akao. 1996. *The university of computer gaming world*. Tokyo: Media Factory.

Ikeo, Kyoichi. 2013. Kyoukyu sinka to marketing taiou: game sangyou wo jirei tosite [Progress in supply and marketing responses: Using the video game industry as a case example]. Kwansei Gakuin University. *Shogakuronkyu*, 60(4): 41–83. http://kgur.kawansei.ac.jp/dspace. Accessed 1 April 2015.

Industry Research Division, Mizuho Corporate Bank. 2014. 5 syou game sangyou [Chapter 5 The video game industry] in Content sangyou no tenbou [Outlook on the content industry]. Tokyo: Mizuho Corporate Bank. 112–144. http://www.mizuhobank.co.jp/corporate/bizinfo/industry/sangyou/m1048.html. Accessed 1 April 2015.

Inoue, Satoru. 2009. *Nintendo "odoroki" wo umu houteishiki [Nintendo's equation for creating "Wow!"]*. Tokyo: Nikkei Publishing Inc.

Institute for Information and Communications Policy, Ministry of Internal Affairs and Communications. 2014. *Media soft no seisaku oyobi ryutsu no jittai nikansuru chousa kenkyuu [A study on the production and distribution of media software]*. http://www.soumu.go.jp/iicp/chousakenkyu/seika/houkoku.html. Accessed 1 April 2015.

Jenkins, David. 2007. Mario tops best selling game franchise list. http://www.gamasutra.com/. Accessed 1 April 2015.

Kobayashi, Osamu. 1990. Nintendo America soft kanri to syouhisya jyouhou no syusyu de 40 okudoru no sijyou wo kizuku [Nintendo of America builds $4 billion market with software management and consumer information collection]. *NIKKEI ELECTRONICS*, September 3: 149–153.

Koei Tecmo Holdings Co., Ltd. 2015. Kaisya gaiyou [Corporate profile]. http://www.koeitecmo.co.jp/company/profile/index.html. Accessed 1 July 2015.

Koei Tecmo saikouekini [Koei Tecmo obtains the highest profit ever]. 2015. *Nikkei (Tokyo)*, July 23.

Konami Corporation. 2015. Kaisya gaiyou [Corporate profile]. http://www.konami.co.jp/ja/corporate/data/index.html. Accessed 1 July 2015.

Koyama, Yusuke. 2006. Is video-game industry in Japan active? – From the analysis of top 100 sales data in 1995–2004. Paper presented at the Japan Society for Management Information, Research Report Session, Tokyo, February 18.

Kyousou housyu ga kasseikasouchi game sangyou no dynamism ni manabou [Vitalizing devices are competition and reward – learning from the dynamism of the video game industry]. 1997. *NIKKEI BUSINESS*, March 17: 29.

Maeda, Hiroyuki. 2014. *Kateiyou gameki kouboushi [The rise and fall of the home video game system industry]*. Tokyo: OAKLA PUBLISHING Inc.

Maki, Keisuke. 2011. *Nihon no video game sangyou niokeru business model no hensen [Business model changes in the Japanese video game industry]*, ed. Tatsuhiko Inoue. Tokyo: Waseda University Asian Service Business Research Institute. ASB Case, no.2. http://waseda-asb.jp/research/. Accessed 1 April 2015.

Matsumura, Takayuki. 2011. *Game sangyou no koremade no doukou to hatten korekara [Trends and the development of the game industry: The past and the future]*. Tokyo: Bunkyo University. http://open.shonan.bunkyo.ac.jp/~hatakama/zemi/matsumura.pdf. Accessed 1 April 2015.

Media and Content Industry Division, Ministry of Economy, Trade and Industry. 2003. Game sangyou no genjyou to kadai [The current state and challenges of the video game industry]. http://www.meti.go.jp/policy/media_contents/downloadfiles/kobetsugenjyokadai/geme200307.pdf. Accessed 1 April 2015.

Ministry of Economy, Trade and Industry (METI). 2006. *Game sangyou senryaku no sakutei ni mukete [Forming game industry strategies]*. Tokyo: METI. http://

www.meti.go.jp/committee/materials/downloadfiles/g60428c03j.pdf. Accessed 1 April 2015.

———. 2013. *Digital content hakusho [Digital content white paper],*. Tokyo: Digital Content Association of Japan.

———. 2014. *Digital content hakusho [Digital content white paper],*. Tokyo: Digital Content Association of Japan.

Ministry of Internal Affairs and Communications. 2003. *Jyouhou tsushin hakusyo [WHITE PAPER information and communications in Japan],* . Tokyo: Ministry of Internal Affairs and Communications.

———. 2005. *Jyouhou tsushin hakusyo [WHITE PAPER information and communications in Japan],*. Tokyo: Ministry of Internal Affairs and Communications.

———. 2014a. *Jyouhou tsushin hakusyo [WHITE PAPER information and communications in Japan],* . Tokyo: Ministry of Internal Affairs and Communications.

———. 2014b. *Jyouhoutushin media no riyoujikan to jyouhoukoudou ni kansuru chyousya houkokusyo [Investigation report on use time and behavior in the information and communication media].* Tokyo: Ministry of Internal Affairs and Communications.

Newzoo. 2015. Top 25 companies by game revenues. http://www.newzoo.com/free/rankings/top-25-companies-by-game-revenues/. Accessed 1 July 2015.

Nichols, Randy. 2014. *The video game business.* London: British Film Institute.

Nikkei Inc. 2005. *Nikkei kaisya jyouhou harugou [Nikkei company information spring].* Tokyo: Nikkei Publishing Inc.

———. 2009. *Nikkei kaisya jyouhou natsugou [Nikkei company information summer].* Tokyo: Nikkei Publishing Inc.

———. 2012. *Nikkei kaisya jyouhou huyugou [Nikkei company information winter].* Tokyo: Nikkei Publishing Inc.

———. 2015. *Nikkei kaisya jyouhou natsugou [Nikkei company information summer].* Tokyo: Nikkei Publishing Inc.

Nintendo Co., Ltd. 2015. Hardware and software sales units. http://www.nintendo.co.jp/ir/en/sales/hard_soft/index.html. Accessed 1 April 2015.

Nintendo sumaho kaitaku he tenkan [Nintendo to cultivate smartphone possibilities]. 2015. *Nikkei (Tokyo),* March 18.

Nintendo theme park sinsyutsu [Nintendo to expand business to theme park management]. 2015. *Kyoto Shimbun News,* May 8.

Nomura, Hirokazu. 2003. Game ha mada owarani [The game continues]. *NIKKEI BUSINESS* February 24: 126–129.

Okamoto, Hajime. 2011. *Kateiyou game sangyou niokeru syuchyu nitsuite [Concentration in the home video game industry].* Tokyo: Research Group of the Japan Society of Information and Communication Research. http://www.jotsugakkai.or.jp/doc/okamoto110215.pdf. Accessed 1 April 2015.

Saeki, Shinya, and Yudai Nishi. 2013. Game wo reset seyo [Reset the game]. *NIKKEI BUSINESS,* July 29: 46–53.

SEGA Sammy Holdings Inc. 2015. Kaisya gaiyou [Corporate profile]. http://www.segasammy.co.jp/japanese/pr/corp/data.html. Accessed 1 July 2015.

Shin, Kiyoshi. 2011. Download game to social game sangyou no kouzou henka ga okiteiru [Download games and social games: The structure of the video game industry is changing]. Tokyo: The Mainichi Newspapers. *Economist* 89(33): 39–41.

Shintaku, Junjiro, Tatsuo Tanaka, and Noriyuki Yanagawa. 2003. *Game sangyou no keizai bunseki [An economic analysis of the video game industry.]*. Tokyo: Toyo Keizai Inc.

Shiragami, Hiroshi. 2011. A perspective research on global trends of the game market. *Annual Review of Tohoku University of Art and Design*, no.18/19: 38–46.

Sony Computer Entertainment Inc. 2015. Sony computer entertainment enkaku [History of Sony Computer Entertainment]. http://www.scei.co.jp/corporate/history/index.html. Accessed 1 April 2015.

Square Enix Co., Ltd. 2015. Kaisya gaiyou [Corporate profile]. http://www.jp.square-enix.com/company/ja/outline/. Accessed 1 July 2015.

Tanaka, Akimasa, and Ryo Sato. 2013. Seicyou sangyou niokeru dynamic capability no kenkyuu [Study of dynamic capability of growing industry]. Paper presented at National Conference 2013 Autumn, The Japan Society for Management Information, Kobe, October 27.

Tanaka, Masaharu. 2008. *Famicom wa koushite umareta saisyukai [The birth of the Famicom last episode]*. Tokyo: Nikkei Business Publications, Inc. http://techon.nikkeibp.co.jp/article/NEWS/20081106/160885/. Accessed 15 March 2016.

The Cabinet Office. 2013. *Heisei 25 nendo keizai zaisei houkoku [Economic and fiscal policy management report FY 2013]*. Tokyo: The Cabinet Office. http://www5.cao.go.jp/j-j/wp/wp-je13/13.html. Accessed 1 April 2015.

The Editorial Office. 2013. 5 nen burini zennen wo uwamawatta kateiyou gameki [Home video game systems higher than last year for the first time in five years]. *Nikkei Entertainment*, January: 60–61.

———. 2014. 3DS to PS3 no two top ga shijyou wo hipparu: kateiyou gameki to sumaho no kakine ga nakunaru [3DS and PS3: The two top devices drive the market – No boundary between home video game systems and smartphones anymore]. *Nikkei Entertainment*, January: 58–59.

The Pokémon Company. 2015. Data ichiran [Data list]. https://www.pokemon.co.jp/corporate/data/. Accessed 1 July 2015.

Uemura, Masayuki, Koichi Hosoi, and Akinori Nakamura. 2013. *Famicom to sono jidai: tv game no tanjyo [The life and times of the Nintendo Famicom: The birth of TV games]*. Tokyo: NTT Publishing Co., Ltd.

Yada, Mari. 1996. *Game rittkoku no miraizou [The future vision of the leading nation in the video game industry]*. Tokyo: Nikkei Business Publications, Inc.

————. 2013. 'Service-oriented games' has become more popular in the game business: 'Service as a game.' Digital Games Research Association Japan. *Journal of Digital Games Research* 6(2): 47–51.

Yanagawa, Noriyuki, and Jyo Kuwayama. 1999. *Kateiyou video game sangyono keizaibunseki [An economic analysis of the home video game industry]*. Tokyo: The Research Institute of Economy, Trade and Industry. http://www.rieti.go.jp/jp/publications/act_dp.html#jp. Accessed 1 April 2015.

Yanotunetakinenkai. 2015. *Nihon kokuseizue [Japan census data book]*. Tokyo: Yanotsunetakinenkai.

Yasuyama, Seiken. 2014. *Game sangyo no doukou [The current state of the video game industry]*. Tokyo: Fukoku Capital Management, Inc.

Zackariasson, Peter, Timothy L. Wilson, Casey O'donnell, Mikolaj Dymek, Aphra Kerr, Ulf Sandxvist, Mirko Ernkvist, et al. 2014. *The video game industry formation, present state, and future*, ed. Peter Zackariasson, and Timothy L. Wilson. New York: Routledge.

CHAPTER 3

It's Dangerous to go Alone! Take this (New Technology): Nintendo's Impact on the Technological Landscape of the Video Gaming Industry

Arielle Goldberg, S. Austin Lee, and Alexis Pulos

INTRODUCTION

As I was walking through the city to work, my phone vibrated in my pocket with a new alert – a wild Pokémon just 200 meters away. So close! I could spare a couple of minutes on my commute to investigate a possible new addition to my line-up. I pulled up the app on my cell phone and gauged the Pokémon's direction … heading just slightly eastward off my normal path. My app ticked off numbers as the distance to the Pokémon kept shrinking; I was getting close. Finally, around a corner, I found a courtyard full of bushes, trees and patio furniture – a perfect hiding spot for a small Pokémon. My app alerted me – the Pokémon was in range. I could see through the foliage that it was a Pikachu! I couldn't believe I hadn't found one of the little creatures yet. Luckily, I had a couple of Pokéballs left in my inventory. I selected one and aimed just right,

A. Goldberg (✉) • S.A. Lee • A. Pulos
Department of Communication, Northern Kentucky University,
Highland Heights, KY, USA

© The Author(s) 2016   65
S.A. Lee, A. Pulos (eds.), *Transnational Contexts of Development History, Sociality, and Society of Play*, East Asian Popular Culture,
DOI 10.1007/978-3-319-43820-7_3

ready to toss the device and catch the wild Pikachu. I held my breath as a few
uncertain seconds passed, until – phew! The Pokéball stopped moving. Got it!

The opening description of this chapter may sound like a scene out of a poorly written piece of Pokémon fan fiction. However, experiences such as this will be reality for players of the upcoming Nintendo game, "Pokémon GO." Rather than control a cartoon avatar searching for Pokémon in a storybook world, as in previous iterations of the popular monster-catching game, players of "Pokémon GO" will become the avatar themselves, exploring the *real* world (or, more specifically, the software-augmented real world) in search of Pokémon, other trainers and specially organized group battle opportunities. "Pokémon GO" is one of several examples covered in this chapter of the way Nintendo creates an innovative, immersive gaming experience via creative interfaces in ways that set Nintendo apart from competitors who focus on the graphic fidelity and processing speed of games instead of the gamer's experience in, and connection with, the game-world. In this chapter, we examine the ways that Nintendo's handheld devices, controller interfaces and multimedia approach to blurring the line between the real world and game-world have laid the groundwork for the augmented reality game, "Pokémon GO."

In Chapter 2, the landscape of the Japanese video game industry was explored from a business and sales data perspective – a quantitative point of view. In this chapter, we begin to explore the qualitative changes in the video game industry, specifically through the lens of Nintendo's interfaces and the ways they facilitate immersion. To that end, we argue that Nintendo uses its essentially static character line-up to create a liminal space between not only reality and the game-world, but also between nostalgia and innovation. In this liminal space, game players' interest and imagination are captured and the experience of the avatar become synonymous with the experience of the player – creating an immersive experience through the physical interfaces that the player manipulates.

In this chapter, we first define the key terms "immersion" and "interface" in order to provide a framework for the analysis. Next, we introduce the concept of innovation in interfaces with an historical example from Nintendo's pre-console days. Then, we look at the way that portability, interfaces and the combination of these two innovations allows Nintendo to provide an immersive experience for players. We examine portability through the lens of the handheld gaming device, in its many Nintendo-made forms; for example, the Game & Watch, Game Boy and

Nintendo 3DS. Then, we discuss interfaces through the way that various controller designs throughout the lifespan of the "Legend of Zelda" series, one of Nintendo's primary intellectual properties (IPs), have facilitated a sense of immersion for players. Finally, we tie the ideas of portability and player dexterity/movement together by examining "Pokémon GO", a foray for Nintendo into both augmented reality and mobile gaming. The chapter concludes by discussing the potential future direction of Nintendo interfaces and the way that Nintendo's interface design facilitates immersion.

Immersion

The concept of immersion is often examined in the context of video games because of their interactive nature. Janet Murray (1997) conceptualizes immersion as entering a "liminal trance." In a well-developed game, all of the nuts and bolts that make the experience work are largely hidden from the player. Occasionally, the intrusion of graphical or technological glitches into the game-world ends up briefly cracking the illusion of immersion for the player. For example, in "The Witcher 3," the player may move the hero's horse down a hill; however, at release time, the horse did not stay attached to the ground as gravity would have us believe is normal. Instead of running downhill, the horse took off into the air and jittered awkwardly above the ground instead. This slight glitch in the graphics was all the more noticeable because of the realism of the rest of the game. The more immersive the game-world, the more one would think these types of "error" would become unacceptable. However, McGloin et al. (2013) found that this was not the case; the greater the sense of immersion a game generates, the more acceptable glitches have become – in fact, gamers even tend not to notice them. Thus, we suggest that immersion, to some degree, is a state of concentration generated by playing a game, rather than a sense of environmentalrealism.

So, what is it that might facilitate this "liminal trance" of immersion? Participation is a key component of video games – unlike other media, such as movies and television shows, the video game player has a role to play in the story they are watching unfold. Without the player-avatar, the game does not progress. The player is not a passive observer; the player exists within the game, represented by their avatar, as well as outside the game, directing the avatar's action through a controller interface. Murray describes the digital game as "participatory narrative," in order to separate it from the experience one has reading a novel or experiencing some other unchangeable text. The player is not just watching the game unfold; the player is concentrating on taking action, making choices by *becoming* the avatar. While experiencing the game, the player exists in a liminal space between the real world and the game-world, simultaneously experiencing the real waving of the controller or pressing of the buttons that signify avatar actions, conversations, actions, triumphs and failures of the avatar in the game-world. Thus, the player's sense of immersion in the game-world is both limited and facilitated by the interfaces – including controllers – that allow them to engage with the game. In the next section, we describe what is meant in this chapter by "interfaces" and briefly explore the present unit of analysis – the controller.

Interfaces

We begin the present examination by focusing on a specific game interface, the Nintendo controller, in order to understand how immersion has been facilitated in video games through its creative design. Games are made up of several interfaces(such as the game code, menus, avatars, and controllers) that work together to deliver the full, immersive experience of playing the game.

The controller is typically the only interface by which the player's actions in the real world translate into actions in the game-world (performed by the player-avatar), and has a measureable effect on the player's conceptualization of realism of the game, as well as spatial presence. McGloin et al. (2011) found that when playing a tennis game ("Top Spin 3"), the more "natural" the type of controller used by players affected perceptions of audio/visual realism and spatial presence (see Fig. 3.1, which depicts the more "natural" Nintendo Wii Remote versus a standard Sony Playstation 3 controller). The players were able to access a mental model of the "tennis" motion they knew to make in the real world – extending the arm, aiming at the incoming tennis ball, and swinging a tennis racket – via the interface of the Wii remote. This gave player's a greater sense of perceived reality, which McGloin and colleagues found contributed to an increase in immersion in the game.

In the next section, we begin to explore the way that Nintendo has facilitated immersion over the last few decades, from 1880s to 1970s, through the controllerinterfaces. In order to demonstrate the range of

Fig. 3.1 Nintendo Wii Remote (*left*) versus Sony Playstation 3 controller (*right*) (Sources: (*Left*) Ashida, Kenichiro, Junji Takamoto, Masato Ibuki, Shinji Yamamoto, Hirokazu Matsui, Daisuke Kumazaki, and Akiko Suga. "Controller for electronic game machine." US Patent D559,254, issued January 8, 2008. (*Right*) Schena, Bruce M. "Device having selective directional tactile feedback capability." US Patent 7,979,797, issued July 12, 2011)

interfaces Nintendo has experimented with, we begin with a brief "analog" game example of immersion from the company's early days as a card manufacturer.

FACILITATING IMMERSION THROUGH INTERFACE INNOVATION

Stacking the Deck

As we learned in the previous chapter, Nintendo's beginnings date back to 1887 in Kyoto, Japan; the company name translates as "leave luck to heaven" (Gregory 2013), which may allude to the element of chance that is found in the card games which Nintendo produced in its early years (Ryan 2012). Until the 1970s, Nintendo's main business was making handmade Hanafuda playing cards (Firestone 2011; Gregory 2013). Toward the end of its playing card reign, Nintendo produced a deck of "Pin-Up Playing Cards" that opened in an unusual way.

The box featured a seated woman and was cut so that it split diagonally across the middle, along the woman's waistline. As the player opened the box, the top half of the woman was pulled away to reveal a nude top half of that same woman underneath (Voskuil 2012). The design of the card box was not only structurally unusual, it also forcibly involved the card player in actually disrobing the woman on the card. In order to access the risqué game, the player was forced to take an active role in, the erotic design. While a small design tweak, this example illustrates that Nintendo had begun tinkering with interface design in gameplay even before the digital age.

Gaming on the Go

Around the same time that this deck of Pin-Up Cards was hitting the market in the 1970s, Nintendo began its foray into video game development and publishing. After a brief success with laser-gun shooting ranges in 1973, Nintendo acquired the rights and began to distribute the Magnavox Odyssey home gaming system in Japan. The popularity of the Odyssey led Nintendo to build on the success of this venture by partnering with Mitsubishi to create the Color TV-Game 6, a home console that allowed players to engage in virtual games of tennis (six variations, hence the name) and, soon afterwards, the Color TV-Game 15. Together, the systems moved two million units and marked Nintendo's entry into the realm of video games and home consoles (Sheff 1994). However, at this time, home consoles were not very lucrative sources of income – the games they could run were technologically limited – and it was not possible for a home player to purchase many to play on a single console.

Nintendo continued to tinker with its product offerings in order to figure out what delivery system would capture the minds and wallets of its consumer base. One of the men now leading a team of game designers at Nintendo was Gunpei Yokoi, who had come up with the hit toy "Ultra Hand," which sold 1.2 million copies in 1970 (Ryan 2012; Crigger 2007). As the story goes, Yokoi noticed a man idly pressing the buttons of an electronic calculator on the bullet train; from this observation burst forth the seed of an idea for a handheld gaming system that ran on a calculator battery (Crigger 2007; Ryan 2012). Yokoi and team turned that seed of an idea into Game & Watch, Nintendo's first handheld gaming device, and preempted a slew of games, sometimes at a rate of one per month (which, in the era of arcade gaming cabinets, was quite a fast pace). In all, the Game & Watch series accounted for 43.4 million units sold (Nintendo 2010) and piqued gaming audiences' interest in the portability of games, leading to the release and success of the Game Boy. The Game Boy, as with Game & Watch, was not remarkable in the way it displayed games or created "realistic" worlds; both devices' technological capabilities were few and the buttons were configured in a very simple layout in order to accommodate the small size of the devices and the resulting technological limits that size imposed. However, the success of the handheld devices normalized gaming "on the go," allowing video games and a sense of immersion in them to be experienced almost anywhere – as long as the battery held up. In turn, this paved the way for the next generation of handheld gaming devices: the Nintendo DS and 3DS.

Nintendo 3DS

The Nintendo DS and its successor, the 3DS, took a page from the old Game & Watch dual screen (hence the moniker "DS"), featuring a clamshell unit designed with both a top and bottom screen (see Fig. 3.2). The

Fig. 3.2 Nintendo 3DS

top screen rendered graphics in 3D and could be adjusted based on user's preference (as the dimensionality did not change the functionality of the game; it merely changed the appearance of the game and, perhaps, was an attempt to create more graphic immersion despite the low-quality images the 3DS produced in comparison to competitor devices). The touch-sensitive bottom screen was designed to be responsive to a stylus.

The DS's portability and Wi-Fi capabilities became a primary way for designers to facilitate immersion in the game-world – even when not playing a game. Each DS owner was asked to create a "Mii;" that is, an avatar that exists on the player's DS system that represents the player to other Nintendo gamers. When two DS units came into close proximity to each other, the systems' Miis would "StreetPass," or virtually meet each other, exchanging greetings and allowing the device owners to engage in visiting Miis in games. The Mii avatars allowed Nintendo DS owners to create a representation of themselves in the gaming device, in a game-world created by Nintendo and independent of any specific gaming software experience – in fact, tied to the controller/console interface itself. The DS device itself becomes a pas-sive way for the player to be present and interact with others in the game-world. By constructing and enabling this passive interaction for the gamer, Nintendo facilitates the player's immersion not in a specific game-world, but in the world of gaming itself, through the interface of the DS.

Moving on to console-dependent interfaces – that is, controller inter-faces which are not also handheld devices – we explore the way specific interface designs have facilitated players' immersion in titles throughout a very particular game-world: "Hyrule," in the "Legend of Zelda" (LoZ) series. Why this franchise? The LoZ series is one of the best-selling of all time, topping 80 million units sold and ranked as one of the top 20 best-selling video game franchises ever (Nintendo 2010; Parton 2004). LoZ is a prime example of some of the most recognizable Nintendo IPs, and because of its longevity, it dovetails nicely with a discussion of the various controller interfaces Nintendo has introduced over its time in the home console market.

"The Legend of Zelda" was introduced in 1986 and, since then, the series has grown to include more than three dozen video game appear-ances, including releases, re-releases, spin-offs and franchise character cameos in other games. However, from release to release, the storyline is basically the same: Link must travel around Hyrule to save a princess; collect important, often mystical items; grab the Master Sword (a recurring key weapon that symbolizes the player-avatar's worthiness of becoming a hero); and defeat several dungeon bosses along the way. The gameplay experience often only varies each time a LoZ game is (re-)released due to the interfaces through which the player experiences and is immersed in this otherwise routine world-saving mission. While the core experience of a Zelda game does not change from release to release, the introduction of new technology interfaces facilitates immersion, revitalizing long-term players' interest in participating in the game and keeping the LoZ series relevant to new players.

The subsequent analysis is divided into three main sections, each corresponding to a significant decade and period of change for the interface used by the player. First, we examine the way that the very "plain" Nintendo Entertainment System controller's interface facilitated immersion in the early LoZ titles (1986–1996). Then, we take a look at 1996–2006, during which the Nintendo 64 interface was introduced, which added several buttons and controls to the mix for the player and did not change significantly with the next console release (Nintendo Gamecube). Finally, we move to the next 10-year period (2006–present) and the introduction of the unique Wii remote, discussed earlier as a facilitator of more "natural" movement (McGloin et al. 2011), and its impact on player immersion.

"The Legend of Zelda"

A Bird's-Eye View (1986–1996)

The LoZ game-world is called "Hyrule;" the world is typically open to the player to explore via an avatar whose default name is "Link" (we refer to avatar and Link interchangeably in this section). Exploration was a definitive feature of the Zelda series from the start, breaking away from the side-scrolling and platforming model. Rather than viewing their avatar from the side, the player controlling Link in the original LoZ viewed their avatar from above. Link could move in any direction on the screen (left, right, up and down were available at the time), uncovering hidden items under bushes and grass and behind exploding rocky walls to reveal cave passages or secret alcoves. The player was rewarded for going off the beaten path and immersing themself in the puzzles that Hyrule had to offer.

The ability to explore in this way facilitates immersion in the game-world but does not require a complex interface. In fact, the original LoZ interface, the basic Nintendo Entertainment System controller, topped

Fig. 3.3   Nintendo Entertainment System controller

out at just four buttons plus a four-directional control pad (see Fig. 3.3). The interface, in conjunction with the top-down view of the world, allowed the exploration of the game-world to become one of the key goals for the player. Rather than simply rescuing a princess, defeating a "bad guy" and saving the world, as a typical hero story would have the player-avatar focus on, the player-avatar was also rewarded in small ways for discovering hidden paths or caves – perhaps an upgrade to a weapon, or an extra piece of heart (unit of health). Often, these discoveries were only achieved by talking to non-playable characters, veering out of the prescribed storyline and otherwise wandering about. In other words, immersing oneself in the game-world without a clear objective besides exploration was rewarded.

This general experience of immersion is necessarily facilitated through the controller interface, rather than a result of it. Despite the simplicity of the interface at this time in video game history, the designers of LoZ were able to focus the gameplay experience on exploration. In fact, the limitations of the rest of the sensory experiences of the gamer and the simplicity of the delivery itself contributed to this sense of immersion. The player could not hear Link's voice; the player could not get a strong sense of what Link or his enemies looked like; thus, the player was forced to focus on the exploration, immersing themselves in the mysteries of the game-world and the basic controls that facilitated exploration.

On Target (1996–2006)

In 1996, the N64 launched without a Zelda title. However, players were hungry for Link's next adventure and, once it was announced, presale numbers attached a significant dollar value to the fever pitch. "Ocarina of Time," the first LoZ game for the N64, launched in 1998 and tripled the presale records set by the previous title-holder, "Diddy Kong Racing," topping out at half a million units (Bulik 1999). Once the game was released, players were introduced to three major interface innovations: the Z-targeting system, a dynamic camera view and context-specific buttons.

The N64 controller contained 10 buttons, as well as a directional pad and a joystick (see Fig. 3.4). The additional buttons on this interface allowed players to customize Link's arsenal, to equip themselves with several items at once, to change the camera angle and to perform several context-specific actions that numbered well beyond the available dozen configurable buttons.

The Z-targeting system redefined the way the player controlled Link and the way Link interacted with his targets. The three-dimensional environment to which the N64 introduced LoZ players was significantly trickier to navigate for the player than the top-down iterations in the previous few games. The player's point-of-view options included one of the first examples of first-person perspectives that was not a first-person shooter. By default, however, the player's view included the avatar and was oriented as though the player were standing behind and slightly above Link. This allowed unseen enemies to creep up behind Link and damage him if the player were not carefully checking all around and rotating the camera using the

Fig. 3.4 Nintendo 64 controller

new array of C-buttons on the N64 controller interface. In addition, the new dimensions and more sophisticated controls complicated the player's attack pattern – no longer could the player simply swing in four main and four diagonal directions on a gridded field. Now, players had a 360-degree, multi-faceted field around which to swing a sword – and several more chances for their swing to be inaccurate. Overall, the feel was much more immersive for the player – they were the center of the action, rather than stuck looking on from above in some omnipotent, God-like top-down view. To ease this transition of perspective for the gamer and to allow the player to feel more naturally in control of their Link, "Ocarina of Time" introduced Z-targeting. This feature allowed a gamer either to hold or press a button on the controller (labeled "Z," hence the name) that would "lock" Link's gaze onto an object, enemy, or conversational partner in the game. The system allowed game players to immerse themselves more fully in the story by taking away the worry that a misplaced sword swing would mean the death of their Link. Instead, players could concentrate on the strategy: what is the boss's attack pattern and when can Link move in to strike? Where is this enemy's weakness? Rather than become bogged down in the mechanics of the three dimensions that were new to the Zelda franchise, the player could simply enjoy the puzzle ahead and focus on saving Hyrule.

In "Ocarina of Time," players were also introduced to context-sensitive buttons. Now a commonplace feature of most role-playing games released today, having context-sensitive buttons simply means that what each button does varies, depending on what Link is doing or what he's targeting. When Link runs up against a hole in the wall, he can crawl into it by pressing B, revealing hidden alcoves. When he targets an enemy, he can attack with B. But, if he's talking to someone, B simply advances the conversation. This contextual variation allows for a wide range of in-game action despite the finite number of button combinations. Moreover, it added to the player's sense of immersion in the game by making Link's movements more natural.

The Z-targeting system, the ability to control the avatar view and switch to first-person, and context-sensitive buttons have all evolved into common features in most adventure or role-playing games. While keeping Link's mission consistent, the developers at Nintendo utilized the new technology of the N64 controller interface to create a more immersive experience for the gamer, one that has proved successful as the tactics used are now expected features of these types of games. Next, we discuss a true game-changer in terms of controller interface design and gamer experience – the Nintendo Wii and Wii Remote.

Flailing in Real Life (2006–Present)

The Nintendo Wii was released in 2006 and, with it, came a new kind of controller: The Wii Remote (see Fig. 3.5). The Wii, argues Lee (2008), was the first console that asked a gamer to perform physical motions with a controller that felt like, and corresponded to, what their avatar was enacting in the virtual space of the video game-world. It is important to note that game interfaces requiring no controller – or specifically using the player's body as a controller, had already come before the Wii Remote. For instance, Sony's Playstation EyeToy in 2003 used a camera to capture the player's movements and translate them into in-game action. However, the webcam approach had both logistic and creative limitations – the room had to be well-lit and free of errant motion (pets and children could pose a problem). In addition, most of the games that first utilized webcam motion capture were made specifically for that purpose and did not immerse the player in a game-world – or, importantly, ask the player to don an avatar. Instead, the player themself was simply displayed onscreen as they performed realistic, tactical tasks such as dancing (see, e.g., the "JustDance" series). While controlling a game with one's body alone can be an immersive experience in a dance game, the parallel between dancing in-game and dancing in real life

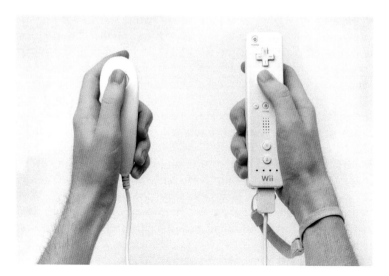

Fig. 3.5 Wii Remote (*right*) and Nunchuck (*left*)

is so close that the two experiences become the same. Consider, instead, a game such as LoZ, in which the player fights monsters with fantastical weapons and is immersed in a fictional world. Without a sword and shield in the living room, the experience of "acting out" the motions Link performs with his sword becomes less convincingly immersive.

Providing a happy medium between the webcam/no-controller combination and the completely fictional, intangible in-game items in Link's arsenal, the Nintendo Wii Remote interface becomes the player's tool both in-game and in the real world – a bow and arrow, sword, or fishing rod, for example. The player can interact with the remote just as the avatar on-screen interacts with the specifically equipped item. The Wii Remote is therefore more than an interesting periphery; it is a useful tool that simultaneously has meaning in the real world and in the game-world, further blurring the divide between player and avatar, and facilitating the player's immersion in the game-world. The interface the player sees and feels truly has meaning as both an in-game and real-life object and, moreover, allows the player more smoothly to enter the liminal trance of immersion in a game.

This idea of interface as in-game object is exemplified by the gameplay experience in "The Legend of Zelda: Twilight Princess." In the Wii version of "Twilight Princess," unlike every LoZ game that came before, the player does not have any button to press that corresponds to a sword attack. Instead, players are asked literally to swing, stab and thrust the Wii Remote in different movement patterns, which cause Link to perform different sword attacks in the game-world. For instance, in order to perform Link's famous spin attack, the player must quickly shake the Nunchuck back and forth. (The Nunchuck is a Wii Remote plug-in that connects a joystick and extra trigger buttons to be held in the player's other hand; see Fig. 3.5). This immersion achieved through movement is also added to pockets of the game that are completely optional, such as fishing. First introduced in "Link's Awakening" (created for the Game Boy, released in 1993), the fishing rod spurred entire mini-quests in "Ocarina of Time," "Twilight Princess" and "Phantom Hourglass," and can even be used to distract Ganon, one of the final bosses in "Twilight Princess." With the advent of the Wii Remote, even this non-essential equippable item got special treatment. Instead of simply pressing a button to cast a line, players arc the Wii Remote backward a bit and then forward, mimicking the way a real fishing line might be cast into a pond.

Following the introduction of the Wii remote, LoZ games also introduced social components similar to the StreetPass Plaza featured in the Nintendo DS system interface and discussed earlier in this chapter. Again, using the console itself (specifically, its connectivity over wireless internet) as facilitator and creator of a game-world independent of game, and as interface itself, the new social aspects of LoZ games on the Wii U served to facilitate the player's immersion in the game and further blur the line between reality and game-world.

The Nintendo Wii U launched in 2012, with a new "Wind Waker" experience following a year later. Similar to the port of "Ocarina of Time" on the 3DS, "The Wind Waker" re-release was essentially the same cell-shaded adventure for the GameCube, only in high definition and sporting some extra features that incorporated a more social aspect to the game. The limited additions to the original GameCube game did not dampen sales, as "Wind Waker" HD remained one of the top selling Wii U games in 2015, with 1.52 million units sold as of March 31, 2015. Harking back to the Nintendo leadership's original vision of the Nintendo Entertainment System (NES) as a communications device first, gaming console second, the Wii U version of "Wind Waker" came equipped with several social features. In general, the Wii U introduced to players the ability to write messages to one another by typing on the Game Pad or using the stylus to "hand write," earn stamps to add to those messages by playing games and add each other as friends for online play. "Wind Waker" HD took advantage of these communicative features of the Wii U by tacking on a "selfie" mode (front-facing camera, perfect for self-portraits) to the classic "Wind Waker" pictograph (a camera item with which Link may equip himself), and allowing users to send and receive messages in bottles to one another via the ocean that Link sails through during the game. The addition of these features changed nothing about the storyline; the communication aspect of the game simply allowed players a new interface – writing messages on the Wii U Game Pad (Fig. 3.6) and sending them via wireless connectivity – with which they could deepen their immersion in the game. Why send a text message to a friend when it's just as easy to send a note via the gaming console? Moreover, this marked the first add-on of social content to a LoZ game, appealing to a younger audience who had grown up with the ability to "share" built into just about every device on every platform they used and therefore appealing to the idea that, in the real world, players were already used to communicating via multiple channels.

Fig. 3.6 Wii U Game Pad
(*Source*: Tokyoship, Wikimedia Commons. "Wii U controller illustration." https://commons.wikimedia.org/wiki/File:Wii_U_controller_illustration.svg, created June 24, 2011)

Nintendo designed the messages in the bottles, then, to be an extension of the real world experience its younger players knew. Thus, this social connectivity is yet one more example of the way that Nintendo has blurred the line between real-world and game-world interaction.

As evidenced by the social additions to "Wind Waker" HD, Nintendo's strategy for immersing players in the worlds of their games is much broader than simply inventing new ways for the hardware to be handled and the way the software looks and sounds. Instead, the developers focus on the feeling a player has – is the gamer connecting with their avatar? Does the player feel as if they are having the same experience that their avatar is having in the game-world? What are the differences between the player's game-world and real-world experiences, and how can they be molded more closely into a one-"world" experience? To that end, immersion is not limited to the experience the player has in the game-world. We argue that the sense of immersion stretches beyond the console, out of Hyrule and into the real world. Nintendo affords its LoZ fans several immersive sensory experiences in the real world; these come not only in the form of merchandise, but also as fictional history books, symphony experiences and toys that bring the player full-circle back to the gaming console, Amiibo. In the next section, I explore these three real-world sensory interfaces further, again through the lens of the LoZ series (in order to rein in the scope of this chapter).

ATTRACTING NEW GAMERS AND DEEPENING EXISTING RELATIONSHIPS

Thinking Outside the Console

This section will expand on the ways Nintendo immerses its fans in game-world elements at all times, through interfaces beyond the handheld systems and console controller interfaces explored earlier in this chapter. In fact, Nintendo is not merely interested in influencing the gaming industry in the traditional sense (consoles, games and so on); the company seeks to change the way mass audiences interact (Bulik 2007). Nintendo is able to create a more immersive sensory experience for fans through real-world "extras" that deepen the relationship while gamers are not actively playing, including symphony experiences, history books and toys that have significance both in-game and in the real world.

First, we consider *Hyrule Historia*, a tome of more than 200 pages featuring information about the Zelda universe and game artwork. The book topped the *New York Times* bestseller list within a week of its release (Pitcher 2013). One of the biggest selling points for fans was its status as the official answer to several theories about whether or not a timeline exists that weaves all Zelda games together into one seamless lore. Nintendo provided an official, comprehensive timeline in *Hyrule Historia*, finally providing an answer as to why Link must continuously save Hyrule and why Hyrule doesn't seem to see Ganon coming each time. Whether they think the timeline makes sense or not, fans took this as the official word and have dubbed this book the "Zelda Bible" (Wenzel 2012). Similar to the repetition of familiar storylines, the LoZ games also feature recurring musical themes in the form of its soundtrack, created by composer Koji Kondo. Nintendo has capitalized on the fan base for this music by literally orchestrating opportunities for fans of the symphony and games alike to experience the LoZ soundtrack together.

The music of the "Legend of Zelda" franchise tells a story as important as that of the game. Fans recognize nearly every note, from the "Overworld Theme" to the triumphant fanfare Link is greeted with on opening a treasure chest or obtaining an item. Nintendo capitalized on this sonic engagement with the Legend of Zelda 25th Anniversary Symphony, a three-city "warm-up'" before the tour "The Legend of Zelda: Symphony of the Goddesses." The concerts were ticketed events in venues around the world that paired live music from the "Legend of Zelda" with pre-recorded footage of gameplay and game imagery. All images and musical arrangements were approved in advance by Nintendo – even as they release their proprietary music into the wilds of the public arena, the company retains control over how their IP is being presented and perceived. As Wenzel (2012) reported, the show's co-creator and music director, Chad Seiter, noted that everything was done "by the book," and all first-party elements were provided directly by Nintendo. But, despite its careful visual and musical orchestration, the symphony was an opportunity for Nintendo not only to deepen relationships with existing fans by providing an immersive experience for concert-goers, complete with Hyrulian crest banners and playable demos, but also to present a project created with musicians, conductors and directors who were fans of the game themselves. In addition, concert-goers who were also fans of the game eschewed normal symphony dress codes and "cosplayed" (amalgamation of costume-play, or dressing-up) as characters from the franchise. In short, it was made by fans, for fans; it facilitated a deeper immersion in this game-world for fans by legitimizing the games as artistic, providing an opportunity to publicly watch gameplay as if it were a film and, finally, to dress up as characters from the series in public – a public setting, the symphony, where such a display would normally be frowned upon.

On the horizon, a potential next step for Nintendo may create paid positions for potential employees to cosplay – think of those "real-life" versions of Mickey and Minnie Mouse at Disney World. Potential Nintendo-themed attractions could be on the horizon in partnership with Universal Parks & Resorts, which currently has international theme park locations (Walton 2015). By continually keeping the focus on the immersive experience of its gamers, rather than the hardware specifications of its consoles, Nintendo is thinking broadly and ahead. All the seemingly superfluous add-ons such as communication via messages-in-bottles in "Wind Waker," and the creation of Mii avatars to represent players in the digital Nintendo-world speak to the continuously blurring line between individuals' digital and physical personas and lay the groundwork for external game-world experiences such as theme parks and symphony concerts.

Next, we turn the lens back to the console by exploring Amiibo. Amiibo are small figurines made to look like Nintendo characters. The figurines first appeared in 2014, timed in conjunction with the "Super Smash Bros." game for Wii U. The figurines are both collectibles and game accessories; while one may think they are simply collectible figurines, and certainly function as such, they are also functional in several Nintendo games. The platform to which each Amiibo character is affixed communicates with the Wii U Game Pad controller, as well as the New 3DS XL and an upcoming peripheral addition to the 3DS, via a near-field communication device (NFC) (a technology commonly used in European banking cards). NFC allows the Amiibo to communicate with games on compatible consoles. In "Super Smash Bros.," for example, touching an Amiibo to the controller or 3DS activates a computer-controlled version of the character that the gamer can fight with or against – or even train to fight against other Amiibo or real-world players (akin to Pokémon, or a less savory comparison, dog fighting). Players may also customize the digital representation of the Amiibo to personalize its fighting style, outfit, name and appearance. Amiibo are a further example of the way Nintendo blurs the line between the game-world and the real world, of how the company creates engaging, immersive experiences via creative interfaces such as figurine-avatars and controllers, and keeps that immersion alive via sensory experiences such as symphony performances.

The Next Adventure: How Will Nintendo Stay Competitive?

Thus far, we have explored the way that Nintendo normalized portable gaming devices, introduced several immersive interfaces, and took the game-world outside the confines of the console (and even software) by engaging fans' senses through histories, symphonies and figurine-avatars that bring the fans right back to the game environment. Next, we explore the ways that Nintendo is poised to use new interfaces to facilitate immersion by combining devices' mobility, innovative interfaces and wireless connectivity. We close the section with a look at a game outside the LoZ franchise that could provide the ultimate immersive experience of augmented reality.

Mobile Games

Historically, Nintendo has been hesitant to allow partnerships with third-party developers to flourish to their fullest extent, and representatives of the company have stated that it would not bring its IP to cell phones in the form of popular, revenue-generating mobile games (Nintendo, Q & A 2015e). At this time, one of the few other groups who still consider these kinds of mobile games to be relatively new comprises scholars (Passmore and Holder 2014). However, in a move that delighted their shareholders by proving

Nintendo had a strategy to embrace this new gaming platform and aim to turn a profit out of the venture, the company announced a partnership with DeNA finally to bring its IP to mobile devices in 2015 (Brown 2015). The first game created with DeNA was called "Miitomo" and utilized the earlier-explored Mii avatars. Nintendo representatives say there will be no "recycling" of content from the NES or Game Boy; instead, the mobile offerings will use Nintendo IP in new, specific games designed for mobile devices, and will be limited to about five mobile titles released by 2017 (Byford 2015). It is a typically slow-paced move for Nintendo, as its late president and CEO Satoru Iwata explained, to allow the developers, designers and testers enough time to produce quality games that truly mesh with the capabilities of today's smartphone devices and mean something to the modern gaming audience. In Iwata's words, "even with highly popular IP, the odds of success are quite low if consumers cannot appreciate the quality of a game" (Byford 2015). In addition to taking the time necessary to produce high-quality games, Nintendo and DeNA have decided to produce smartphone games that fall into a variety of genres (Grubb 2015) in order to reach a diversified audience.

While it is unclear how the games will specifically function, we argue that these games by nature will be immersive. As anyone who has played – or read about – "Candy Crush" can attest, even the simplest mobile games have the potential to absorb players quickly. Rougeau (2014) lamented Nintendo's late entry into the mobile gaming arena: "This is the company that launched an HD console a generation later than everyone else, and still hasn't proven it can do online multiplayer right … Nintendo comes late to every trend that it itself doesn't start." However, we argue that Nintendo, having begun in the handheld gaming market with the Game & Watch, understood the appeal of mobile games long before they were played on cell phones, when the company took a chance on that handheld device born from the observation of a man playing idly with a calculator on a train. That scene seems quite similar to the modern commuter, absorbed in his cell phone on the subway.

Hardware

Hardware is another area where Nintendo tends to make decisions that separate its offerings from the pack, rather than capitalizing on things it knows gamers on a whole want to see, or have come to expect. For example, the only difference between the experience of playing the Wii and Wii U, besides a long-awaited upgrade to HD for the graphics display of the console, was the Wii U Game Pad. This is a comparatively large controller that features a screen and a stylus, in addition to a suite of buttons, that more closely resembles the organization of the Game Cube controller than the Wii Remote. The Wii U Game Pad functions in Zelda games as a permanent pause/menu screen, similar to the way that the 3DS games utilized the lower screen on the unit. While it can be said that other consoles do not provide an experience like that of the Wii U, with a second screen on the Game Pad, it has also been compared directly to the DS, which hampers the Wii U being seen as an innovative offering.

Nintendo hopes to change this with the next console, the Nintendo Switch. According to the Latino Post staff (2015), the console will be developed as an entirely new brand concept, rather than yet another update to the same type of console features (e.g. processing speed, graphics capabilities, storage) that gamers have come to expect with each new generation. At the time of going to press, Nintendo has confirmed via marketing trailers that the console will be a portable home console - a hybrid of the systems they've built so far. The console will have detachable and interchangeable controllers, and support multiplayer games played between two console units. Other features are yet to be revealed at press time. In addition, the current weakness of the existing online multiplayer gaming offerings from Nintendo, coupled with the release and marketing campaign behind 2015's Wii U game, "Splatoon," seems to indicate that online gaming could become a more serious area of focus for Nintendo. "Splatoon" is an online multiplayer game that features squid-like children in competitions that include "turf battles" wherein players on competing teams must use paint guns, rollers and other devices to cover an arena with more ink than the other team. Essentially, it is a family-friendly take on the frenzy and teamwork required of a cooperative shooter game or military simulator such as the "Call of Duty" or "Halo" franchises.

Putting It All Together: "Pokémon GO"

In this chapter, we have focused on handheld gaming, console controller interfaces, and both in-game wireless connectivity experiences and out-of-game sensory experiences that blur the line between the game-world and the real world in order to facilitate immersion, mainly through the lens of one of its landmark IPs, LoZ. To conclude, we turn our analytical lens to the future and discuss "Pokémon GO," the game previewed at the beginning of this chapter that, we argue, ties it all together.

The Wii Remote helped facilitate a connection between player and avatar that was missing from technologically bare-bones games such as the original LoZ. The line between what the player was doing in their living room and what the avatar was doing on-screen was blurred – while the player was probably not holding a sword, the Wii Remote functioned as an approximation of the on-screen weapon in order to deepen the sense of immersion the player experienced in the game-world. Player moves the remote to the right, Link moves his sword to the right. Player equips a fishing rod and flicks the remote back, then forward; Link casts his line into the pond. The bond formed between player and avatar was made tighter by connecting real-world actions to game-world actions (again, see McGloin et al. 2011).

In "Pokémon GO," players have even fewer tools – just a cell phone and - as indicated in original marketing trailers, perhaps a later addition ofa small, Pokéball-shaped, clip-on device. Instead of using these tools in the living room to facilitate some kind of on-screen experience, the tools are taken out into the real world. The gaming experience is no longer limited geographically to the console, the machine or the handheld device. Instead, the gaming experience is facilitated by a mobile phone and brought out into the real world via augmented reality experiences.

Nintendo has already laid groundwork for this type of experience and normalized the idea of meeting other gamers in the game-world. With the handheld systems described earlier in this chapter, as well as the social functionality introduced in games such as "Wind Waker," gamers expect to "meet" other gamers virtually in their DS StreetPass Plazas. In"The Legend of Zelda: A Link Between Worlds," a game for the DS, "Shadow Links" appeared throughout Hyrule. These ghostly figures represented other gamers' Link avatars. The avatars "arrived" in-game via StreetPass and could be engaged in battle for the chance to win a bounty. Other games, including "Shin Megami Tensei" and "Bravely Default," featured similar StreetPass functionality in which other players could "visit" a player's DS system in the game-world and provide helpful tips, battle assistance, or competitive gameplay outside the regular storyline.

In "Pokémon GO," the trailer suggested that players will have the ability to meet not just in the game-world, but in the real world as well, in order to carry out tasks in-game. In the trailer, an example is shown in which Mewtwo, a rare Pokémon, will appear in Times Square at a specific time for a certain length of time. "Pokémon GO" players are encouraged to meet at that location and, as a group, battle the rare

Pokémon. This blending of the in-game communication system, game-world and real world, may contribute to an even more tangible sense of immersion for players. Nintendo mirrors the way that players meet people in StreetPass, but now asking them to meet in person to play games and overcome in-game challenges – at once virtually, through the device or game, and in-person, through the shared physical experience of augmented reality. However, several months post-launch of the game, these simulated experiences in the trailers have yet to come to fruition in gameplay.

While "Pokémon GO" had a great surge in popularity at launch, the game lost steam quickly due to its incongruity with marketed game simulations. Nonetheless, the idea of moving away from the console, away from the controller, to a more purely immersive experience – is worth further examination. What will happen when Nintendo, and perhaps other developers, no longer need to create the game-world from scratch and limit its visual representations to a screen of some kind – when, instead, they are able to augment our real world in ways that facilitate immersion in their imagined game-worlds?

Conclusion

Nintendo is different from its video game console-offering peers. At Nintendo, perhaps because of its historical focus on developing mainly first-party content (in contrast to its peers), the creative process encompasses the whole of the gaming experience. Cindy Gordon, Nintendo's vice president of corporate affairs, described the creative process at the company: "Usually the way it works at Nintendo is, someone comes up with a great software idea, and that enables a particular hardware experience. Very often at Nintendo, software and hardware are intrinsically tied together" (Peckham 2012). The formula has continued to move the dial in terms of innovative interfaces, but the company's financial situation has been somewhat unclear for the past few years, as it dragged its feet entering the mobile gaming market and wrestled with leadership changes. In 2015, after the company's first profitable quarter in four years (Nintendo, Investor Relations Information 2015b; Walton 2015), Nintendo is exploring new ways to connect with its fan base and deepen the gaming experience for new and old fans alike.

Rather than race to create the most popular games, the most realistic graphics or sound quality, or even the most robust online multiplayer experience, Nintendo is focusing on the way that gamers interact with its IP both in and outside the game-world, knitting the player and avatar experience tightly together. In this chapter, we have provided an overview of the way that Nintendo has historically tied together the experience of the player, both in and outside the game-world. we have discussed how, more recently, the company has begun to use that groundwork to blend those two worlds with immersive projects such as "Pokémon GO," using the real world as game-world and asking the player to take on the role of avatar (or perhaps removing the need for an avatar entirely).

Pokémon are not new; the idea of repackaging familiar characters in new interface experiences is important to the understanding of Nintendo's role in the video game industry. Rather than focus on delivering the best graphics, the biggest games, or the fastest response times for players, Nintendo focuses on creating an immersive world in which players are able to embody familiar avatars – such as Link in LoZ, or their own self-designed Mii avatars, or to interact with familiar characters such as Pokémon. By keeping its suite of characters consistent, Nintendo is then able to focus on delivering a new experience with each interface; Nintendo fans know that there will be another LoZ game with the launch of the next Nintendo console. The excitement lies in the reveal of how the player will inhabit the avatar of Link this time around. With the release of "Pokémon GO," and its minimalistic interface that turns the real world into the game-world, Nintendo continues to push the envelope in terms of interface design but, at the same time, recycle familiar, popular IP.

Bibliography

Brown, Mark. 2015. #PGCSanFran: DeNA and Nintendo will make 5 games, from 5 IPs, by April 2017 [Update]. *Pocket Gamer,* July 8, 2015. http://www.pocketgamer.co.uk/r/Android/Nintendo+news/news.asp?c=66380. Accessed 26 July 2015.

Bulik, Beth Snyder. 2007. Nintendo is ad age's marketer of the year. *Advertising Age*, October 13, 2007. http://adage.com/article/news/nintendo-ad-age-s-marketer-year/121039/. Accessed 19 July 2015.

Byford, Sam. 2015. Nintendo will release five smartphone games by 2017. *The Verge*, My 7, 2015. http://www.theverge.com/2015/5/7/8571827/nintendo-smartphone-games-release-schedule. Accessed 26 July 2015.

Cheng, Kevin, and Paul A. Cairns. 2005. Behaviour, realism and immersion in games. *CHI'05 Extended Abstracts on Human Factors in Computing Systems.* ACM: 1272–1275. doi: 10.1.1.127.5030.

Crigger, Lara. 2007. *The rainmakers: Searching for Gunpei Yokoi.* Last modified March 6, 2007. http://www.escapistmagazine.com/articles/view/videogames/issues/issue_87/490-Searching-for-Gunpei-Yokoi. Accessed 18 July 2015.

Duffy, Owen. 2014. Board games' golden age: Sociable, brilliant, and driven by the internet. *The Guardian,* November 25, 2014. http://www.theguardian.com/technology/2014/nov/25/board-games-internet-playstation-xbox. Accessed 19 July 2015.

Ernkvist, Mirko. 2008. Down many times, but still playing the game: Creative destruction and industry crashes in the early video game industry 1971–1986. In *History of insolvency and bankruptcy from an international perspective,* ed. Karl Gratzer, and Dieter Stiefel, 161–191. Sweden: Södertörns högskol.

Firestone, Mary. 2011. *Nintendo: The company and its founders.* Edina: ABDO.

Gregory, Tony. 2013. *Freelancers! A revolution in the way we work.* Durham: Strategic Book Publishing.

Grubb, Jeff. 2015. Nintendo working on five mobile games, according to DeNa. *Venturebeat,* July 8, 2015. http://venturebeat.com/2015/07/08/nintendo-working-on-5-mobile-games-all-in-different-genres-according-to-dena/. Accessed 26 July 2015.

Kent, Steven L. 2001. *The ultimate history of video games: The story behind the craze that touched our lives and changed the world.* Roseville: Prima Publshing.

Latino Post Staff. 2015. Nintendo 'NX' console facts & features: What we know about the Wii U's successor so far. *Latino Post,* March 29, 2015. http://www.latinopost.com/articles/16263/20150329/nintendo-nx-console-facts-features-what-we-know-about-wii-u-s-successor-so-far.htm. Accessed 26 July 2015.

Leavitt, David. 2015. The legend of zelda: Symphony of the goddesses' producer on video game music. *Boston Examiner,* March 4, 2015. http://www.examiner.com/article/the-legend-of-zelda-symphony-of-the-goddesses-producer-on-video-game-music. Accessed 26 July 2015.

Lee, H. 2008. *Welcome to the Brain Age: How culture industry transforms videogames into mental training tools in the neoliberal society.* Conference papers – National Communication Association.

McGloin, Rory, Farrar, Kirstie M., and Marina Krcmar. 2011. The impact of controller naturalness on spatial presence, gamer enjoyment, and perceived realism in a tennis simulation video game. *Presence* 20(4): 209–324.

———. 2013. Video games, immersion, and cognitive aggression: Does the controller matter? *Media Psychology* 16(1): 65–87. doi:10.1080/15213269.2012.752428.

Mewes, Trey. 2014. Joystick: 'Hyrule Warriors' is a Love Letter to the 'Legend of Zelda.' *Austin Daily Herald*, October 4, 2014. http://www.austindailyherald. com/2014/10/joystick-hyrule-warriors-is-a-love-letter-to-the-legend-of-zelda-series/. Accessed 19 July 2015.

Murray, Janet. 1997. *Hamlet on the holodeck: The future of narrative in cyberspace*. New York City: Simon and Schuster.

Nintendo. 2015a. *Amiibo*. Last modified 2015. http://www.nintendo.com/amiibo/what-is-amiibo. Accessed 23 July 2015.

———. 2015b. *Investor relations information*. Last modified June 26, 2015. http://www.nintendo.co.jp/ir/en/stock/meeting/index.html. Accessed 26 July 2015.

———. 2015c. *Iwata asks*. Last modified April 2010. http://iwataasks.nintendo.com/interviews/#/clubn/game-and-watch-ball-reward/0/0. Accessed 19 July 2015.

———. 2015d. *Iwata asks*. Last modified 2009. http://iwataasks.nintendo.com/interviews/#/wii/punchout/0/0. Accessed 19 July 2015.

———. 2015e. *Nintendo Co., Ltd. DeNA Co., Ltd. Business and capital alliance announcement Q & A*. March 17, 2015. http://www.nintendo.co.jp/corporate/release/en/2015/150317qa/index.html. Accessed 26 July 2015.

———. 2015f. *Sales data*. Last modified March 31, 2015. http://www.nintendo.co.jp/ir/en/sales/index.html. Accessed 19 July 2015.

Nintendo Co., Ltd. *Financial results briefing for fiscal year ended March 2010 supplementary information*. Retrieved from http://www.nintendo.co.jp/ir/en/library/events/100507/

Parton, Rob. 2004. Xenogears vs. Tetris. *RPGamer*. Last updated March 31, 2004. Retrieved from http://www.rpgamer.com/news/japan/rp033104.html

Passmore, Holli-Anne, and Mark D. Holder. 2014. Gaming for good: Video games and enhancing prosocial behavior. *Journal of Communications Research* 6: 199–224.

Peckham, Matt. 2012. Nintendo: Wii U is core enough and it's the most innovative game system ever made. *Time*, September 17, 2012. http://techland.time.com/2012/09/17/nintendo-wii-u-is-core-enough-and-its-the-most-innovative-game-system-ever-made/. Accessed 26 July 2015.

Pitcher, Jenna. 2013. The Legend of Zelda: Hyrule Historia is a New York Times bestseller. Polygon, February 11, 2013. http://www.polygon.com/2013/2/11/3975630/the-legend-of-zelda-hyrule-historia-is-a-new-york-timesbestseller. Accessed 23 July 2015.

Rougeau, Michael. 2014. Nintendo Amiibo: Everything you need to know about Nintendo's toys-to-life figures. *Tech Radar*, November 3, 2014. http://www.techradar.com/us/news/gaming/nintendo-amiibo-everything-you-need-to-know-about-nintendo-s-toys-to-life-figures-1271347. Accessed 23 July 2015.

Ryan, Jeff. 2012. *Super Mario: How Nintendo conquered America*. New York: Penguin.

Sheff, David. 1994. *Game over: How Nintendo conquered the world*. New York: Vintage Books.

Sutherland, Adam. 2012. *The story of Nintendo*. New York: The Rosen Publishing Group.

Voskuil, Erik. 2012. Nintendo Pin-up Playing Cards (ca 1970). Last modified September 2, 2012. http://blog.beforemario.com/2012/09/nintendo-pin-up-playing-cards-ca-1970.html. Accessed 17 July 2015.

Walton, Mark. 2015. Nintendo turns a profit, reveals plans for real-life theme park. *Ars Technica*, May 7, 2015. http://arstechnica.com/gaming/2015/05/nintendo-turns-a-profit-reveals-plans-for-real-life-theme-park/. Accessed 26 July 2015.

Wenzel, John. 2012. Video games as art: 'Symphony of the goddesses' tour features legend of Zelda video games. *The Denver Post*, April 6, 2012. http://www.denverpost.com/ci_20327775/symphony-goddesses-tour-features-legend-zelda-video-games. Accessed 23 July 2015.

PART II

Mobile Social Games

CHAPTER 4

In-Game Purchases and Event Features of Mobile Social Games in Japan

Akiko Shibuya, Mizuha Teramoto, and Akiyo Shoun

INTRODUCTION: MOBILE GAME PLAYERS ON TRAINS

On board commuter trains, many passengers can be seen using their smartphones or mobile phones and moving their fingers on the screens. This scene has become common in industrial countries in recent years, and many passengers are playing mobile games in Japan. Some play games on smartphones, while others play video games on handheld consoles. Game players include middle-aged men and women, as well as children, and adolescents. Since the 1990s, children have been playing video games on handheld consoles on trains in Japan, but recent changes in mobile games

---

A major part of this study was first presented in Japanese at the Summer Research Conference of Digital Games Research Association Japan (DiGRA, Japan), at Tokyo University of Technology on August 24, 2014. It was later presented in English at the Digital Games Research Association 2015 Conference (DiGRA2015) and is available in its digital library.

A. Shibuya (✉)
Department of Humanities, Soka University, Tokyo, Japan

M. Teramoto • A. Shoun
Department of Humanities and Sciences, Ochanomizu University, Tokyo, Japan

© The Author(s) 2016   95
S.A. Lee, A. Pulos (eds.), *Transnational Contexts of Development History, Sociality, and Society of Play*, East Asian Popular Culture,
DOI 10.1007/978-3-319-43820-7_4

are attracting busy, young and middle-aged adults, as they occupy their spare time while traveling in trains.

On the popularity of mobile games, some parents, educators and policy makers are concerned that many children and adolescents are addicted to game play and spend too much time and money on games. Since these mobile social games on smartphones or mobile consoles adapt a relatively new business model, called freemium, or free-to-play model, its in-game and in-app purchases and other features, known as *gacha*, have become controversial.

Considering the social background, this study aims to assess the kinds of monetary features of mobile social games that are more likely to lead to game addiction in adolescents and young adults. Additionally, the study looks at the psychological and social contexts that can mediate or moderate the effects by combining a systematic game analysis and a longitudinal study. Firstly, we report the systematic analysis of in-game purchases, event features and lottery features of mobile social games.

Rapid Growth of the Japanese Mobile Social Game Market

The market for mobile social games is growing rapidly in Japan, and its market size in 2015 was 945 billion yen in gross sales (approximately 7.8 billion USD), which includes the market for smartphone games.[1] As shown in Fig. 4.1, the Japanese game market dramatically changed within this decade.[2]

Behind the rapid growth, some markets have shrunk. For example, the console and handheld market, which includes video game hardware and software (e.g., PlayStation 4, PlayStation Vita, Nintendo Wii, Nintendo 3DS and Xbox 360), was at its highest in 2007. However, the console market has shrunk in recent years. Prior to the rapid expansion of the smartphone market in 2012, the game market of feature phones (e.g., cell phones and mobile phones, excluding smartphones) had been developing from 2005 until 2010. Although PC and online game markets and the console and handheld software market continue to retain similar market size, the feature phone game market and the hardware market for console and handheld games have become smaller. The smartphone market, including games within social networking services (SNSs), is now the largest in-game software markets, and the Japanese game market, in total, has been rapidly expanding in recent years.

In 2014 and 2015, Japan was the number one country in terms of Android Google Play revenue and the number two country in the iOS App Store. Four Japanese games and three game publishers in Japan were ranked in the top 10 games in the world, even though those games have been played almost solely in Japan.[3] This market information suggests that Japanese social game publishers and developers, especially for smartphones, have been extremely successful as gaming business.

Background of Mobile Social Game Market in Japan

The rapid expansion of mobile social games in Japan can be attributed to specific social, cultural, historical, economic and psychological contexts. Although this chapter focuses on monetary features of the games such as *gacha* and events, there are a number of other features worth mentioning.

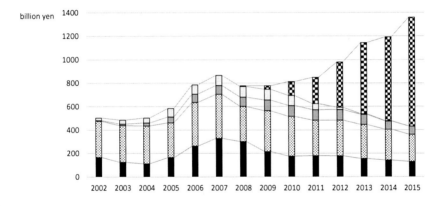

Fig. 4.1 Changing market of digital games in Japan (Sources: Data from カドカワ [Kadokawa dwango], ファミ通ゲーム白書 2016 [Famitsu game white paper 2016] (Tokyo: Kadokawa dwango, 2016), 330–331; 総務省情報通信政策研究所調査研究部[Institute for Information and Communications Policy (IICP) Ministry of Internal Affairs and Communications (MIC)], 平成25年度ICT新興分野の国際展開と展望に関する調査研究報告書 [A survey research report on ICT international development and outlooks of new ICT areas] (IICP 2014), 16, accessed May 31, 2015, http://www.soumu.go.jp/iicp/chousakenkyu/data/research/survey/telecom/2014/2014game.pdf)

Mobility and Social Networking Features

One reason for the rapid expansion of these social games is the mobility feature, making possible for players to play games while engaging in other activities such as commuting on public transport, eating lunch, watching TV or getting ready for bed. The availability of the games leads individuals to play more frequently.

Another reason for this rapid growth could be attributable to SNS connections, especially in combination with mobility. Through these SNSs, social games can become more popular with players introducing friends to the games or sharing with friends. From this perspective, social games can be narrowly defined as games played within SNS. In Japan, GREE, Mobage (SNS operated by DeNA), mixi, Ameba (SNS operated by Cyber Agent), LINE and Facebook are all popular SNSs, or social apps, for social games. Mobage and GREE saw rapid expansion when they started social games in 2006 and 2007, respectively, especially as mobile phone-based SNSs, and both have created large SNS platforms for mobile games.[4] As shown in Fig. 4.1, these developments and success in mobile phone markets are important factors prior to the onset of the smartphone.

Through these SNSs, social games have developed, with the definition of social games referring to games based on web browsers that are found through SNSs,[5] including on mobile phones, smartphones and PCs. However, social games in the Japanese setting often include games in smartphones and referred to as "social game apps,"[6] or *soshage* (a shortened combination of the Japanese pronunciation of the words 'social' and 'game'), partly because some games have been developed with mobile SNSs or social apps, such as LINE or mixi.[7]

Monetary Features of Games

Another reason for the rapid expansion of the mobile market in Japan is the monetary feature as a business model. Mobile social games often adapt the freemium model, which was popularized by venture capitalist Fred Wilson and writer Chris Anderson, a word that combines the words "free" and "premium."[8] Unlike packaged games, the freemium model, or free-to-play model, allows players to start playing games for free, but the game then prompts players to purchase useful game items. Social games present players with alerts to purchase useful items for continual play, stamina-restoring items, weapons and costumes, by spending real money (or coins used in SNSs, which correspond to real money).

A project team, consisting of industry and academic leaders in Japan, has summarized social game mechanics as a business model with the following features[9]: (1) games are basically free of charge, (2) they are easy to play at the outset (e.g., gaming skills are not usually required), (3) players can expand play by making in-game purchases, (4) player retention and satisfaction occur through the creation of a community or social networking, (5) game publishers keep players active by planning events and (6) game publishers analyze player data to improve satisfaction and retention rates. Nojima (2011) also described three stages of social game services: *hook* (providing a chance to play), *retention* (keeping players playing continuously) and *monetization* (motivating players to pay for game features).[10]

The social game experience has been discussed in terms of player perspectives in Finland.[11] In Japan, some studies have focused on players' motivations for playing social games, and business models of social games have been examined.[12] Among these features of social games, we focused on monetary features, especially in-game purchases, the *gacha* system and event features. Such in-game purchases are not new to the game industry.[13] However, the rapid expansion of mobile phones and smartphones, as well as mobile social games among teenagers, has begun to cause social problems in Japan,[14] and criticism was particularly strong concerning certain types of *gacha* in 2012.

Gacha

In social games, players can use *gacha*, which are similar in screen appearance to vending machines that dispense children's toys, and lucky players can win valuable gaming items this way. *Gacha* is onomatopoeia; the sound of the word imitates the sound of a crank on a toy vending machine. *Gacha* can be free to play; however, rare and/or valuable gaming items often need to be obtained through special *gacha* with monetary purchasing. Unlike gambling, players cannot obtain real money as a reward within the context of games. However, the perception of reward from obtaining rare and special items, such as strong weapons or cards from *gacha*, can be similar to that of gaining monetary rewards from gambling. Players can experience the sensation of a "big win" by paying increasingly larger amounts of money. Therefore, *gacha* can be compared to gambling as it represents a lottery within the context of a game, and it is often referred to as simulated gambling.

We use the phrase *gacha* throughout this study because *gacha* (or *gachagacha, gachapon, gashapon*) are commonly found in Japan, in places such as toy stores and supermarkets. Children use real money, usually 100 to 500 yen, to purchase toys from *gacha* machines. Invented in the United States as a gum machine, *gacha* was first introduced in Japan in 1965[15] becoming a popular form of toy capsule machine. As shown in Fig. 4.2, *gacha*, or toy capsule machines, are available in toy stores, supermarkets and gift shops. Some toy stores stock dozens of *gacha* machines. Not only children and adolescents but also young and middle-aged adults buy their favorite or unique characters or items just for fun, which are used as topics of conversation or memories of travels. In 2015, the toy capsule industry reached 3.16 billion yen (approximately 259 million USD).[16]

"Kompu Gacha"

One particular type of *gacha*, the so-called *kompu gacha*, was criticized. This *kompu gacha* (an abbreviation of "complete *gacha*,") provided players with opportunities to obtain especially rare and valuable items by

Fig. 4.2 Examples of toy capsule machines, often called *gacha, gachagacha, gachapon* or *gashapon*. Each costs usually 100 yen–500 yen. These toy capsule machines are often found in arcade, toy stores and supermarkets in Japan. Children and adults can obtain small toys or figures from the toy capsule.

collecting complete sets of cards, items with *different* marks or numbers. When *kompu gacha* was on the market, some players became far too involved in collecting all the cards and spent a great deal of money.[17] The mechanics dramatically increased the revenue, partly because it provided players with some cognitive biases through the perception of "reaching the goal" or "I have nearly completed the collection except for one card," which is similar to the perception of "nearly winning" in gambling.[18] In addition, some players earned real money by trading valuable cards or duplicating cards.[19]

In 2012, the media criticized *kompu gacha*, as did the Consumer Affairs Agency in 2012. Because of the criticism, major social game platforms and developers decided to restrict *kompu gacha*. The mobile game industry in Japan set a monetary limit of less than or equal to 5000 yen (approximately 50 USD) for players aged 15 years or under and 10,000 yen (approximately 100 USD) for players aged 18 or under. Some games in smartphones also set monetary limits for minors of up to 20,000 yen per month or 5000 yen for 15 years and under. Additionally, minors are requested to obtain the permission of parents or guardians. Moreover, mobile console companies and consumer agencies started to recommend that parents discuss the game system with their children, set passwords and not link any credit cards or phone bills to the games.[20] However, the effects of these measures have not yet been empirically tested.

Limited-Time Events

In addition to the in-game purchases and *gacha* discussed above, this study also focused on features of limited-time events. These types of events are of interest because they motivate players to pay large amounts of money during limited periods in order to obtain rare and valuable items or cards.[21] For example, events can be scheduled on weekends, and if a player is ranked within the top 1000 players, that player can obtain special cards or items. If the player is within the top 100, then he/she receives cards or items that are even more valuable. Some players collect items that restore stamina or health when events are not held and "run for an event," which means working hard and achieving high scores for the event in order to obtain high-ranking awards. Events can vary, and some events offer limited-time *gacha* or limited-time only discounts.

A number of other industries in Japan frequently use these limited-time campaigns and products. Some food companies provide "limited-time only increased amount" on products such as of potato chips or "limited-time only" flavors. Some drink companies collaborate with an animation company or a dinnerware maker, and consumers can obtain valuable items by buying a certain numbers of products during limited-time events. As in other countries, Japanese companies use these limited-time strategies to help attract the attention of consumers and motivate them to buy more of their products. Japanese food and drink companies are always looking for innovative ways to offer products, and Japanese social games often use limited-time only event strategies in the same way.

Limited-Time Gacha

In limited-time events, players can draw limited-time *gacha* or *gacha* that is only available for a limited time. For example, *Puzzle and Dragons* (GungHo Online Entertainment 2012b), one of the most popular mobile games in Japan, has several different *gacha*, including special *gacha* (e.g., a rare egg machine) in which special stones, called Magic Stones, need to be obtained by the player. Also in this game, players can obtain rare and valuable characters for limited periods (e.g., during a special festival). Although players can collect Magic Stones through other means (e.g., logging in to the game every day or completing a series of adventures), players are able to continue playing *gacha* until they obtain the characters they want through making monetary purchases.[22] There are many other games that feature this type of limited-time *gacha*, and, as yet, the degree of its availability and psychological effects remain unknown.

"Step-Up Gacha" in Limited-Time Events

Other types of *gacha*, the so-called step-up *gacha* or box or package *gacha*, are designed to attract players and are offered as limited-time events. While players can draw the *gacha* only once, game companies provide players with chances to draw the gacha multiple times (e.g., 10 times) in order to obtain rare and valuable items for sure. The contexts of "step-up *gacha*" vary. For example, in some games, 100 cards are packaged as a box set, with the pack containing one extremely rare and valuable card and some moderately important cards. Whenever a player draw the *gacha*, the probability of obtaining the extremely rare and valuable cards increases or "steps-up" (e.g., 1/100, 1/99, 1/98…1/3, 1/2, 1/1). In this "step-up" *gacha* (sometimes referred to as "box *gacha*"), enthusiastic players sometimes draw all 100 *gacha*. This type of "step-up gacha" can be more problematic than normal and limited-time *gacha* because players are strongly encouraged to spend more money by giving the biased impression of being "very close to the goal."

Since 2012, when the problems and criticism relating to social games arose, the amount of media coverages regarding "*gacha*" has decreased. However, as seen in Fig. 4.3, the number of consulting cases involving minors has not decreased, partly because of the expansion of smartphones and the attraction of social games for young individuals.[23] According to a survey conducted by CESA in 2013 and 2015, teenagers aged 15–19 were the most frequent mobile social game players among all age groups.[24] While the limits imposed on the amount of money that can be used by minors have helped to minimize problems relating to in-game purchases, the freemium model has remained opaque. The model is poorly understood and has not gained acceptance by society in general, nor within the game

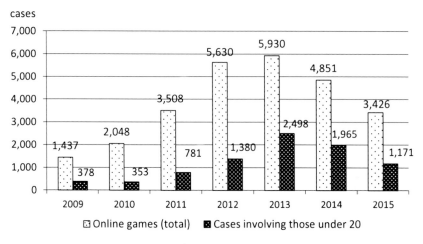

Online games (total)   Cases involving those under 20

Fig. 4.3   The number of consumer problems with online game involving minors (registered with PIO-NET, registration by February 28; the number of 2015 does not include consultation cases from local consumer centers) (Sources: Data from 国民生活センター相談情報部情報通信チーム[National Consumer Affairs Center of Japan, Consultation Information Division, Information Technology Team]. "オンラインゲームに関する消費生活相談[Consumer affairs consultation information on online games]," 9, accessed August 18, 2016 http://www.caa.go.jp/adjustments/pdf/160324shiryo2.pdf). PIO-NET is Practical living Information Online-NETwork, which is an online network connecting NCAC and local consumer centers (http://www.kokusen.go.jp/e-hello/ncac_work.html)

industry and among players. Therefore, empirical studies that specify the mechanics,[25] or *real* features of games, in terms of in-game purchases are now necessary.

In order to establish empirical findings regarding monetary and event features of mobile social games, we developed four research questions based on the social backgrounds of the games in Japan:

RQ1: What are the most frequently made in-game purchase categories in mobile social games in Japan?

RQ2: (1) What is the ratio of social games that have in-game purchases where players are asked to report their age? (2) When players are minors, what is the ratio of social games that have in-game purchases where players are asked to obtain permission from a parent or guardian?

RQ3: What are the most frequently occurring limited-time events in mobile social games in Japan?

RQ4: Are there any differences between limited-time only *gacha* and normal *gacha* in terms of availability, probability of obtaining the rarest items, and the highest cost?

A Systematic Analysis of Interactive and Online Game Mechanic

This study used a content analysis method that had been previously used in the analyses of violent content and gender representation in video games.[26] However, the content of games can vary according to the players, as well as when and how long a game is played and traditional methods of content analysis do not necessarily reflect interactive and online features of the game experience.[27] Social games are usually based on online services, and their content can change depending on the amount of time the game is played and the choices made by players. Moreover, the mechanics of online services are subject to change by game publishers and developers. This study attempts to assess these interactive and online features in terms of game mechanics, by assigning multiple coders to play the games for multiple days. Regarding game mechanics, Elson et al. (2014) explained the game experience using three components: narrative, mechanics and context.[28] The present study focuses on elements of mechanics, which can be seen as *real* features of games, or rules of play.[29] On the other hand, traditional content analyses of video games have previously dealt with the narrative aspect, or *fictional* features, of games.

SELECTION OF GAMES AND ANALYSIS OF CONTENTS: METHOD

Survey for Sampling Games

Participants as Game Informants

Teenagers (n = 950, 475 men and 475 women) and young adults (n = 1710, 508 men and 1202 women) participated in the study in the role of game informants. They were volunteers, registered with a mobile online research company, who had agreed to participate in studies such as the current study.

Survey Procedure

In order to select popular social games played by young people, we conducted a survey in November 2013, with the game informants described above. They were asked whether they had played social games, including smartphone games such as *Puzzle and Dragons* (GungHo Online Entertainment 2013), or *LINE POP* (LINE 2012a), in which players are able to cooperate or compete with other players by using mobile devices, such as cell phones, smartphones or mobile terminals (excluding game consoles) within the last month. Participants who responded "yes" to the above question, and who were between 15 and 29 years old, were requested to provide further responses to the subsequent questionnaires.

One of the purposes of this study was to investigate the effects of monetary features of games on the psychological characteristics of users. We therefore used a quota system and assigned a greater number of players that paid additional money during social games to participate in the survey. Among 2600 game informants, there were 570 non-paying (NPPs) and 380 paying teenage players (PPs)[30], in a total of 950 teenagers. In the young adult group of 1710 players, there were 1140 PPs, which was double the number of NPPs.

The ethical committee of the first author's university approved this survey. The informed consent of participants was considered unnecessary, as they had volunteered to participate in such studies. They were free to withdraw from the study at any time. The anonymity of all participants was also assured.

Sampling Popular Games

All the game informants were asked to list up to three games that they had played most frequently within the last month. Table 4.1 lists the 30 most popular social games played by young people. Two games tied as the 30th most popular game, and as such, 31 games representing the most popular social games in Japan were analyzed.

Coding Procedure of Game Analysis

Participants as Game Coders

Coders ($N = 11$) with experience in playing social games (8 male university students and 3 male graduate students) were recruited for this study in February and March 2014.

Coding Process

First, we held training sessions for all coders and explained the game coding procedures, operational definitions and coding categories. Then, we asked the coders to analyze one game after watching the play screen and made sure that they correctly understood the coding categories. After the training sessions, we randomly assigned three coders to each of the 31 games. The mean number of games analyzed by each coder was 8.45 games. Since the coders needed to understand the game mechanics,[31] the coders played the social games while recording the play screens for 30 minutes per day over 3 days. Each coder was then asked to fill out a coding sheet after playing each game. All game play and analyses were conducted in the first author's laboratory.

The 31 games included apps obtained from Google Play and App Store. We used two Android OS terminals and two iPhone terminals and four smartphones for which we signed service contracts with a mobile phone service provider. In order to keep the social features active among the coders, four new accounts (e.g., GREE, Mobage, LINE, Twitter and Google+) were created for each terminal.[32] All four accounts were registered as friends or followers. Coders were asked to write comments, or "tweets," when an action was requested by an app. While playing, coders were asked to make in-game purchases for up to 1000 yen when it was required for accurate coding. The coders used prepaid cards that were funded by this research project to pay for in-game purchases.

Table 4.1   Samples of social games analyzed

Rank	Game title	Frequency	Platform[a]	Publisher/Developer
1	Puzzle and dragons	910	Google[b]	GungHo[c]
2	LINE pop	325	LINE	LINE
3	LINE pokopang	313	LINE	LINE
4	LINE bubble	202	LINE	LINE
5	Quiz RPG: The world of mystic Wiz	128	Google	COLOPL/Kuma the Bear
6	LINE windrunner	124	LINE	LINE
7	Puyopuyo! quest	73	App Store	SEGA
8	Idolm@ster Cinderella girls	60	Mobage	DeNA
9	Love live! school idol festival	59	App Store	Bushiroad/Klab
10	Princess punt sweets	54	Google	GungHo
11	Rage of Bahamut	50	Mobage	Cygames
12	Girl friend (beta)	48	Ameba	Cyber Agent
12	Dragon collection	48	GREE	Konami[d]
14	Clash of clans	40	App Store	Supercell
15	Chain chronicle	38	Google	SEGA
16	Hay day	37	App Store	Supercell
16	Battle cats	37	App Store	PONOS
18	Sengoku collection	36	Mobage	Konami
19	AKB stage fighter	35	GREE	Ateam
20	Hakoniwa [miniature garden][e]	31	GREE	GREE
21	Candy crush saga	30	Google	King[f]
21	Gundam card collection	30	Mobage	Bandai Namco[g]
23	Nouen hokkorina [cozy farm][e]	29	Mobage	DeNA
24	Divine gate	27	Google	GungHo/Acquire
24	Tanken [adventure][e] driland	27	GREE	GREE
26	Moba pro [mobile online pro baseball game][e]	27	Mobcast	Mobcast
26	Animal boyfriend	27	GREE	Ambition
28	Fairy doll	24	GREE	Ambition
29	Solitaire	23	Google	Mobility Ware
30	One piece grand collection	21	Mobage	Bandai Namco
30	My forged wedding	21	GREE	Voltage

[a]Platform: Most frequently cited platform in the survey. Certain games can be obtained in multiple platforms

[b]Google: Google Play

[c]GungHo: GungHo Online Entertainment

[d]Konami: Konami Digital Entertainment

[e]English translation or explanation was added by the first author in [...]

[f]King: King Digital Entertainment

[g]Bandai Namco: Bandai Namco Entertainment.

Four digital video camera recorders mounted on four tripods recorded the play screens. Coders referred to their play screen while they filled out the coding sheets. The coders completed two sets of coding sheets, one for the first day and the other for the second and third days, based on the operational definitions and coding categories of the study. The unit of analyses was each social game.

Operational Definitions and Coding Categories

In-Game Purchases

In order to answer RQ1, in-game purchases were operationally defined as "purchasing costumes, weapons, items for restoring-stamina, proceeding with the story, and further battle time, and multi-purpose items within the games and apps, paid for with game coins or gold, which were obtained through actual monetary payments. Additionally, in-game purchases included playing paid *gacha*, which could involve playing roulette or a lottery, by the use of game coins or gold obtained through monetary payment." The in-game purchase features were coded according to the presence or absence of the following nine categories: (1) restoring stamina or health or proceeding with the story or adventure[33]; (2) continuing battles with other players; (3) recommencing the game by starting over at the final stage after the game was over (e.g., "continue?"); (4) increasing the number of items that players owned; (5) increasing the number of friends; (6) purchasing other items, such as weapons, costumes and tools; (7) watching a special story; (8) obtaining rare cards or other items through *gacha*, roulette or a lottery; and (9) purchasing multi-purpose items that could be used for more than three of the purposes (1)–(8) above. In addition, when *gacha* was present, coders were requested to provide information about (a) the availability of information on the probability of obtaining the rarest items, (b) the probability that players could obtain the rarest items and (c) the highest cost for playing *gacha*.

Moreover, in order to answer RQ2 (1) and (2), when in-game purchases were possible, a questionnaire was used to inquire (a) whether players had been asked to report their age and (b) whether players had been asked to obtain permission from their parents or guardians.

Limited-Time Events

To answer RQ 3 and 4, we requested the following information about limited-time events: (1) the availability of limited-time events in general (e.g., 1-hour open adventures, limited-time *gacha*, battles, rankings and discounts); (2) the availability of limited-time only *gacha*, any additional information for available limited-time *gacha* regarding (a) the availability of information about its probability that players could obtain the rarest items, (b) the probability that players could obtain the rarest items, (c) the highest prices for using *gacha* and (d) the presence of step-up *gacha*, in which players are able to increase the probability of obtaining rare items by paying more (e.g., when the number of items to draw is limited or when all players can obtain specific rare items or cards by playing paid *gacha* continuously 10 times); (3) the availability of limited-time only rankings, in which top-ranking players are able to obtain rare items; and (4) finally, availability to purchase limited-time only discounts.

Reliability

For all 31 games, reliability coefficients of six results (two coding sheets from each of the three coders) were calculated by using the multiple coder version of Scott's pi[34] for all 18 categories. Nearly all the median reliability coefficients were above 0.86. For one variable, the median coefficient was less than 0.80, which was "limited-time only discounts" (0.56). Since this feature was often found in limited-time events and was only available to certain players, all the categories were considered as having acceptable validity for conducting a systematic analysis of online services and interactive media.[35]

RESULTS OF THE SYSTEMATIC ANALYSIS

In-Game Purchases Were Present in 97% of the Games

In-game purchases were possible in 30 (97%) of the 31 games. Two types of payment appeared to be most frequent: one was for *gacha*, including payments for playing roulette or lotteries, that were found in 27 games (87%) and the other was "payments for restoring stamina or health, or proceeding with the story or adventure," found in 27 games (87%). As shown in Fig. 4.4, "purchasing other items," and "purchasing multi-purpose items," also occurred frequently.

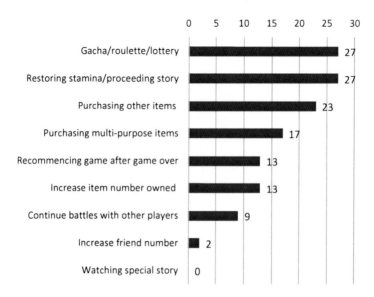

Fig. 4.4 Frequencies of in-game purchases

Table 4.2 The comparison of *gacha* in amount and probability

Average (range)	Normal gacha	Limited-time gacha
Number of games	27 games	26 games
Average amount of most expensive *gacha*	430 Yen (4 USD)	911 Yen (9 USD)
(Range)	(40–1200 yen)	(40–4883 yen)
Probability information	14 games	17 games
Average probability of obtaining the rarest items	2.85%	5.15%
(Range)	(0.05–8.33%)	(0.05–36.67%)

As described in Table 4.2, the average cost of the most expensive *gacha* was 430 yen (approximately 4 USD), with prices ranging from 40 yen to 1200 yen. Among the 30 games facilitating in-game purchases, five games (17%) inquired as to the age of players. In four of these five games (13% of 30 games), minors were requested to obtain the permission of a parent or guardian before making purchases. Children under 13 years were not permitted to make in-game purchases in only one of the games.[36] For normal *gacha*, information on the probability of obtaining rarest items was observed in 14 games; the mean probability was 2.85% (SD = 3.07%), with a range between 0.05% and 8.33%, depending on the game.

Limited-Time Events Were Found in 90% of Games

Limited-time events were found in 28 games (90%) and limited-time *gacha* was the most common in these categories, found in 26 games (84%). "Limited-time only discounts" were second (65%, 20 games), whereas "limited-time ranking" was found in less than half the games (48%, 15 games).

Comparisons of Normal and Limited-Time Gacha

Among the games featuring "limited-time only *gacha*," the most expensive *gacha* (M = 911, SD = 1096) cost significantly more than normal *gacha* (M = 430, SD = 1200; $t(24)$ = 2.15, p = .042). The mean cost of limited-time only *gacha* in each game ranged from 40 to 4883 yen. Information on the probability of obtaining the rarest items in limited-time only *gacha* was provided in 17 of the games. Although the probability of obtaining the rarest items (M = 5.15%, SD = 8.88%) was higher than it was in normal *gacha* (M = 2.85%, SD = 3.07%), this number was not statistically significant ($t(13)$ = 1.05, p = .315). The average probability of gaining items from limited-time only *gacha* in each game ranged from 0.05% to 36.67%. Finally, step-up *gacha*, in which the probability of obtaining rare items increases through higher payments, was found in 17 games (55%).

DISCUSSION

This study systematically analyzed the contexts of in-game purchases and event features in mobile social games. The study found that *gacha*, and "stamina-restoring or proceeding with the story," were the most frequent categories that required in-game purchasing. Teramoto et al. (2014) found the highest positive correlation between the tendency to use *gacha* and the monthly payment for mobile social games.[37] Therefore, the results of the current study suggest that the presence of *gacha* helps to monetize these games and that extensive use of *gacha* could lead to players spending more money.

"Stamina-restoring or proceeding with the story" was found as often as *gacha*. By continuing to buy and use items, players can continue playing the game for longer periods. Therefore, exposure to this feature should focus on analyzing the time and money spent on game play. However, Teramoto et al. (2014) found weaker positive correlations between the "stamina-restoring or proceeding with the story" feature and the amount of money players spend monthly on games.[38] This type of feature alone may not lead to increased monetary purchases. That is, there are other motivations or mechanisms (e.g., obtaining rare items in limited-time events, advancing faster through a story in limited-time events) that may lead players to buy items to restore stamina and proceed with the story.

Regarding the age question, only 13% of social games where in-game purchases were possible requested minors to obtain the permission of a parent and guardian. Although other games requested passwords or had monetary limits for minors, these games might prevent children or adolescents from making additional purchases in social games. Further studies about their effects would provide the necessary empirical evidence.

During limited-time events, limited-time *gacha* was offered in a number of games. The average probability of obtaining the rarest items was somewhat higher than that of normal *gacha*, although the maximum cost of this type of *gacha* was higher than for normal *gacha*. Teramoto et al. (2014) found that players who frequently use this limited-time *gacha* spent more money on mobile social games.[39] Therefore, these types of limited-time events may motivate some players to use *gacha* more frequently because players might assume that they are being presented with "an ideal time to make in-game purchases!"

More interestingly, this study also found that the limited-time events were *not* limited to a certain period in a literal sense because the reliability of event-related categories, with the exception of limited-time discounts, was consistent among coders. If the limited-time events were rare, and truly available only for a limited time, their reliability could be considered low because coders played for 3 days, and they should have been presented with the event for one day or one player only. Although coders found different events at different times, the consistent results of this study (e.g., nearly all 3 days or three players) indicated that game publishers present events on a near-constant basis, in order to keep players active.[40] This infers that had the coders played for more days (e.g., 10 days), the reliability of limited-time events could be considered even lower than it was for 3 days.

There were several limitations to this study. First, the results were based on a playing period of only 3 days on for each coder. Some games may require a certain number of days of play before a player can buy some items or use certain *gacha*. Second, although this study found many games included *gacha*, step-up *gacha* and limited-time only *gacha*, these features did not always lead players to spend additional money. In further empirical studies, interactions between game mechanics and age, gender, personality-types, motivations and psychological characteristics of players could be considered. In addition, this study did not assess other important features (e.g., social features, attractive characters, stories, voices and other game design aspects). These features can also affect players' level of satisfaction and monetization.[41]

In spite of these limitations, this study highlighted the mechanics of in-game purchases and event features of mobile social games in Japan and found that the mechanics vary among games. Behind the successful game business, Japanese game publishers, developers, social platform companies, mobile console makers, consumers and governments seem to be struggling to balance revenue, player motivations and social acceptance of this relatively new form of entertainment. We, as authors, hope this research will provide insight into the mobile game industry and mechanisms based on empirical evidence and that it will assist with the building of socially acceptable gaming mechanics.

The final purpose of this study was to analyze the effects of monetary features of social games on game players by combining systematic analysis and survey data. This chapter is only the first step, and we cannot make any suggestions or solve any social conflicts based only on this analysis. However, the results might help reveal relatively unknown mechanics of social games in a Japanese cultural and social context to non-Japanese readers through the empirical analysis presented. We are unsure whether Japanese mobile social games will continue to be successful, but it might depend on how well new game mechanics are understood and accepted among game players in Japan and throughout the world. We hope this chapter provides some insight and understanding.

NOTES

1. See Computer Entertainment Supplier's Association, CESA, (2016) "*2016 CESA games white paper.*" (Tokyo: CESA, 2016), 138.
2. See カドカワ[Kadokawa dwango], "ファミ通ゲーム白書2016 [Famitsu game white paper 2016]," (Tokyo: Kadokawa dwango, 2016), 330–331.
3. See "*App Annie Index: 2014年総括 アプリ市場動向レポート*[App Annie Index: 2014 summary; A report about trends of application market]."

App-Annie-Index-2014-Retrospective-jp. pdf. Received this pdf file by signing up for App Annie; *"App Annie 2015 retrospective."* App-Annie-2015-Retrospective-EN. Received this pdf file by signing up for App Annie.

4. See 田中辰雄山口真一[Tatsuo Tanaka and Shinichi Yamaguchi], ソーシャルゲームのビジネスモデル:フリーミアムの経済分析[Business model of social games] (Tokyo: Keisoshobo, 2015), 227–235.

5. Computer Entertainment Supplier's Association (CESA). *2014 CESA games white paper*, 137.

6. エンターブレイン[Enterbrain]. ファミ通ゲーム白書2014 [*Famitsu game white paper 2014]*, 322–323.

7. For social mechanics, see Akiko Shibuya, Mizuha Teramoto and Akiyo Shoun. "Toward individualistic cooperative play: A systematic analysis of mobile social games in Japan." In D.Y. Jin (ed.) *Mobile Gaming in Asia, Mobile Communication in Asia: Local Insights, Global Implications* (Dordrecht: Springer, 2017), 207–225.

8. See Chris Anderson, *Free: How today's smartest businesses profit by giving something for nothing.* (New York: Hyperion, 2009), 26.

9. See 三菱総合研究所[Mitsubishi Research Institute], 平成24年度コンテンツ産業強化対策支援事業(ネットワーク系ゲーム環境整備研究事業)報告書 [A report about a project of supporting strategies of content industry (a research project of reconstructions of environment of networking games)]. March, 2013, accessed June 1, 2015. http://www.meti.go.jp/meti_lib/report/2013fy/E002770.pdf.

10. See 野島美保[Miho Nojima], "ソーシャルゲームにおける日本型データ・ドリブンのあり方とは [How should the Japanese model of data-driven in social games?]," Business Media Makoto. September, 2011, accessed March 4, 2014. http://bizmakoto.jp/makoto/articles/1109/22/news015.html.

11. See Janne Paavilainen et al., "Social Network Games: Players' Perspectives." *Simulation and Gaming*, 44, no.6 (December 2013): 794–820, accessed May 31, 2015. http://sag.sagepub.com/content/44/6/794.

12. See 新井範子[Noriko Arai], "ソーシャルゲームにおけるユーザーの心理特性と課金行動の関連性について [The analysis of the social psychological factors that influence the enthusiasm of social game]," 上智経済論集 [Sophia Economic Review], 58 (March 2013): 277–287; 山口真一[Shinichi Yamaguchi], "ソーシャルゲームユーザの行動決定要因:ネットワーク効果の実証分析 [Behavioral determinants of social game users: Empirical analysis of the network effect]," *InfoCom Review*, 62 (March 2014): 2–17; 寺本水羽渋谷明子秋山久美子[Mizuha Teramoto, Akiko Shibuya, and Kumiko Akiyama]. "ソーシャルゲームの利用動機と利用状況:モバイルインターネット調査の報告 [Game playing motivations and micro-transactions: A mobile-Internet survey on social game players]." Proceedings of

the 2014 Spring Conference of Japan Association of Simulation and Gaming (JASAG), 10–15. Chiba- Matsudo, Japan, May 31, 2014.

13. See 野島美保[Miho Nojima], 人はなぜ形のないものを買うのか:仮想世界のビジネスモデル [Why do people buy shapeless items?: A business model of virtual worlds] (Tokyo: NTT publishing, 2008), 95–125.

14. See 井上 理[Osamu Inoue], "行き過ぎたソーシャルゲームGREEで不正行為の内幕:無法の「換金市場」と「射幸性」 [Excessive social games: Cheating found inside games of GREE: Outlaw 'real money trade market' and 'nature that arouses speculative spirit']." Nikkei, February 25, 2012, accessed May 31, 2015, http://www.nikkei.com/article/DGXBZ O39032660T20C12A2000000/; 新清士[Kiyoshi Shin], "ソーシャルゲームが抱える潜在的リスク:「射幸心」あおる仕組みとは [Potential risks of social games: A system that arouses 'speculative spirit'], *Nikkei*. January 25, 2012, accessed May 31, 2015, http://www.nikkei.com/article/DGXZZO38258340U2A120C1000000/?df=4.

15. See 上原茂樹[Shigeki Uehara], "「ガチャ」ビジネスの創業者として、お客さまに夢を提供する:カプセル玩具運営事業(株)ペニイ" [As a founder of "gacha" business, a capsule toy management business company Penny has provided dreams to customers]," アミューズメント産業 *[Amusement Industry]*, 41 (December 2012): 36–38.

16. See 日本玩具協会[Japan Toy Association], 2015年度国内玩具市場規模 [Domestic market size in 2015], June, 2016, accessed August 3, 2016. http://www.toys.or.jp/pdf/2016/2015_sijyoukibo_zenpan.pdf. The average exchange rate of 1 US dollar (USD) for the year 2015 was taken as 122.05 Japanese yen (JYN). Source: Mitsubishi UFJ Research and Consulting, Exchange quotations – Yearly Averages, accessed August 3, 2016, http://www.murc-kawasesouba.jp/fx/year_average.php.

17. See Kathleen De Vere, "*Japan officially declares lucrative kompu gacha practice illegal in social games,*" Social Times, May 18, 2012, accessed September 20, 2015, http://www.adweek.com/socialtimes/japan-officially-declares-lucractive-kompu-gacha-practice-illegal-in-social-games/525608?red=im; Consumer Affairs Agency, Government of Japan. *White paper on consumer affairs 2014 summary*, Accessed May 30, 2015, http://www.caa.go.jp/en/pdf/.

18. See a review about biased evaluations and erroneous perception of gambling, by Mark Griffiths, "*Adolescent Gambling,*" (London: Routledge, 1995), 22 and 23; 井上理[Osamu Inoue], 14.

19. See 井上理[Osamu Inoue], 14.

20. See 井上理[Osamu Inoue], "続行き過ぎたソーシャルゲーム 依然残る「射幸心」:「ガチャ依存」か「脱ガチャ」か 健全化への分水嶺 [Excessive social games 2: 'Dependence on gacha' or 'departs from gacha' watershed for social acceptance]. Nikkei, May 22, 2012, accessed May 31, 2015, http://

www.nikkei.com/article/DGXZZO41687870S2A520C1000000/; 国民生活センター [National Consumer Affairs Center of Japan (NCAC)], "大人の知らない間に子どもが利用！　オンラインゲームのトラブルにご注意を"[Adults do not notice that children are playing! Be careful of troubles in online games]." Press Release, December, 2013, accessed on August 6, 2015, http://www.kokusen.go.jp/pdf/n-20121220_2.spdf.; National Consumer Affairs Center of Japan (NCAC). Online gaming troubles involving children continue to grow: Discuss gaming as a family, and carefully manage your credit cards! *NCAC news*, 25(6) (March, 2014), 4–5, accessed August 6, 2015, http://www.kokusen.go.jp/e-hello/data/ncac_news25_6.pdf.

21. 走り続ける男たち:モバマス廃人 [Men who continue running (for events):Addicts of Idolm@ster for Cinderella girls in Mobage]. (2013). 三才ムック[Sansai mook], 622. 三才ブックス[Sansai books]. [Kindle version], accessed September, 2013, http:// www.amazon.co.jp/; 井上理[Osamu Inoue], "行き過ぎたソーシャルゲーム [Excessive social games], 14.

22. See Gunho Online Entertainment, Puzzle & Dragons Guide & Tutorials, 2013, Accessed August 6, 2015 http://puzzleanddragons.us/guides-tutorials/introduction/; *Puzzle & Dragons* 究極攻略データベース [Puzzle & Dragons Ultimate Strategy DB], 2012, accessed August 6, 2015, http://pd.appbank.net/guide/top.

23. Consumer Affairs Agency, Government of Japan. *White paper on consumer affairs 2014 summary*, 18, Accessed May 30, 2015, http://www.caa.go.jp/en/pdf/whitepaper2014_1.pdf;　国民生活センター相談情報部情報通信チーム[National Consumer Affairs Center of Japan, Consultation Information Division, Information Technology Team]. オンラインゲームに関する消費生活相談[Consumer affairs consultation information on online games]. (March, 2016), accessed August 18, 2016, http://www.caa.go.jp/adjustments/pdf/160324shiryo2.pdf.

24. CESA. *2014 CESA games white paper*, 97; CESA. *2016 CESA games white Paper*, 88.

25. Malte Elson et al., "More than stories with buttons: Narrative, mechanics, and context as determinants of player experience in digital games." *Journal of Communication*, 64, no. 3 (June 2014): 521–542, accessed June 1, 2015, http://onlinelibrary.wiley.com/doi/10.1111/jcom.12096/.

26. See Stacy L. Smith, Ken Lachlan and Ron Tamborini, "Popular video games: Quantifying the presentation of violence and its context." *Journal of Broadcasting & Electronic Media*, 47, no. 1 (January 2003): 58–76, accessed May 31, http://www.tandfonline.com/doi/abs/10.1207/s15506878jobem4701_4; Dmitri Williams et al., "The virtual census: Representations of gender, race and age in video games." *New Media & Society*, 11, no. 5 (August 2009): 815–834, accessed May 31, 2015, http://nms.sagepub.com/content/11/5/815.full.pdf+html.

27. Mike Schmierbach, "Content analysis of video games: Challenges and potential solutions." *Communication Methods and Measures*, 3, no. 3 (August 2009): 147–172, accessed May 31, 2015, http://www.tandfonline.com/doi/abs/10.1080/19312450802458950#.VWss3pUw_IU.

28. See Malte Elson et al., 521–542.

29. Jesper Juul, *Half-real:Video games between real rules and fictional worlds* (Cambridge, Mass: MIT Press, 2005), 55–120.

30. The ideal number of paying teenage players was 1140, but the number of game players that made in-game purchases was limited to those under 20 years of age.

31. See Mike Schmierbach, 147–172.

32. We ensured that creating multiple accounts for this study did not cause problems or violate the rules and guidelines of SNS, and social apps, and we obtained oral or written permissions from certain SNSs when it was considered necessary.

33. Originally, "restoring stamina or health" and "proceeding with the story" were coded separately. They were combined later because players could restore stamina and health when proceeding with the story or in adventure modes of some social games.

34. William A. Scott, "Reliability of content analysis: The case of nominal scale coding." *Public Opinion Quarterly* 19, no. 3 (Fall 1955):321–325; Barbara J. Wilson, et al., "Violence in the television programming overall: University of California, Santa Barbara study." In *National Television Violence Study* Vol.1 (Newbury Park, CA: Sage, 1997), 3–268.

35. The reliability of "limited-time only discount sale" was .56 because the discount sale was literally available "limited-time only" (e.g., for one day for certain players).

36. For game apps obtained through Google Play and App Store, players or their parents, or guardians, could set passwords for making additional payments. In other browser games in certain SNSs, such as GREE and Mobage, the social game industry set the maximum amount of payments that could be made by minors (e.g., 5000 yen or less for a month for those under 16 years of age).

37. See Mizuha Teramoto et al., 12. The Teramoto's study is based on the same survey data as explained in the "Survey for Sampling Games." Teramoto analyzed game users' experiences, and we used the results of the study in the discussion part of this chapter.

38. Ibid, 12.

39. Ibid, 12.

40. Mitsubishi Research Institute. 9.

41. We also measured social mechanics, connections to SNSs, cooperation and competition, in this systematic analysis. Some major results were reported at the DiGRA2015. More detailed report was published as Shibuya et al. (2017).

Acknowledgments This study was funded by JSPS KAKENHI Grant Number JP25380857.

GAME REFERENCES

Acquire. 2013. *Divine gate* [Google Play/App Store], GungHo Online Entertainment, Tokyo Japan: Played February and March, 2014.

Ambition. 2011. *Animal boyfriend* [GREE], Ambition, Tokyo Japan: Played February and March, 2014.

———. 2012. *Fairy doll* [GREE], Ambition, Tokyo Japan: Played February and March, 2014.

Ateam. 2011. *AKB stage fighter* [GREE], GREE, Nagoya Japan: Played February and March, 2014.

Bandai Namco Entertainment. 2011. *Gundam card collection* [Mobage], Bandai Namco Entertainment, Tokyo Japan: Played February and March, 2014.

———. 2012. *One piece grand collection* [Mobage], Bandai Namco Entertainment, Tokyo Japan: Played February and March, 2014.

Cyber Agent. 2012. *Girl friend (beta)*. [Ameba], Cyber Agent, Tokyo Japan: Played February and March, 2014.

Cygames. 2011. *Rage of Bahamut* [Mobage], Cygames, Tokyo Japan: Played February and March, 2014.

DeNA. 2010. *Nouen hokkorina* [Mobage], DeNA, Tokyo Japan: Played February and March, 2014.

———. 2011. *Idol m@ster Cinderella girls* [Mobage], DeNA, Tokyo Japan: Played February and March, 2014.

GREE. 2008. *Hakoniwa* [GREE], GREE, Tokyo Japan: Played February and March, 2014.

———. 2011. *Tanken driland* [GREE], GREE, Tokyo Japan: Played February and March, 2014.

GungHo Online Entertainment. 2012a. *Princess punt sweets* [Google Play/App Store], GungHo Online Entertainment, Tokyo Japan: Played February and March, 2014.

———. 2012b. *Puzzle and dragons* [Google Play/App Store], GungHo Online Entertainment, Tokyo Japan: Played February and March, 2014.

King Digital Entertainment. 2012. *Candy crush saga* [Google Play/App Store], *King Digital Entertainment*, London UK: Played February and March, 2014.

Klab. 2012. *Love live! School idol festival* [App Store/Google Play], Bushiroad, Tokyo Japan: Played February and March, 2014.

Konami Digital Entertainment. 2010a. *Dragon collection* [GREE], Konami Digital Entertainment, Tokyo Japan: Played February and March, 2014.

———. 2010b. *Sengoku collection* [Mobage], Konami Digital Entertainment, Tokyo Japan: Played February and March, 2014.

Kuma the Bear. 2013. *Quiz RPG: The world of mystic Wiz* [Google Play/App Store], COLOPL, Japan: Played February and March, 2014.

LINE. 2012a. *LINE POP* [LINE], LINE, Tokyo Japan: Played February and March, 2014.

———. 2012b. *LINE bubble* [LINE], LINE, Tokyo Japan: February and March, 2014.

———. 2013a. *LINE pokopan* [LINE], LINE, Tokyo Japan: Played February and March, 2014.

——— 2013b. *LINE windrunner* [LINE], LINE, Tokyo Japan: Played February and March, 2014.

Mobcast. 2010. *Moba pro* [Mobcast], Mobcast, Tokyo Japan: Played February and March, 2014.

Mobility Ware. 2010. *Solitaire* [Google Play /App Store], Mobility Ware, Irvine USA: Played February and March, 2014.

PONOS. 2012. *Battle cats* [App Store/Google Play], PONOS, Kyoto Japan: Played February and March, 2014.

SEGA. 2013a. *Puyopuyo! quest* [App Store/Google Play], SEGA, Tokyo, Japan: Played February and March, 2014.

———. 2013b. *Chain chronicle* [Google Play/App Store], SEGA, Tokyo Japan: Played February and March, 2014.

Supercell. 2012a. *Clash of clans* [App Store/Google Play] Supercell, Helsinki Finland: Played February and March, 2014.

———. 2012b. *Hay day* [App Store/Google Play], Supercell, Helsinki Finland: Played February and March, 2014.

Voltage. 2011. *My forged wedding* [GREE], Voltage, Tokyo Japan: Played February and March, 2014.

BIBLIOGRAPHY

Anderson, Chris. 2009. *Free: How today's smartest businesses profit by giving something for nothing*. New York: Hyperion.

App Annie. 2015. "App Annie Index: *2014年総括 アプリ市場動向レポート [App Annie Index: 2014 summary; A report about trends of application market]*." Obtained as "App-Annie-Index-2014-Retrospective-jp. pdf" by signing up for App Annie.

———. 2016. "*App Annie 2015 retrospective*." Obtained as "App-Annie-2015-Retrospective-EN" by signing up for App Annie.

新井範子[Arai, Noriko]. "ソーシャルゲームにおけるユーザーの心理特性と課金行動の関連性について [The analysis of the social psychological factors that influence the enthusiasm of social game]," 上智経済論集 [Sophia Economic Review], 58 (March 2013): 277–287.

Computer Entertainment Supplier's Association (CESA). 2014. *2014 CESA games white paper*. Tokyo: CESA.

———. 2016. *2016 CESA games white paper*. Tokyo: CESA.

Consumer Affairs Agency, Government of Japan. 2015. *White paper on consumer affairs 2014 summary*, Accessed 30 May 2015, http://www.caa.go.jp/en/pdf/whitepaper2014_1.pdf

De Vere, Kathleen. 2012. Japan officially declares lucrative kompu gacha practice illegal in social games, Social Times. http://www.adweek.com/socialtimes/japan-officially-declares-lucractive-kompu-gacha-practice-illegal-in-social-games/525608?red=im. Accessed 20 Sept 2015.

Elson, Malte et al. 2014. More than stories with buttons: Narrative, mechanics, and context as determinants of player experience in digital games. *Journal of Communication* 64(3): 521–542. http://onlinelibrary.wiley.com/doi/10.1111/jcom.12096/. Accessed 1 June 2015.

エンターブレイン[Enterbrain]. 2014. ファミ通ゲーム白書2014 [Famitsu game white paper 2014], Tokyo: Kadokawa.

Griffiths, Mark. 1995. *Adolescent gambling*. London: Routledge.

GungHo Online Entertainment, Puzzle & Dragons Guide & Tutorials, 2013. http://puzzleanddragons.us/guides-tutorials/introduction/. Accessed 6 Aug 2015.

井上理[Inoue, Osamu]. 2012a. "行き過ぎたソーシャルゲーム GREEで不正行為の内幕:無法の「換金市場」と「射幸性」[Excessive social games: Cheating found inside games of GREE; Outlaw 'real money trade market' and 'nature that arouses speculative spirit']." Nikkei. http://www.nikkei.com/article/DGXBZO39032660T20C12A2000000/. Accessed 31 May 2015.

———.2012b. "続行き過ぎたソーシャルゲーム 依然残る「射幸心」:「ガチャ依存」か「脱ガチャ」か 健全化への分水嶺[Exessive social games 2: 'Dependence on gacha' or 'departs from gacha' watershed for social acceptance]. Nikkei. http://www.nikkei.com/article/DGXZZO41687870S2A520C1000000/. Accessed 31 May 2015.

総務省情報通信政策研究所調査研究部   [Institute   for   Information   and Communications Policy (IICP) Ministry of Internal Affairs and Communications (MIC)]. 2014. 平成25年度ICT新興分野の国際展開と展望に関する調査研究報告書*ICT*[A survey research report on ICT international development and outlooks of new ICT areas], IICP. http://www.soumu.go.jp/iicp/chousakenkyu/data/research/survey/telecom/ 2014/2014game.pdf. Accessed 31 May 2015.

日本玩具協会[Japan   Toy   Association].   2016.   2015年度国内玩具市場規模 [Domestic market size in 2015], June, 2016. http://www.toys.or.jp/pdf/2016/2015_sijyoukibo_zenpan.pdf. Accessed 3 Aug 2016.

Juul, Jesper. 2005. *Half-real: Video games between real rules and fictional worlds*. Cambridge, MA: MIT Press.

カドカワ[Kadokawa dwango]. 2016. ファミ通ゲーム白書2016 [Famitsu game white paper 2016]. Tokyo: Kadokawa dwango.

走り続ける男たち:モバマス廃人[Men who continue running (for events). 2013. Addicts of Idolm@ster for Cinderella girls in Mobage]. 三オムック[Sansai mook], 622. 三オブックス[Sansai books]. [Kindle version]. http://www.amazon.co.jp/. Accessed Sept 2013.

三菱総合研究所[Mitsubishi Research Institute]. 2013. 平成24年度コンテンツ産業強化対策支援事業(ネットワーク系ゲーム環境整備研究事業)報告書[A report about a project of supporting strategies of content industry (a research project of reconstructions of environment of networking games)]. http://www.meti.go.jp/meti_lib/report/2013fy/E002770.pdf. Accessed 1 June 2015.

国民生活センター [National Consumer Affairs Center of Japan (NCAC)]. 2013. "大人の知らない間に子どもが利用! オンラインゲームのトラブルにご注意を"[Adults do not notice that children are playing! Be careful of troubles in online games]." Press Release, December, 2013. http://www.kokusen.go.jp/pdf/n-20121220_2.spdf. Accessed 6 Aug 2015.

National Consumer Affairs Center of Japan (NCAC). 2014. Online gaming troubles involving children continue to grow: Discuss gaming as a family, and carefully manage your credit cards! *NCAC News* 25(6): 4–5. http://www.kokusen.go.jp/e-hello/data/ncac_news25_6.pdf. Accessed 6 Aug 2015.

国民生活センター相談情報部情報通信チーム[National Consumer Affairs Center of Japan, Consultation Information Division, Information Technology Team]. 2016. オンラインゲームに関する消費生活相談[Consumer affairs consultation information on online games]. http://www.caa.go.jp/adjustments/pdf/160324shiryo2.pdf. Accessed 18 Aug 2016.

野島美保[Nojima, Miho]. 2008. 人はなぜ形のないものを買うのか:仮想世界のビジネスモデル[Why do people buy shapeless items?: A business model of virtual worlds]. Tokyo: NTT publishing.

———. 2011. "ソーシャルゲームにおける日本型データドリブンのあり方とは[How should the Japanese model of data-driven in social games?]," Business Media Makoto. http://bizmakoto.jp/makoto/articles/1109/22/news015.html. Accessed 4 Mar 2014.

Paavilainen, Janne, Hamari, Juho, Stenros, Jaakko, and Kinnunen, Jani. 2013. Social network games: Players' perspectives. *Simulation and Gaming* 44(6): 794–820. http://sag.sagepub.com/content/44/6/794. Accessed 31 May 2015.

Puzzle & Dragons. 2012. 究極攻略データベース [Puzzle & Dragons Ultimate Strategy DB], http://pd.appbank.net/guide/top. Accessed 6 Aug 2015.

Schmierbach, Mike. 2009. Content analysis of video games: Challenges and potential solutions. *Communication Methods and Measures* 3(3): 147–172. http://www.tandfonline.com/doi/abs/10.1080/19312450802458950#.VWss3pUw_IU. Accessed 31 May 2015.

Scott, William A. 1955. Reliability of content analysis: The case of nominal scale coding. *Public Opinion Quarterly* 19(3): 321–325.

渋谷明子寺本水羽祥雲暁代[Shibuya, Akiko, Teramoto, Mizuha, and Shoun, Akiyo]. 2014. "ソーシャルゲームにおける課金とソーシャル性:人気モバイルゲームの系統的分析[Micro-payments and social features of social games: A systematic analysis of popular mobile games in Japan-]," (paper presented at the Summer Research Conference of Digital Games Research Association Japan (DiGRA JAPAN), Tokyo, August, 24). http://digrajapan.org/summer2014/S09B.pdf. Accessed 19 Aug 2016.

Shibuya, Akiko, Teramoto, Mizuha, and Shoun, Akiyo. 2015. Systematic analysis of in-game purchases and social features of mobile social games in Japan. (paper presented at Digital Games Research Association 2015 Conference (DiGRA2015), Luneberg, Germany, May, 16. http://www.digra.org/wp-content/uploads/digital-library/137_Shibuya_etal_Systematic-Analysis-of-In-game-Purchases.pdf. Accessed 19 Aug 2016.

Shibuya, Akiko, Mizuha Teramoto, and Akiyo Shoun. 2017. Toward individualistic cooperative play: A systematic analysis of mobile social games in Japan. In *Mobile gaming in Asia, mobile communication in Asia: Local insights, global implications*, ed. D.Y. Jin, 207–225. Dordrecht: Springer.

新清士[Shin, Kiyoshi]. 2012. "ソーシャルゲームが抱える潜在的リスク:「射幸心」あおる仕組みとは[Potential risks of social games: A system that arouses 'speculative spirit'], *Nikkei*. http://www.nikkei.com/article/DGXZZO38258 340U2A120C1000000/?df=4. Accessed 31 May 2015.

Smith, Stacy L., Lachlan, Ken, and Tamborini, Ron. 2003. Popular video games: Quantifying the presentation of violence and its context. *Journal of Broadcasting & Electronic Media* 47(1): 58–76. www.tandfonline.com/doi/abs/10.1207/s15506878jobem4701_4 /. Accessed 31 May.

田中辰雄山口真一[Tatsuo Tanaka, and Shinichi Yamaguchi]. 2015. ソーシャルゲームのビジネスモデル:フリーミアムの経済分析[Business model of social games]. Tokyo: Keisoshobo.

寺本水羽渋谷明子秋山久美子[Teramoto, Mizuha, Shibuya, Akiko, and Akiyama, Kumiko]. 2014. "ソーシャルゲームの利用動機と利用状況:モバイルインターネット調査の報告[Game playing motivations and micro-transactions: A mobile-Internet survey on social game players]." Proceedings of the 2014 Spring Conference of Japan Association of Simulation and Gaming (JASAG), 10–15. Chiba-Matsudo, Japan.

上原茂樹[Uehara, Shigeki]. 2012. "「ガチャ」ビジネスの創業者として、お客さまに夢を提供する:カプセル玩具運営事業(株)ペニイ" [As a founder of "gacha" business, a capsule toy management business company Penny has provided dreams to customers]," アミューズメント産業 *[Amusement Industry]*, 41: 36–38.

Williams, Dmitri et al. 2009. The virtual census: Representations of gender, race and age in video games. *New Media & Society* 11(5): 815–834. http://nms.sagepub.com/content/11/5/815.full.pdf+html. Accessed 31 May 2015.

Wilson, Barbara J., et al. 1997. Violence in the television programming overall: University of California, Santa Barbara study. In *National Television Violence Study*, vol 1, 3–268. Newbury Park, CA: Sage.

山口真一[Yamaguchi, Shinichi]. 2014. ソーシャルゲーム・ユーザの行動決定要因:ネットワーク効果の実証分析" [Behavioral determinants of social game users: Empirical analysis of the network effect]. *InfoCom Review* 62: 2–17.

CHAPTER 5

Bowling Online: Mobile Social Games for Korean Teen Girls

Hogeun Seo and Claire Shinhea Lee

The ways in which people communicate in online and offline spaces are increasingly converging. Especially, the everyday socializing activities of young people are expanding from physical places to online places. For instance, they make friends in online communities, communicate with each other via mobile messengers, and play together through online games. With a plethora of smartphone uses infiltrating many facets of our daily lives, the complex relationship among mobile media, online games, and social activities is becoming increasingly important. To understand some of these dynamics, this article focuses upon a case study of playing mobile social games among teen girls in South Korea (hereafter 'Korea'). On the basis of its highly developed information and communication technology, Korean young people are actively adopting digital culture to their everyday lives; they now enjoy online leisure activities with their offline friends by playing mobile social games. As a pioneer of mobile social games, and as one of the centers for technological innovation and tech-savvy youth (Hjorth 2012), Korea provides a suitable case study for these issues.

H. Seo (✉) • C.S. Lee
Department of Radio-Television-Film, University of Texas at Austin, Austin, TX, USA

© The Author(s) 2016
S.A. Lee, A. Pulos (eds.), *Transnational Contexts of Development History, Sociality, and Society of Play*, East Asian Popular Culture, DOI 10.1007/978-3-319-43820-7_5

123

In Korea, a recent notable social phenomenon is the playing of mobile social games via the smartphone messenger application KakaoTalk. The traditional game sphere seemed to cater to the limited population of boys and young male adults. Today, however, it seems that almost everybody in Korea plays games with their smartphones. The two most popular mobile social games in 2013, *Anipang for Kakao* and *Dragon Flight for KaKao*, have more than 20 million downloads (Korea Creative Content Agency 2013). The enormity of this number becomes even more salient when one considers that the total population of Korea is approximately 50 million. In addition, six other mobile social games have more than 10 million downloads. More than 30 million Koreans have downloaded at least one Kakao game (Korea Creative Content Agency 2013). A majority of Koreans are attracted to KakaoTalk's mobile social games.

Meanwhile, in 2013, Korea recorded the second highest smartphone penetration rate—73%—in the world (Richter 2013). The two most popular genres of smartphone applications for Koreans are communication and game applications (Korea Internet and Security Agency 2013). Along with the spread of smartphones, the mobile messenger, KakaoTalk, with approximately 35 million users in Korea, and its mobile social game platform KakaoGame are at the center of a national fever to play mobile social games (Kim 2013b). KakaoTalk is a mobile application which provides instant messaging service along with various communication functions. KakaoTalk became the most popular mobile messenger in Korea for certain reasons; it provides direct connections with a mobile social network service, KakaoStory, and a mobile social game platform, KakaoGame; it also enables diverse communication functions such as video chat, voice call, file transfer, and group chat. These services are closely interdependent with one another, which creates synergy effects by locking the users within their boundaries.

Thanks to its advanced Internet infrastructure, the Korean game sphere has been dominated by PC-based online games. However, it is shifting to mobile games, and the shift is being propelled by the spread of smartphones and the advent of KakaoGame. A recent nationwide survey (2014) revealed that Korean gamers play mobile games (87.2%) more than online games (61.5%). Though the number of online gamers is not deceasing, that of mobile gamers has increased dramatically, which caused this change in the ratio. Meanwhile, mobile gamers are reported to prefer social games to stand-alone games (Korea Creative Content Agency 2014). The characteristics of mobile social games are similar to those of existing mobile casual games. Nevertheless, the fact that they are connected to one's contacts within mobile messengers, such as KakaoTalk, delivers huge additional value to mobile gamers. Indeed, the gamers become more interested in these games since they provide diverse elements that catalyze frequent interactions between the gamers and their contacts, which makes the gamers feel as if they synchronously play the games with their contacts.

Leading this trend are Korean high school students, those early adopters of new communication technologies and cultural practices. To understand why we chose to investigate high school girls, we need to look at their everyday lives. According to Statistics Korea, eight out of ten Korean youths attend afterschool academic programs and after their official school schedules, seven out of ten attend private institutes. For many high school students, their daily routine usually starts around six in the morning and ends at midnight or later. Over two-thirds (67%) of Korean students feel under stress about their school records. Of those who have felt suicidal impulses, more than half point to the cause as being school-related pressure. Life for a Korean high school student is very demanding, both physically and mentally. Forty-five percent of Korean students referred to lack of time as their main complaint (Statistics Korea 2012).

Due to their arduous schedules, Korean high school students have little time to enjoy their leisure activities with peers. Though they are always with their peers at school or in private institutes, they spend most of their time taking classes. They have 10 minutes' recesses between classes, but they are too short for students to enjoy specific leisure activities together. While these everyday limitations apply both to boys and girls, it is important to recognize that high school girls are even more marginalized in Korean society. Older generation still regard teen girls as one of the most vulnerable and unsafe groups who are too sensitive and easily exposed to various kinds of potential crimes including sexual assault. Korean high school girls, who are often prohibited by parents from getting together with their friends in public, are thus gradually socializing in online environments. It has been more common for Korean high school boys to socialize with each other by playing PC online games both publicly in PC bangs and privately at homes (Ministry of Gender Equality and Family 2012).[1] However, such an avenue seems to be untenable for high school girls for some reasons: (1) they feel relatively little attraction to PC online gaming; (2) the environments of PC bangs generally are not friendly to young females; and (3) their personal activities of using computers at home could be easily disclosed to their parents. Thus, high school girls are more and more often relying on smartphones to play games because a smartphone is the only device they can use anytime and anywhere (Kim 2013a). For teen girls, smartphones are much more liberating. They stay with the girls all the time, providing seamless access to online communities through smartphone messengers such as KakaoTalk. Smartphones also enable girls to play mobile social games with their friends. Using smartphones, Korean high school girls are creating their own cultural practices as they socialize.

How then do Korean high school girls use smartphones and socialize through mobile social games? What are the benefits or the harms of their smartphone use? To explore Korean high school girls' mobile social gaming, we use the concepts of social capital and social networks, particularly strong and weak ties. In exploring these phenomena, we pose three research questions:

1) What makes Korean high school girls, who were rather marginalized in the traditional video game sphere, actively participate in the mobile social game sphere?
2) How is Korean high school girls' mobile social gaming related to their strong ties and bonding social capital?
3) How is Korean high school girls' mobile social gaming related to their weak ties and bridging social capital?

To answer these research questions, we reviewed the existing studies about the effects of communication technologies on social capital and social networks, especially on teenagers' social capital and social networks. For the current study, we conducted focus group interviews with 23 Korean high school girls about their smartphone gaming, and then, we analyzed interview data to provide a clearer understanding of Korean high school girls' online socializing behaviors via mobile social gaming.

Social Capital, Social Networks, and Communication Technology

Bourdieu (1985) defined social capital as "the aggregate of the actual or potential resources which are linked to possession of a durable network of more or less institutionalized relationships of mutual acquaintance and recognition" (248). Coleman (1998) defined it as "a variety of entities with two elements in common: They all consist of some aspect of social structures, and they facilitate certain action of actors whether persons or corporate actors within the structure" (Coleman 1988, 98). Putnam (1995) referred to social capital as "features of social organization such as networks, norms, and social trust that facilitate coordination and cooperation for mutual benefit" (67). Baker (1990) defined social capital as "a resource that actors derive from specific social structures and then use to pursue their interests" (619), and Burt (2009) as "friends, colleagues, and more general contacts through whom you receive opportunities to use your financial and human capital" (9).

While some scholars, such as Baker (1990) and Burt (2009), consider social capital as individuals' resources that can be manipulated to create their interests or opportunities, other scholars, such as Putnam (1995), regard it as social features that generate mutual benefit. Though it seems that scholars are using the concept of social capital in many different ways, Portes (1998) argued that 'the consensus is growing in the literature that social capital stands for the ability of actors to secure benefits by virtue of membership in social networks or other social structures' (6). Based on this scholarly agreement, we (i.e., the study authors) embrace Portes' definition of social capital for this research.

As many scholars have tried to establish their own definitions of social capital, they have also paid a great deal of attention to the influence of communication technologies on social capital. The kinds of arguments basically come down to three: Scholars, such as Putnam or Turkle, cast doubt on the role of communication technology, asserting that it decreases social capital by reducing the time and the portion of offline communication (Kraut et al. 1998; Putnam 2001; Turkle 2012). On the other hand, according to other scholars such as Boase or Hampton, communication technologies increase or reinforce social capital (Boase et al. 2006; Hampton et al. 2011). Meanwhile, still other scholars, such as Ellison or Wellman, insist that communication technologies, rather than increase or decrease social capital, compensate for the absence of it (Ellison et al. 2007; Wellman et al. 2002).

If researchers focus on social networks as a whole when investigating the fluctuation of social capital, they can overlook important details. For example, a specific technology can influence positively one's homogeneous network or close relationships and yet at the same time negatively affect one's heterogeneous network or distant relationships. For this reason, researchers have tried to categorize social relationships and the types of social capital within each relationship. Carefully conceptualizing these fundamental ideas should help clarify the effects of communication technologies on different relationships.

Granovetter (1983) divided social networks into strong ties and weak ties. Strong ties are located at the core of a network, related to emotional bonds and trust, requiring more time and energy to maintain. Weak ties lie along the periphery, are more heterogeneous, and require less intensive maintenance. Other scholars have added their ideas about the characteristics of both ties, based on the concepts of Granovetter (Erickson 1996; Hurlbert et al. 2001; Uzzi 1996). Hurlbert et al. (2001) argued that strong ties provide emotional, instrumental, and financial support. Uzzi (1996) claimed that refined information and valuable resources could be exchanged between close people due to the trust and the obligation of strong ties. Meanwhile, Erickson (1996) insisted that diverse contacts lead people to fresh information, allowing them to develop cognitive flexibility and cultural capital.

Putnam (2001) conceptualized the types of social capital that are generated by the two sorts of network ties. He argues that homogeneous networks, which imply strong ties, create bonding social capital. A value more often created by heterogeneous people, which means weak ties, is bridging social capital (Putnam 2001). Bonding social capital is based on exclusive networks that provide emotional or substantive supports; bridging social capital is related to inclusive networks that provide new information and resources (Putnam 2001). Studies about the relationships between communication technologies and strong ties are somewhat inconclusive, yielding three types of hypotheses: reinforcement, displacement, and no impact (Chen 2013). First, scholars supporting the reinforcement hypothesis insist that communication technologies influence strong ties positively and therefore increase bonding social capital (Boase et al. 2006; Boase 2008; Brooks et al. 2011; Ellison et al. 2007; Jones et al. 2013). Second, according to the displacement hypothesis, technology-mediated communication reduces time for existing offline communication and therefore decreases the bonding social capital (Itō et al. 2006; Jones et al. 2009; Olds and Schwartz 2009; Turkle 2012). Third, the no-impact hypothesis maintains that communication technologies are not directly related to the fluctuation of strong ties and bonding social capital (Bargh and McKenna 2004; Kennedy et al. 2008).

Most of the existing studies about weak ties claim that communication technologies positively influence weak ties and therefore increase bridging social capital (Constant et al. 1996; Donath and Boyd 2004; Ellison et al. 2007; Steinfield et al. 2009). Many scholars have argued in particular that using social network sites is positively related to the manageability of weak ties and an increase of bridging capital. On the other hand, there are also a small number of studies asserting that communication technologies negatively influence weak ties (Dunbar 2003; Gergen 2008; Roberts et al. 2009). Scholars who support this hypothesis argue that communication technologies make people more focused on their strong ties and pay little attention to their weak ties (Gergen 2008; Haythornthwaite 2002).

To sum up, scholars generally agree with the ideas that communication technologies, especially new media technologies, enhance bridging social capital, while there is no scholarly consensus on the effects of communication technologies on bonding social capital. However, instead of concluding these debates, scholars have to pay attention to individual technologies and the contextual practices with them because the features of communication technologies are ever changing, and the same technology can cause different results according to the contexts.

The Effects of Mobile Phones and Games

Many scholars are conducting studies about the effects of mobile phones on one's social capital and social networks. Rettie (2008) has argued that mobile phones support users to develop or maintain network ties by increasing access to networks. Other scholars have insisted that using mobile phones strengthens social bonds (Geser 2006; Ling 2004; Rivière and Licoppe 2005). Ling (2004) maintained that mobile phones nurture social capital. However, the previous studies on mobile phones tend to focus on strong ties. Using mobile phones has been revealed to affect strong ties because people usually communicate with their close friends or family members through mobile phones (de Gournay 2002; Matsuda 2006; Reid and Reid 2005). Many scholars have also argued that communicating via mobile phones enhances strong ties at the cost of weak ties (Gergen 2002; Katz 2006; Ling 2004; Rivière and Licoppe 2005). These results might be found since scholars have focused on the basic functions of mobile phones such as calling or texting.

Scholars explored the effects of mobile phone calling and texting on one's social networks; for example, Igarashi et al. (2005) have revealed that relations supported by mobile phone calls and text messages are more intimate than relations maintained only by face-to-face communication. Licoppe (2004) argued that the connectedness enabled by text messages and mobile phone calls develops into 'connected presence' in close relationships. However, recent mobile devices, including smartphones and tablets, enable diverse practices in addition to phone calls and text messages. People send email, upload postings on social network sites, or play mobile games with their smartphones. Though diverse social and cultural practices with mobile phones were explored in a limited number of studies (Itō et al. 2006), these kinds of studies are still insufficient to keep up with the ever-changing mobile technology. For this reason, more studies have to be conducted to thoroughly understand the influences of recent mobile phones on one's social capital and social networks.

Meanwhile, the number of studies on the relationship between video gaming and one's social capital or social networks is increasing. As Williams (2006b) argued that video gaming can be a space where the practices of young people can be analyzed, it is important to explore young people's video gaming and the effects of their virtual practices. Some scholars have found that specific types or elements of video games are related to one's social capital and social networks. Skoric and Kwan (2011) insisted that massively multiplayer online games (MMOGs) are related to bonding social capital, while civic gaming experiences in MMOGs are associated with bridging social capital. Steinkuehler and Williams (2006) claimed that the gaming environment of MMOGs has the potential of stimulating the building of bridging social capital by making gamers play games together while these games do not increase bonding social capital. However, many of these studies focus on PC online games, especially MMOGs, while studies on the effects of mobile games or social games on gamers' social capital are few. Since the number of mobile gamers is increasing dramatically, there is a great potential of these games to affect the gamers' social capital or social networks. Indeed, a great deal of mobile games have socializing functions that allow gamers to interact with their friends, which makes the potential even greater. Thus, scholars have to pay more attention to the relationship between mobile games and social capital or social networks.

Scholars also have conducted studies on the relationships between video games and adolescents' social capital or social networks. Orleans and Laney (2000) suggested that computer gaming promotes sociality when computers are networked or when adolescents use computer gaming as a topic of talk. Suoninen (2013) insisted that children create networks relying on mutual interest and exchange knowledge about gaming and game software as well. However, studies on the effects of mobile gaming on adolescents' social capital have not been conducted thoroughly.

Recently, playing games with mobile devices, such as smartphones or tablets, has become one of the most prevalent leisure activities among children and adolescents. Moreover, while traditional video gaming was generally an activity for boys, now the number of girl gamers is increasing dramatically due to the spread of smartphones. However, the existing studies on the relationships between children's gaming and social capital or social networks have focused on boys' online gaming behaviors. Thus, more studies on girls' gaming via smartphones and its influences on their social capital or social networks should be conducted thoroughly to understand this newly emerged cultural phenomenon and its implications.

METHODOLOGY

For this study, we conducted focus group interviews with 23 Korean high school girls aged 16–19. Thirteen participants were interviewed in the summer of 2013, and the rest ten were interviewed in the summer of 2014. We used a snowball method to select the sample, which minimizes the potential reactive effects since all the participants are from the moderators' strong or weak social ties. This technique was followed because in a Korean cultural context it is necessary, in recruiting sensitive and vulnerable high school girls, to use trustworthy bridging networks and thereby gain parental approval. Two recruiters—teachers at a public school and a private educational institute—helped recruiting the interviewees. The teachers recruited the initial interviewees since the recruiters observed them using smartphones frequently. Then, the recruiters asked the initial interviewees to introduce other students possessing smartphones and playing mobile games for the further interviews. In that way, we conducted focus group interviews with 8 groups composed of 2–4 students.

Focus group interviews were conducted instead of individual interviews to allow the high school girls a level of comfort that they might not otherwise feel. The goal was to make the interviews similar to chatting among close friends, with the hope of eliciting authentic responses. The interviews were conducted by two interviewers; one of these two participated in each interview. The interviews took place in a classroom, which made them comfortable. We used the semi-structured interview method, so the interviewees could be more at their pace; though we had the list of questions, we moved the conversation away from certain topics, if they made the sensitive high school girls uncomfortable. The interviews were recorded using a voice recorder embedded in the interviewers' smartphones. Based on these files, we made a transcript for each interview for research analysis.

The analysis of the interview data was conducted over seven steps. First, we classified the comments from the interviewees into groups by meaning. Second, we mapped these groups of comments on the research questions. Third, we analyzed the interview comments on the basis of the theories and the concepts applied to each question. Fourth, we figured out the significance of each group by counting the amount of repeated comments. Fifth, in accordance with the significance, we organized the answers for each research question in order to elaborate the arguments of this research. Sixth, we compared the findings of this research with the results of the existing studies, whether the findings supported or contradicted the existing studies or if there were original findings. Lastly, we figured out the implications and the limitations of the current research.

Though many of the existing studies related to the influences of media use on social networks are based on quantitative methods, this study employs the qualitative method. Indeed, the purpose of this study is not to generalize findings but to understand new and rapidly changing practices that might provide grounds for further research. We believe this approach of the present study would somewhat justify the relatively small sample size. Finally, this method enables the current study to create an initial understanding of the outlines of emergent cultural practices such as high school girls' mobile social gaming.

Results

Results of the current study illustrate some unexpected relationships within girls' social networks as well as the significance of specific platforms for social networks. How does video gaming influence a gamer's social networks and social capital? Though many scholars have conducted studies to answer this question, they paid more attention to PC online games oriented to males such as massively multiplayer online games (MMOGs) (Huvila et al. 2010; Kobayashi 2010; Skoric and Kwan 2011; Trepte et al. 2012; Williams 2006a). As noted earlier, most of these studies argued the positive relationship between online games and gamers' social networks or social capital, especially their bridging social capital. In addition, the existing studies on the adolescents' gaming also suggest an increase in their social capital because of the games (Orleans and Laney 2000; Suoninen 2013).

Meanwhile, the relationship between other kinds of new gaming platforms including smartphones or tablets and gamers' social capital is rather unclear. For this reason, exploring the effects of mobile social games that have become one of the most popular leisure activities for Korean adolescents will provide an opportunity of understanding the relationship between using smartphones as a gaming device and gamers' social capital. If a game applies diverse socializing functions, will it increase the social capital of Korean high school girls whose offline social interactions lack?

In the interviews, we found that mobile social games enable the gamers to interact with the members in the mobile messenger contact list while playing games by providing specific socializing functions interlocked with mobile messengers. In Korea, a mobile social game platform, KakaoGame, was launched, based on the nationwide popularity of the mobile messenger, KakaoTalk. Recently, numerous smartphone users, especially females, became rigorous mobile gamers who enjoy various social games offered by KakaoGame with their friends or even just acquaintances (Kim 2013b). A survey revealed that more than a half female mobile gamers (57%) download mobile games from the mobile game platform, KakaoGame (Korea Creative Content Agency 2014). Unlike other platforms, such as Google Play or App Store, KakaoGame mostly provides social games that are connected to their mobile messenger, KakaoTalk.

From the interview data, we could find that mobile social games offered by KakaoGame share three common core factors: cooperation, competition, and diffusion. 'Cooperation' is realized in games by specific game items such as 'life' or 'heart.' Gamers can send these items to the messenger contacts who also play the same game. If gamers receive these items, they can play additional games with these items, while gamers cannot play more games for a specific period of time without them. 'Competition' is usually realized with the in-game ranking board and the function named 'boasting.' The ranking board stimulates the competition between gamers by notifying where they are ranked among the messenger contacts who play the same game. Moreover, when gamers move up in the rankings, they can send boasting messages to other gamers via the mobile messenger, KakaoTalk, which causes more competition. We found that these two components—cooperation and competition—were designed to raise the game usage rates by attracting the interviewees to play more games.

In the meantime, 'diffusion' is realized by the function named 'invitation.' This function enables gamers to send invitation messages to any of the messenger contacts through the mobile messenger. Since the interviewees were rewarded with gaming items or avatars in accordance with the number of sending invitations (even when invitees did not download those games), they played a huge role in promoting the games voluntarily. This viral marketing tool is very efficient in recruiting new gamers, so many gamers begin to play specific games after they receive invitation messages. According to a report on Korean gamers, almost two out of three (65.4%) begin to play mobile social games due to the invitations or recommendations from other gamers (DIGIECO 2013). Basically, the interactions between gamers, or between gamers and non-gamers, through mobile social games consist of these three limited components.

KakaoGame marks the beginning of mobile social games as one of the main leisure activities for Korean high school girls. For the first research question asking what makes Korean high school girls actively participate in the mobile social game sphere, our findings indicate that Korean high school girls actively play these games for three reasons. First, it allows them to socialize with one another. Second, these games are relatively suited to the tastes of female gamers compared to other online games. Third, Korean high school girls have an easy accessibility to the gaming device itself—the smartphone.

First, the interviewees stated that while teen boys are interested in the game itself, teen girls are fascinated by mobile social games because they can enjoy them with their friends. What is meaningful to them is not just playing games for fun but feeling a sense of belonging and communicating with one another. A small number of heavy gamers among the interviewees stated that they would play PC online games more often if they played those games with their friends since PC online games were more amusing than mobile games. Twenty out of 23 interviewees mentioned that they would be much less interested in mobile social games if those games did not provide any interactions with their friends. Interviewee V emphasized the importance of the socializing functions for her mobile gaming.

> I really like playing mobile games and I play them much more than my friends, but I prefer playing with my friends because competing with and beating them is so exciting. I never play games if I cannot play them with others. Even when I used to play PC games, I played them only when I could play with my friends. It's not just playing games. It's more like interacting with my friends.

While we could expect that teen girls would play various games in their smartphones in turn since rather simple mobile games could easily become boring, the interviewees played only a couple of games that were also played by their close friends. A survey also revealed that female gamers play fewer mobile games (3.7) on average than male gamers (5.5) (Korea Creative Content Agency 2014). In other words, teen girls consider playing with friends or interacting with them is more important than the amusement from gaming itself. The interviewees seem to support their limited offline social activities with mobile social gaming, which is in line with the previous studies arguing that communication technologies compensate for the lack of social capital (Ellison et al. 2007; Wellman et al. 2002). They interact, cooperate, and compete with one another by playing mobile social games. One survey also revealed that people played mobile social games because they could play them with their friends rather than because those games were interesting (Korea Internet and Security Agency 2013). This tendency appeared more clearly from the interviewees who had fewer opportunities for socializing and placed more value on it. One of the interviewees stressed the importance of the socializing function by mentioning that interesting games become uninteresting when her friends stop playing them.

Secondly, the interviewees preferred mobile social games due to the distinct features and the genres of these games. Korean high school girls seem to be put off with games that require a high level of involvement and long playing time. They want games that can be played casually during a short recess. PC online games usually have a higher level of difficulty than mobile games, which makes most high school girls hard to commit since their main purpose of gaming is not just gaming but interacting while gaming. Chan (2008) points out that the ease of play is paramount in mobile games since game developers and industry analysts try to attract new casual gaming audiences rather than the hard-core gamers. A nationwide survey also supports this finding by revealing that the rate of female gamers who prefer easy and simple casual games (44.8%) is much higher than that of male gamers (25.5%) (Korea Creative Content Agency 2014). Interviewee G clarified the reason that she preferred mobile games to PC games.

> I think most girls do not play PC games. Boys play those games, but those games are too brutal or gross. I saw boys shooting one another, playing Sudden Attack. It was too sensational, and looked somewhat too difficult for me to play. Girls seem to enjoy different kinds of games. Something cute and not too serious. Something simple and casual.

Moreover, as interviewees confessed, high school girls inevitably have lower competitiveness compared to high school boys in the PC online game sphere since they can rarely spend time at PC bangs due to parental surveillance, where high school boys play games together for hours. A national survey also revealed that teen boys play games longer than girls and that boys' level of participation was meaningfully higher than that of Korean high school girls (Korea Creative Content Agency 2012). In the meantime, high school girls are able to increase their competitiveness in the mobile game sphere more easily since the number of in-game social activities results in the level of competitiveness in mobile social games. The girls can play these games more frequently at any minute of the day or night. These 'pick up and play' mobile social games are 'geared for intermittent bouts of mobile play, ostensibly for 'killing time' or while traveling on public transport networks' (Chan 2008, 16). Moreover, the major genres of mobile social games such as puzzle and quiz suit the tastes of high school girls. Industry analyst Amy Jo Kim (2004) acknowledges that mobile games manage to attract comparable gender equity in terms of their player demographics by privileging communication and collaboration rather than fighting. As a result, although more and more sophisticated networked games are available nowadays, casual game genres, such as puzzle and quiz, are still the most popular mobile games. Teen girls stated that the easy and intuitive gaming mechanism and cute game characters of mobile social games allowed them to enjoy these games more than other genres of video games. To sum up, the features of the mobile social games that require less participation and the simple and casual genres allow the interviewees to play these games more actively.

Lastly, Korean high school girls' accessibility to smartphones adds more value to mobile social games. One interviewee, L, mentioned that the portability of smartphones made her play more, while the spatial limitations of computers made her play PC games infrequently. They played PC-based social games less frequently than their smartphone social games, meaning the media delivering the games are important. Interviewee F emphasized the value of smartphones as a gaming device. She preferred playing social games through smartphones since she could play them at any time she wanted. Bell et al. (2006) recognize that one of the vital factors in the mobile game's success and longevity is this kind of flexibility of when and where to play which allows people to fit it into home life, commuting, and work. Since smartphones were always around them—in their pockets, bags, on the desk, or in their hands—the interviewees formed a habitual use of smartphones. They used their smartphones at every opportunity, even when they do not have any specific purpose for using it. Their habitual use of smartphones obviously increased the total amount of time spent using smartphone applications, including mobile social games or other communication applications. Our analysis lies in the same line with the findings of Itō et al. (2006) on the importance of paradigmatic characteristics like the 'personal' and the 'portable' in patterns of Japanese mobile phone use.

> I always carry my smartphone. I do Internet surfing or see what's happening on the SNSs. But I cannot repeat these limited patterns of behaviors endlessly. I need something more to do with my smartphone. Then, I search popular games in Google Play. I download some of the most popular games. I play games more than before because I use my smartphone all the time.

Meanwhile, by competing and cooperating with each other, the interviewees are socializing with one another and maintaining their relationship through these mobile social games. Interviewee V elaborated how she socializes by playing mobile social games.

> Kakao games usually show the rankings among my friends. I only play those kinds of games. If my friend takes first place, I want to defeat her. I really want to beat her. While playing those games, we also share game items. We enjoy playing games together. Some recent mobile social games are even like PC online games. We can meet online to play these games synchronously.[2]

These gaming activities are interconnected through mobile messengers, wielding huge influence on their social networks. Though many mobile social games provide asynchronous gameplay environments, it is not a critical issue for Korean high school girls because they did not have enough time to play games together anyway. While mobile messengers provide Korean high school girls a good place to gather together, mobile social games enable them to play with one another. These two virtual spaces interlocked with each other are settling as alternative communities for Korean high school girls experiencing severe constraints on socializing in real spaces. Around these communities, Korean high school girls are forming their unique peer culture by shifting between offline spaces and online spaces in order to gather and play together.

Girl gamers prefer to play games with others they already know (Lenhart et al. 2008). In this sense, mobile social games are more suitable for the interviewees since they allow the interviewees to play games with others they know. Interviewee A admitted that she played Kakao games since she could play games with her friends or acquaintances by inviting them to play games together. By playing these mobile social games with existing networks, they maintain and also develop their relationships. They cooperate with one another by exchanging game items such as 'heart' or 'life,' while they also stimulate others' competitive spirit by sending 'boasting' messages.

Sometimes, the more the interviewees were immersed in mobile social games, the more disconnected they became from one another even when they were in the same physical place. This phenomenon was somewhat contradictory to their arguments mentioning that they used smartphones more actively since they could not interact sufficiently in offline spaces. Interviewee G described this paradox.

> When we all were excited about playing *CookieRun*, all of my classmates just played that game in their seats with earphones. They didn't talk to each other. They were overly sensitive. When I said something to one of my friends playing the game, she got angry and told me that she lost the game because of me. When they play games, they don't really care about others at all.

For the second and third research questions asking how Korean high school girls' mobile social gaming is related to their social networks and social capital, this research revealed that playing mobile social games influences strong ties and weak ties differently. Most of the mobile social games provided by mobile messengers such as KakaoTalk commonly reveal the ranking between one's messenger networks in order to ignite competition between gamers on the network. To win the competition, the interviewees cooperate with their strong ties by exchanging gaming resources. For example, when they need game items to defeat higher rankers, the interviewees would ask their strong ties in the messenger group chat rooms for help.

> I play a KakaoTalk game, *CookieRun*, these days. A couple of days ago, a friend of mine boasted that she broke my record. I was really annoyed. I became highly competitive and kept playing the game to beat her. But we have only five lives, so if I die five times, I have to wait ten minutes to have one more life. But I cannot wait for ten minutes for a life. So, I asked my friends in the group chat rooms to send me lives because we can send lives to each other. So, they sent me lives and I kept playing to defeat her.

According to the interviewees, both the allies with whom they cooperate and the rivals with whom they compete in mobile social games are their close friends, in other words, strong ties. In that manner, they are utilizing and increasing their bonding social capital by communicating and interacting with their strong ties constantly. To some extent, this finding supports Putnam's (1995) definition of social capital which emphasizes coordination and cooperation for mutual benefit. However, this research also found that the competition between strong ties also works to maintain or increase bonding social capital by creating constant interactions and amusement. Meanwhile, it is noticeable in particular how these games affect weak ties. Since the gamers can acquire more valuable and powerful items as rewards in proportion to their social activities, the more the users contact their network ties by sending invitations, the more competitive they become. To receive better rewards, the interviewees would try to make their networks broader and contact more people in their networks. They sent invitations to their friends with whom they did not keep in touch for a while or even to just acquaintances in their messenger list, which would exercise great influence on their weak-tie relationships. One of the interviewees, Interviewee M, had been disconnected from her friends after transferring to another school. However, she began to communicate with them again via a mobile social game. Interviewee B provided her experience of restoring relations with a disconnected friend.

> There was a promotion which gave a special game character if one sent 30 invitations. I invited everyone that I knew because I really wanted that character. At that time, I sent an invitation to my middle school friend who I hadn't contacted for a long time. Then she complained about my using her only for a reward. So I apologized to her and then we began to communicate with each other again.

However, this kind of positive results seldom happened. The interactions between weak ties tend to be designed for commercial purposes and exploited as an efficient viral marketing tool by the game publishers. While the interviewees rarely interacted with their weak ties for the purpose of true communications, they frequently contacted them to earn game rewards. Moreover, interactions are limited to several activities permitted within the games. Mobile social games are designed to make users reach a limit unless they constantly market the game to their network. Thus, the interviewees kept reaching out to their weak ties with no intention of communication.

Considering that many of the interviewees began playing a specific game only after receiving an invitation from their friends or weak ties, the gamers' weak-tie networks are well exploited as a strong viral marketing tool.

Sending invitations is the most typical and effective viral marketing tool of using the gamer's social networks, especially those made up of weak ties. The interactions with weak ties tend to be conducted in a couple of limited ways, with the 'invitation' functioning as a means of being competitive, not as a purpose of communication. Thus, unlike the existing studies that report a positive relationship between playing video games and weak ties (Huvila et al. 2010; Kobayashi 2010; Trepte et al. 2012; Williams 2006b), this research revealed a series of socializing activities conducted through mobile social games sometimes negatively affecting the interviewees' social networks, especially those made up of weak ties. Though in some exceptional cases the interviewees recovered relationships with their once-intimate friends with whom they temporally lost contact, the frequent interactions with weak ties through mobile social games usually did not develop the relationship, which remained superficial without true interactions. Indeed, these social activities sometimes severed relations instead of increasing or maintaining bridging social capital.

> When I send invitations to someone that I haven't been in touch with quite a while, some of these people send me snarky messages or others ask me not to send any more. After getting those messages, I don't contact them again. And some girls who don't play games block those invitations by changing the KakaoTalk settings. Many girls do that because they get too many invitations.

In conclusion, Korean high school girls' mobile social game playing complements their insufficient offline socializing and also affects their social networks. The interviewees stated that they were playing mobile social games in order to socialize with their peers. Since they had easy accessibility to their smartphones, and the games fit the tastes of the interviewees, they could actively participate in the mobile game sphere. This research also revealed two significant findings about the relationship between Korean high school girls' mobile social gaming and their social network and social capital. First of all, we found that the relationship between the interviewees' gaming and their weak-tie relations was not strong. While many of the previous studies claimed the positive relationship between communication technologies or video games and weak-tie relations (Constant et al. 1996;

Donath and Boyd 2004; Ellison et al. 2007; Huvila et al. 2010; Kobayashi 2010; Skoric and Kwan 2011; Steinfield et al. 2009; Trepte et al. 2012), though mobile social games generated frequent interactions between the interviewees and their weak-tie relations, these interactions tended to happen as limited ways allowed in the games, and thus, the interactions rarely led to additional communication. These limited interactions sometimes restored the relations. However, at worst, they caused the dissolution of relationships. These limited interactions with weak ties were one of the core elements for the game publishers to spread the mobile social games. Moreover, these superficial interactions were conducted voluntarily since the gamers could be more competitive in accordance with their interactions. To sum up, it was unusual for the interviewees to improve their weak-tie relations through mobile social gaming, and those relations usually remained as weak ties as they were before. This means, at least, the effects of communication technologies on weak ties are still inconclusive in a specific sociocultural context.

Second, the present study found that it is their close friends, that is to say strong ties, with whom Korean high school girls are interacting through mobile social games by cooperating or competing with one another. The interviewees of this research were creating their own digital peer culture by complementing the realistic constraints that prevented them from gathering together in the same place at the same time. Along with using mobile messengers, they were communicating with their close friends or exchanging mutual benefits to increase their bonding social capital by playing mobile social games together. In summary, Korean high school girls' mobile social gaming is more closely related to their bonding social capital, rather than bridging social capital. However, the fact that the interviewees sometimes denied interactions even with their close friends who were just beside them while they were immersed into mobile gaming was contradictory to their argument stressing that they interacted with one another through mobile messengers or mobile social games because they could not have enough opportunities for offline socializing.

DISCUSSION

By conducting focus group interviews with 23 Korean high school girls, this research found the answers for three research questions: (1) What makes Korean high school girls, who were marginalized in the traditional video game sphere, actively participate in the mobile social game sphere?

(2) How is Korean high school girls' mobile social gaming related to their strong ties and bonding social capital? (3) How is Korean high school girls' mobile social gaming related to their weak ties and bridging social capital? In particular, the present study revealed different findings from the existing studies on the relationship between playing video games and the gamers' social network and social capital.

For the first research question, the current study found that Korean high school girls, by playing mobile social games, emerged as a competitive group in the game sphere which was dominated by young males. It was possible because the interviewees had scarce opportunities for offline socializing, while they liked the characteristics of mobile social games and the gaming device. This result contradicts the common belief emphasizing male adolescents' dominance in the traditional video game sphere. Here, we acknowledge that Pierre Bourdieu's formula for studying social practices, '[(habitus) (capital)] + field = practice,' can be helpful in understanding theses girls' active participation in the mobile social game sphere (Bourdieu 1986, 101). As the concept of habitus explains a system of dispositions that influences individuals to become who they are or how they act in a way, we believe that our analysis reveals how South Korean social structures and the process of teen girls' socialization form these girls' habitus. Thus, Korean teen girls' social position lacking economic and cultural capital and dispositions preferring social relationship combined with the field of mobile gaming technology/industry may produce a particular practice of mobile social gaming.

For the other two research questions asking how Korean high school girls' mobile social gaming is related to their social networks and social capital, the interviewees answered that playing mobile social games is helpful for them to maintain or develop their strong-tie relations rather than weak-tie relations. This result conflicts with the earlier studies arguing that communication technologies or video games such as MMOGs affect one's weak-tie networks more than one's strong-tie relationship. As a common and efficient promotion tool, mobile social games give more rewards to the gamers who make more in-game interactions, such as sending invitations, with their social networks. This gaming mechanism successfully made the interviewees interact more with weak ties in their mobile messenger contact list and lure the non-gamers to the games. However, those interactions with the weak ties were conducted only for the in-game rewards which will increase their competitiveness in the games, and those behaviors rarely developed the relations or caused constant communication. Instead, the mobile social game publishers seemed to exploit the interviewees' week tie networks to increase the number of users. Here, we need to realize that what matters is not only the quantity of social networks among strong or weak ties but also the quality of those ties. In this study, we argue that through qualitative methods, we could investigate more in detail the purpose and the quality of the bridging social capital developed by teen girls' mobile gaming.

On the other hand, the interviewees constantly interacted with their strong ties by cooperating or competing with one another through mobile social games. Unlike the interactions with their weak ties, the interactions with their strong ties tended to trigger constant online and offline interactions among the interviewees. Overall, our result supports the existing studies on the relationship between mobile phone use and social capital which argue that the activities with mobile phones enhance bonding capital (De Gournay 2002; Igarashi et al. 2005; Rettie 2008). However, contrasting to some studies that argue this reinforcement of strong tie is at the cost of weak ties (Ling 2004), we argue that mobile social gaming provides potential opportunities for stimulating weak-tie relationships although very limited and risky.

Overall, we suggest two significant implications throughout the study. First, we suggest that Korean high school girls are creating their own digitalized peer culture by accepting virtual spaces in order to supplement the restrictions in reality. For Korean high school girls, the dichotomous thinking of space—whether it happens online or offline——seems to be meaningless with the boundary between the two beginning to blur. By shifting between the real world and the virtual world frequently, they are forming their own peer communities, communicating with one another, and developing their peer relationship. To sum up, the smartphone as a gaming device surely became an essential and exceptional alternative space for Korean high school girls, profoundly affecting various social relationships. Second, as the title of this research shows, we contend that Korean high school girls are 'bowling online' with one another, actively utilizing the new media technology/culture of mobile social gaming rather than 'bowling alone.' Using the metaphorical term 'bowling alone,' Putnam (1995) once worried that media technology would make American people isolated and decease their social capital. However, this research revealed the possibilities that new media technology increases social capital in a specific sociocultural context.

This research has the limitation in its relatively small sample size. However, the purpose of this research was not to generalize the effects of using smartphones or demonstrate causal relations by analyzing statistical data. Rather, it seeks to establish a foundation and propose a direction for further studies by probing in-depth discussions with teenage girls. This study is a qualitative research providing deep insights into the interactions between devices (smartphones), content (the games), and social conditions of use (sheltered teenage girls, somewhat deprived of opportunities for offline social interactions). Unlike traditional media with its limited functions, the recent technologies for smart devices allow many different functions on one device and thus how people use these devices is very diverse. Further studies may be able to produce meaningful results as the researchers focus on the various sociocultural contexts of using new media and the effects on users' social capital.

NOTES

1. A PC bang is a unique cultural place of South Korea which is equipped with a number of high-performance computers. Since the hourly fee is inexpensive and the computer hardware is optimized for gaming, PC bangs maintain popularity as a social meeting place for young gamers. Main patrons are males in their teens and twenties, while only 13.8% of females use PC bangs. Most of PC bang users (86.7%) generally play online games there, and many of them (43.9%) mainly use PC bangs in order to hang out with their friends or colleagues (Korea Creative Content Agency 2014).
2. Mobile social games used to have asynchronous gaming environments. Though game publishers provided social functions, such as invitation and boast, gamers could not play those games synchronously with other gamers. However, due to the development of mobile game technologies, mobile social games began to provide synchronous gameplay.

BIBLIOGRAPHY

Baker, W.E. 1990. Market networks and corpo- rate behavior. *American Journal of Sociology* 96(3): 589–625.

Bargh, John A., and Katelyn Y.A. McKenna. 2004. The internet and social life. *Annual Review of Psychology* 55(1): 573–590. doi:10.1146/annurev. psych.55.090902.141922.

Bell, Marek, Matthew Chalmers, Louise Barkhuus, Malcolm Hall, Scott Sherwood, Paul Tennent, Barry Brown, et al. 2006. "Interweaving mobile games with everyday life." In *Proceedings of the SIGCHI Conference on Human Factors in Computing Systems*, 417–26. CHI '06. New York: ACM. doi:10.1145/1124772. 1124835.

Boase, Jeffrey. 2008. Personal networks and the personal communication system. *Information, Communication & Society* 11(4): 490–508. doi:10.1080/136911 80801999001.

Boase, Jeffrey, John B. Horrigan, B. Wellman, and Lee Rainie. 2006. "The Strength of Internet Ties. Pew Internet and American Life Project." http:// www.pewinternet.org/~/media//Files/Reports/2006/PIP_Internet_ties. pdf.pdf.

Bourdieu, Pierre. 1985. The forms of capital. In *Handbook of theory and research for the sociology of education*, ed. Jacues G. Richardson, 241–258. New York: Greenwood.

———. 1986. *Distinction: A social critique of the judgement of taste*, 1st edn. London: Routledge.

Brooks, Brandon, Howard T. Welser, Bernie Hogan, and Scott Titsworth. 2011. Socioeconomic status updates. *Information, Communication & Society* 14(4): 529–549. doi:10.1080/1369118X.2011.562221.

Burt, Ronald S. 2009. *Structural holes: The social structure of competition*. Cambridge, MA: Harvard University Press.

Chan, Dean. 2008. Convergence, connectivity, and the case of Japanese mobile gaming. *Games and Culture* 3(1): 13–25. doi:10.1177/1555412007309524.

Chen, Wenhong. 2013. "Internet use, online communication, and ties in Americans' networks." *Social Science Computer Review*, 31(4), 404–423. March, 0894439313480345. doi:10.1177/0894439313480345.

Coleman, James S. 1988. Social capital in the creation of human capital. *The American Journal of Sociology* 94: S95–120.

Constant, David, Sproull Lee, and Sara Kiesler. 1996. The kindness of strangers: The usefulness of electronic weak ties for technical advice. *Organization Science* 7(2): 119–135. doi:10.1287/orsc.7.2.119.

De Gournay, Chantal. 2002. Pretence of intimacy in France. In *Perpetual contact: Mobile communication, private talk, public performance*, ed. James E. Katz, and Mark Aakhus. Cambridge: Cambridge University Press.

DIGIECO. 2013. "소셜네트워크게임(SNG) 이용행태 조사." DIGIECO.

Donath, J., and D. Boyd. 2004. Public displays of connection. *BT Technology Journal* 22(4): 71–82. doi:10.1023/B:BTTJ.0000047585.06264.cc.

Dunbar, R.I.M. 2003. The social brain: Mind, language, and society in evolutionary perspective. *Review of Anthropology* 32: 163–181.

Ellison, Nicole B., Charles Steinfield, and Cliff Lampe. 2007. The benefits of facebook 'Friends:' Social capital and college students' use of online social network sites. *Journal of Computer-Mediated Communication* 12(4): 1143–1168. doi:10.1111/j.1083-6101.2007.00367.x.

Erickson, B.H. 1996. Culture, class, and connections. *American Journal of Sociology* 102(1): 217–251.

Gergen, K.J. 2002. The challenge of absent presence. In *Perpetual contact: Mobile communication, private talk, public performance*, ed. James E. Katz, and Mark Aakhus. Cambridge: Cambridge University Press.

———. 2008. Mobile communication and the transformation of the democratic process. In *Handbook of mobile communication studies*, ed. J.E. Katz, 297–310. Cambridge, MA: MIT Press.

Geser, Hans. 2006. Towards a sociological theory of the mobile phone. In *E-Merging media: Communication and the media economy of the future*, ed. Axel Zerdick, Jean-Claude Burgelman, Klaus Schrape, Valerie Feldmann, Roger Silverstone, Christian Wernick, and Carolin Wolff. New York: Springer.

Granovetter, Mark. 1983. The strength of weak ties: A network theory revisited. *Sociological Theory* 1: 201. doi:10.2307/202051.

Hampton, Keith N., Lauren F. Sessions, and Eun Ja Her. 2011. Core networks, social isolation, and new media. *Information, Communication & Society* 14(1): 130–155. doi:10.1080/1369118X.2010.513417.

Haythornthwaite, Caroline. 2002. Strong, weak, and latent ties and the impact of new media. *The Information Society* 18(5): 385–401. doi:10.1080/01972240290108195.

Hjorth, Larissa. 2012. "Relocating the mobile: A case study of locative media in Seoul, South Korea." *Convergence: The International Journal of Research into New Media Technologies*, December, 1354856512462360. doi:10.1177/1354856512462360.

Hurlbert, J.S., J.J. Beggs, and V. Haines. 2001. Social networks and social capital in extreme environments. In *Social capital theory and research*, ed. N. Lin, K.S. Cook, and R.S. Burt, 209–231. New York: Aldine de Gruyter.

Huvila, Isto, Kim Holmberg, Stefan Ek, and Gunilla Widén-Wulff. 2010. Social capital in second life. *Online Information Review* 34(2): 295–316. doi:10.1108/14684521011037007.

Igarashi, Tasuku, Jiro Takai, and Toshikazu Yoshida. 2005. Gender differences in social network development via mobile phone text messages: A longitudinal study. *Journal of Social and Personal Relationships* 22(5): 691–713. doi:10.1177/0265407505056492.

Itō, Mizuko, Daisuke Okabe, and Misa Matsuda. 2006. *Personal, portable, pedestrian: Mobile phones in Japanese life*. Cambridge, MA: The MIT Press.

Jones, Steve, Camille Johnson-Yale, Sarah Millermaier, and Francisco Seoane Pérez. 2009. U.S. College Students' internet use: Race, gender and digital divides. *Journal of Computer-Mediated Communication* 14(2): 244–264. doi:10.1111/j.1083-6101.2009.01439.x.

Jones, Jason J., Jaime E. Settle, Robert M. Bond, Christopher J. Fariss, Cameron Marlow, and James H. Fowler. 2013. Inferring tie strength from online directed behavior. *PLoS ONE* 8(1): e52168. doi:10.1371/journal.pone.0052168.

Katz, James E. 2006. Mobile communication and the transformation of daily life: The next phase of research on mobiles. *Knowledge, Technology & Policy* 19(1): 62–71. doi:10.1007/s12130-006-1016-4.

Kennedy, T., A. Smith, A. Wells, and B. Wellman. 2008. *Networked families*. Washington, DC: Pew Internet & American Life Project.

Kim, A. J. 2004. "The network is the game: Social trends in mobile entertainment." Presented at the online proceedings of the Game Developers Conference (GDC '04).

Kim, Hyosil. 2013a. "채팅愛 빠져... 여학생 스마트폰 중독 남학생의 3배." 세계일보.http://www.segye.com/content/html/2013/03/26/20130326005787.html.

Kim, Nari. 2013b. "Kakao talk, leaping to global open platform with domestic success." *Digital Times*. http://www.dt.co.kr/contents.html?article_no=2013101502010831789003.

Kobayashi, Tetsuro. 2010. Bridging social capital in online communities: Heterogeneity and social tolerance of online game players in Japan. *Human Communication Research* 36(4): 546–569. doi:10.1111/j.1468-2958.2010.01388.x.

Korea Creative Content Agency. 2012. "Gamer Survey Report 2012." Naju: KOCCA.

———. 2013. "Report on Smart Content Market 2012." Naju: KOCCA.

———. 2014. "Gamer Survey Report 2014." Naju: KOCCA.

Korea Internet & Security Agency. 2013. "Second Half, Smartphone Using State Survey 2012." Seoul: KISA.

Kraut, Robert, Michael Patterson, Vicki Lundmark, Sara Kiesler, Tridas Mukophadhyay, and William Scherlis. 1998. Internet paradox: A social technology that reduces social involvement and psychological well-being? *American Psychologist* 53(9): 1017–1031. doi:10.1037/0003-066X.53.9.1017.

Lenhart, Amanda, Joseph Kahne, Ellen Middaugh, Alexandra Rankin, Chris Evans, and Jessica Vitak. 2008. "Teens, video games, and civics." http://www.pewinternet.org/~/media/Files/Reports/2008/PIP_Teens_Games_and_Civics_Report_FINAL.pdf.pdf.

Licoppe, Christian. 2004. 'Connected' presence: The emergence of a new repertoire for managing social relationships in a changing communication technoscape. *Environment and Planning D: Society and Space* 22(1): 135–156. doi:10.1068/d323t.

Ling, Rich. 2004. *The mobile connection: The cell phone's impact on society*. San Francisco: Morgan Kaufmann.

Matsuda, Misa. 2006. Mobile communications and selective sociality. In *Personal, portable, pedestrian: Mobile phones in Japanese life*, ed. Mizuko Ito, Daisuke Okabe, and Misa Matsuda. Cambridge, MA: The MIT Press.

Ministry of Gender Equality & Family. 2012. "Report on Youth Media Use 2011." MOGEF.

Olds, Jacqueline, and Richard S. Schwartz. 2009. *The lonely American: Drifting apart in the twenty-first century.* Boston: Beacon Press.

Orleans, Myron, and Margaret C. Laney. 2000. Children's computer use in the home isolation or sociation? *Social Science Computer Review* 18(1): 56–72. doi:10.1177/089443930001800104.

Portes, Alejandro. 1998. Social capital: Its origins and applications in modern sociology. *Annual Review of Sociology* 24: 1–24.

Putnam, Robert D. 1995. Bowling alone: America's declining social capital. *Journal of Democracy* 6(1): 65–78. doi:10.1353/jod.1995.0002.

———. 2001. *Bowling alone: The collapse and revival of American community.* New York: Simon and Schuster.

Reid, Donna J., and Fraser J.M. Reid. 2005. Textmates and text circles: Insights into the social ecology of SMS text messaging. In *Mobile world,* Computer supported cooperative work, ed. Lynne Hamill, Amparo Lasen, and Dan Diaper, 105–118. London: Springer http://link.springer.com/chapter/10.1007/1-84628-204-7_7.

Rettie, Ruth. 2008. Mobile phones as network capital: Facilitating connections. *Mobilities* 3(2): 291–311. doi:10.1080/17450100802095346.

Richter, Felix. 2013. "The United States ranks 13th in smartphone penetration." *Statista.* http://www.statista.com/topics/840/smartphones/chart/1405/the-united-states-ranks-13th-in-smartphone-penetration/.

Rivière, Carole Anne, and Christian Licoppe. 2005. From voice to text: Continuity and change in the use of mobile phones in France and Japan. In *The inside text,* The Kluwer International Series on computer supported cooperative work 4, ed. R. Harper, L. Palen, and A. Taylor, 103–126. Dordrecht: Springer http://link.springer.com/chapter/10.1007/1-4020-3060-6_6.

Roberts, Sam G.B., Robin I.M. Dunbar, Thomas V. Pollet, and Toon Kuppens. 2009. Exploring variation in active network size: Constraints and ego characteristics. *Social Networks* 31(2): 138–146. doi:10.1016/j.socnet.2008.12.002.

Skoric, Marko M., and Grace Chi En Kwan. 2011. Platforms for mediated sociability and online social capital: The role of facebook and massively multiplayer online games. *Asian Journal of Communication* 21(5): 467–484. doi:10.1080/01292986.2011.587014.

Statistics Korea. 2012. "Report on youth." Statistics Korea.

Steinfield, Charles, Joan M. DiMicco, Nicole B. Ellison, and Cliff Lampe. 2009. "Bowling online: Social networking and social capital within the organization." In *Proceedings of the fourth international conference on communities and technologies,* 245–254. C&T'09. New York: ACM. doi:10.1145/1556460.1556496.

Steinkuehler, Constance A., and Dmitri Williams. 2006. Where everybody knows your (screen) name: Online games as 'Third Places'. *Journal of Computer-*

Mediated Communication 11(4): 885–909. doi:10.1111/j.1083-6101. 2006.00300.x.

Suoninen, A. 2013. The role of media in peer group relations. In *Children and their changing media environment: A European comparative study*, ed. Sonia Livingstone, and Moira Bovill, 353–389. New York: Routledge.

Trepte, Sabine, Leonard Reinecke, and Keno Juechems. 2012. The social side of gaming: How playing online computer games creates online and offline social support. *Computers in Human Behavior* 28(3): 832–839. doi:10.1016/j. chb.2011.12.003.

Turkle, Sherry. 2012. *Alone together: Why we expect more from technology and less from each other*. First Trade Paper Edition. Basic Books.

Uzzi, Brian. 1996. The sources and consequences of embeddedness for the economic performance of organizations: The network effect. *American Sociological Review* 61(4): 674. doi:10.2307/2096399.

Wellman, B., J. Boase, and W. Chen. 2002. The networked nature of community: Online and offline. *IT & Society* 1(1): 151–165.

Williams, Dmitri. 2006a. On and off the 'Net: scales for social capital in an online era. *Journal of Computer-Mediated Communication* 11(2): 593–628. doi:10.1111/j.1083-6101.2006.00029.x.

———. 2006b. Why game studies now? Gamers don't bowl alone. *Games and Culture* 1(1): 13–16. doi:10.1177/1555412005281774.

CHAPTER 6

Database Production: Planners and Players in a Japanese Mobile Game Studio

Bryan Hikari Hartzheim

The commercial development of mobile video games has existed in Japan in some form for over three decades since the early days of Nintendo's Game & Watch. Mobile gaming, however, has rapidly accelerated in the last several years with new companies entering the video game industry to produce content for the exploding market of smartphones and electronic tablets.[1] Most of these companies are staffed by Japanese developers who make games primarily for the domestic market of Japan. Some of these companies are also comprised of foreign residents who can speak Japanese and have the skills or aptitude for handling the tasks required for certain jobs in the game industry. In some cases, teams of Japanese and foreign developers work side by side to create games for both the domestic and global markets. It is the latter particular environment that is the central focus of this chapter which, in its observation and analysis, seeks to answer the following questions. Who are the game developers today most responsible for shaping and directing our experiences in dynamic game worlds? What tools or elements do developers use to organize and shape our experiences of and participation in the most commonly played games? And

B.H. Hartzheim (✉)
English and Liberal Arts, Reitaku University, Kashiwa, Japan

© The Author(s) 2016
S.A. Lee, A. Pulos (eds.), *Transnational Contexts of Development History, Sociality, and Society of Play*, East Asian Popular Culture, DOI 10.1007/978-3-319-43820-7_6

151

finally, how does having an understanding of game developers help us better comprehend how games come together or fall apart?

This chapter will look at collaborative global/local production among mobile game creators in Japan, primarily through examining the international culture of production in a single video game studio. In order to show how the creative labor of both foreign and Japanese developers circumstantially and directly affect and alter the game experiences, actions, and responses of players, I will look at how developers engage in and players respond to what I label—borrowing from the theoretical framework of Azuma Hiroki— *database production*. Database production is, I argue, one of the essential methods of media construction for free-to-play mobile games in the casual, non-core gaming segment, relying on databases of design elements and assets centered largely around characters.

To best illustrate this idea, this chapter will employ a critical lens and methodology from the field of "production studies," a subset of critical media industry studies that emphasizes the labor of "below-the-line" workers in the process of media creation. I will focus on a critically unexamined role in the production chain of Japanese game studios that is, nevertheless, fundamentally important to the construction and operations of mobile online games today. This role is the *planner*, and I will first describe the similarities and differences in this role to its Western equivalent, the game "designer." To help frame this analysis of creative decision-making and substantiate the definition of database production, I will employ new media theory that dissects the relationship between consumption and production in the Japanese creative industries in order to show how planners go about constructing Japanese multiplayer, free-to-play (F2P) card-battle games.

To this end, this chapter looks at the construction and operations of a single game and how players react to the design choices that planners implement, based on fieldwork in a Japanese mobile game company conducted over a 6-month period from 2012 to 2013. In some ways, this final aspect takes inspiration from "game ethnographies" of virtual worlds, where researchers simultaneously play and observe the actions and behaviors of participants with one another in the virtual game space.[2] However, rather than strictly focus on how players interact with one another, or on the angle of consumption and player agency, this chapter will organize its analysis around actions and responses of game developers first, and game players second, in order to shed light on how production and play can become an active and changing process, especially when play becomes organized around issues of control over player agency. By focusing on how both planners and players react and respond to attempts at corralling and directing the behavior of one another, this chapter will show how the competitive ethos of planner-based operations is reflected in the players who struggle to locate power and control within the game itself. This struggle illuminates the processes of production in mobile gaming today that rely less on any single designer, but more on teams of task workers to carry out game operations and implement designs.

PLANNERS VS. DESIGNERS

The word "planner" has some different connotations between how it is used in Japan and in other parts of the world. One might think of planners as people who prepare elaborate events (such as wedding planners) or analyze business strategies (such as financial planners). In Japanese console game development, the planner is a title used to describe what is its closest Western equivalent: the video game "designer." Designers in American or European game studios are frequently immersed in various aspects of game design, what Katie Salen and Eric Zimmerman define as "the process by which a *designer* creates a *context* to be encountered by a *participant*, from which *meaning* emerges."[3] The construction of forms (spaces, narratives) to create meaningful play experiences for players is the role of the designer or team of designers. These forms can involve the construction and organization of tools and functions such as menu interfaces, level designs, and battle systems, while the meaning comes in the rules and goals of the play itself.

In console gaming in Japan, teams of planners are typically less responsible for designing large aspects of gameplay than their counterparts in the West.[4] Instead, they are confined to creating or refining core aspects of the gameplay, such as banners in the menu interface, or enemy balancing within the battle system. The sort of macro design that regulates the direction of the entire game is often the responsibility of the game's director and/or producer, who shepherd a team of planners to follow and communicate their instructions to the programmers, artists, or sound/audio technicians involved in game development. Console game planners' main job duties, echoed by James Kay, boil down to asset and naming convention management, software list construction, level design, and attending lots of meetings.[5] As JC Barnett puts it, "Microsoft Excel is their main weapon and tool."[6] In any downtime, they pitch their own game designs/concepts to their superiors, with the hopes of designing a gameplay element, or even an entire game, of their own.

With F2P mobile gaming, however, planners now have a more active role in the day-to-day development of a game. This is actually a throwback to how planning was conducted in the first generation of console and arcade game design in Japan, where those in the planning department took on a variety of tasks such as game design, story writing, character design, and in some cases even music or sound composition. One of the most famous examples of this is Shigeru Miyamoto's iterative design of the levels, characters, and even supposedly the music in *Donkey Kong*.[7] Planners for mobile games now design levels, events, characters, and even entire world maps for some games. Foreign planners for mobile games, a concept that is rare in console gaming but increasingly common in mobile gaming companies, translate scripts, create story, and help localize gameplay elements and character designs for Japanese mobile games that hit the English-language market.

Where designers for console games, or games with few online components, make games that have a discrete set of tasks, goals, and design concepts for a finished product, F2P social and mobile games constantly evolve and create new levels and designs in order to engage a base of continuously playing consumers. This is not a new concept for Western game designers, accustomed to producing massive multiplayer online (MMO) games for players on personal computers. Japanese online play existed in some form on PCs, grew in popularity through the PlayStation 3 and its online components, and has spread rapidly in the last several years with the proliferation of mobile devices that feature free casual games. Thus, Japanese video game studios are now being created for the sole purpose of producing games that can only be played on mobile app platforms such as the App Store or Google Play, with a focus on perpetual gameplay designs where players can play a continually renewable, rather than enclosed, gameplay experience. At the forefront of the people running these unceasing game engines are the task robots once heretofore known as planners, and the core of their work now consists of operating a game once it goes "live."

Planners for F2P mobile games are now responsible for three additional areas as part of their workload of implementing the gameplay designs of the director or producer. First, they must figure out ways to *monetize* or incorporate a pay channel into the game's engine. Monetization is a fact of games since the earliest arcade machines.[8] Monetization in online games can take many forms, such as subscriptions, where players pay a monthly fee to access the game's world, or micropayments, where players make in-game purchases to unlock a previously locked level, upgrade to a special item, or, in most cases, simply to continue playing the game when their "energy" has run out. Players who become addicted to a game can easily rack up hundreds or thousands of dollars in micropayments each month.

One easy to understand example of the micropayment monetization model is featured in the Electronic Arts produced mobile game, *The Simpsons: Tapped Out*. The F2P title, based on the popular animated sitcom, is a city-building game that is tailor-made for monetization. The game first introduces a gameplay hook—rebuilding the Simpsons' neighborhood through acquiring and building simple structures—that is easy to understand and accomplish. The player is provided with an immediate accomplishment for completing goals, which are more akin to simple tasks. At the start of the game, players are provided with game currency to continue playing and accomplishing these tasks, but the currency is finite and requires actual money to continue playing. As players progress in the game, it becomes more and more difficult to progress or stay competitive without the purchase of game currency. Finally, after this bait and switch, players are encouraged to come back through random gifts, continuous events, and the encouragement of other players who they have befriended within the game. This is the core difference of planners who design for free mobile games versus console games and even most MMOs: planners must design their games to get players to pay for the game *after* playing the game, not before. Instead of simply tracking sales of game copies in a given week, planners must take into account metrics such as the average revenue per user (ARPU), the amount of daily active users (DAU), the customer acquisition cost (CAC), and, most importantly, the lifetime value (LTV) or the average total revenue expected from any given player.[9] By analyzing these metrics, planners can have a stronger idea of what types of events, assets, or rewards to include in the game to attract new players and retain old ones.

Related to the concept of monetization, planners must also continue to *build* the game after its core engine is complete, developing value for players to entice them to pay for a better experience. What this means is that planners must create events for the game to continue to draw in players. Most planners must create a *shiyōsho*, or specification document, that encapsulates the salient themes and gameplay features of the event. These events are contingent on the game, and Japanese mobile games are particularly reliant on such methods to draw revenue and player engagement. Often, these events revolve around familiar cultural or trendy tropes, such as fairytales, new films, national holidays, or even other popular game titles in elaborate "collaborations," promotions where content from one game appears in another in order to advertise the content in both games.[10] Such events allow players who download or start up the game to receive limited-time in-game gifts that feature designs from the worlds of other games. These promotions continue to draw players into new events with the hope of obtaining the newest rewards with increased power levels or stats that can give the player an advantage over other players in the game.

Finally, planners must *manage* the games they design, often through asset lists, in what is called "operations." With console games, once the game was completed, the planner could have a brief respite until the next project while thinking of new game pitches. With mobile gaming, the planner's work is only beginning once the designs are completed and the game debuts on a platform. Planners must continue to compose *shiyōsho* and build new assets, as well as oversee the game's events in real time, in order to make returns off the upfront efforts of the game's developers. New assets such as characters, items, and even specially ordered music and cinematic cut scenes must be incorporated into the game, sometimes through events and oftentimes through pay-to-play slot machines. For example, the goal in Square-Enix's homage to RPG battles, *Final Fantasy Record Keeper*, is to acquire new characters and weapons through completing all the battles in individual story chapters based on famous scenes in the *Final Fantasy* franchise. Each event requires digital assets in the form of characters, items, backgrounds, and music designed by digital graphics artists, as well as specific gameplay goals and narration. Planners must oversee the production of all of this, incorporate each asset into the engine's server, and test the event for errors with debuggers. With ambitious game concepts such as this one, these events can occur every week, meaning that teams either need to have one or two energetic and creative planners or a team of a half dozen to continue coming up with and managing fresh concepts.[11]

In sum, the planners' role now is to keep a game running in perpetuity, since this means it is continuously generating revenue. This is achieved in largely two ways: by appealing to a core group of high-spending players or a broad base of players who each spend a little bit. In casino gambling terms, this approach is called appealing to the "whales" and "minnows" of the gaming pool.[12] Because of this, games tend to start small, appealing to a broad user base, and then gradually narrow the funnel to only allow big spenders to squeeze through to the next stages and highest ranks. Ramin Shokrizade has called this structural push for players to spend "coercive monetization." Coercive monetization makes players feel they must pay for "premium currency" to go through "progress gates" and continue a game in which they've invested ample time and emotional attachment, essentially "putting the consumer in a very uncomfortable or undesirable position in the game and then offering to remove this 'pain' in return for spending money."[13]

Coercive monetization is a key difference between the micropayments of arcade machines or even the subscription-based model of MMORPGs of yore, such as *World of Warcraft* and *Everquest*: players could only purchase "upgrades" through transactions with players outside the game, such as paying Chinese players to harvest gold, or avid semi-pro players for their leveled-up characters on eBay.[14] With app-based mobile games, the purchasing of upgrades is encouraged, and often necessary, through the design of the game system itself. This is most obviously seen in the popular mobile F2P puzzle game, *Candy Crush Saga*. As the game's difficulty incrementally rises to a point where it requires immense investment in time for the player to progress, players are encouraged to purchase extra "moves" or "power ups" to be able to pass tough levels when they have run out of lives. Each purchase is only a dollar or two, thus encouraging players to overcome short-term psychological frustration through a (seemingly) painless and minimal financial exchange.

FRAGMENTED CONSUMPTION AND DATABASE PRODUCTION

One way this planner-centric model affects the experience of F2P mobile games is through a fragmentation of the gameplay. Whales might spend to progress in any given game, but the majority of players in a given F2P mobile game do not pay to advance. Instead, the game engine forces them to wait a set number of hours in order for their energy or stamina to recharge and continue playing. Gameplay is chopped up into bite-sized chunks of only several minutes for most players, thus leading to game experiences that are focused on the completion of quick goals and immediately rewarding actions. Fragmentation for F2P mobile games is seen as ideal for the typical player of casual games who open the app on their phone while riding a train to or waiting in line at the bank. Experiences that can be started and ended within a span of a few minutes are easier to absorb, rely less on narratives that focus on developing plot or character, and, importantly, are conducive to long-tail monetization tactics that ask the player to continually invest in the game in small increments over a spread-out period versus a large amount up front.

This fragmentation, however, does not stop at the level of player consumption but also extends to the process of the game's construction. Nearly all F2P games that are released are not finished products, as by definition F2P games need to constantly create new ways for players to return to the core gaming loop and invest money to continue playing or improving their game's experience. As most F2P games are unfinished, they are designed in a similarly piecemeal and additive process, where planners, artists, and programmers are constantly creating new events, designs, and mechanisms that will consistently attract and engage new and returning players. As games are designed to be infinitely expandable, moreover, creators are expected to introduce new narrative and gameplay elements and designs that take the original game in multiple directions.

A simple set of examples can be found in the aforementioned *Final Fantasy Record Keeper*, where only a set number of dungeons are available for players to complete in the beginning of the game. If players immediately pass all the dungeons, they must then wait for additional dungeons to be added at a later date. Hence, the importance placed on weekly timed "event" dungeons—based off of famous areas or scenes in the *Final Fantasy* lineage—where players must climb the dungeon levels and compete against one another, rather than the game's AI, to reap the highest rewards. However, other facets of the game—from the interface to background music—undergo facelifts and updates at periodic junctures as well, effectively adding a fresh coat of digital paint in order to keep the game popular in a competitive platform environment. The production of such F2P games is thus a fragmented process, where designers and developers must constantly read and react to how players respond to previous events or game additions in order to deliver an optimal experience for the purpose of continually monetizing the audience.

Fragmentation of consumption and production is not unique to mobile gaming or Japan, as audiences all over the world have begun regularly consuming serial literature and comics since the early twentieth century and adventure serials and daytime soap operas through radio and television from the mid-twentieth century. Mobile game companies in Japan, however, are uniquely positioned industrially due to the fact that they are frequently developed as part of a larger media ecology known as a *media mix*. In Japan, the media mix is a commonly used expression to denote the serial interconnection of media in Japanese print and visual culture.[15] Under this system, a dense network of media allows for multiple manifestations and cross-media promotions of a single media property. The media mix system affects both producers and consumers to different degrees.

For producers, as Marc Steinberg has observed, the media mix of Japan has many similarities with Henry Jenkins' concept of "transmedia story-telling," where media is developed across a range of formats that are, ide-ally, able to uniquely bring out aspects of a particular narrative.[16] Such multimedia seriality is a more recent phenomenon in the West but has a long lineage in Japan. Steinberg argues that the core elements of a media mix system of media production have been in place in some form since the early 1960s with television animation and further developed as a produc-tion strategy by the Kadokawa Publishing Company in the early 1980s.[17] By considering popular anime series through the multiple-worlds theory of Geoffrey Leibniz in popular anime series, Steinberg further argues that the media mix of Japan—in its use of spreading single properties across multiple media formats—also creates a tolerance for divergence within discrete worlds. These types of media work best, as Steinberg puts it, "when they imagine worlds differently, deploying divergence as a creative practice, and embracing bifurcation at the narrative as well as visual lev-els."[18] Since media networks in the country are so interconnected with one another, producers have become adept at handling distinct segments of a larger media world.

Consumers are, similarly, equally capable of tracking their favorite series across a long chain of distributed media forms. This is most nota-bly seen among *otaku*, or fans of Japan's forms of commercial anima-tion and comics called, respectively, anime and manga. Viewers of anime and manga grew accustomed to consuming serial narratives through television and magazines during the 1960s. Consumption of serial nar-ratives began in weekly installments in manga through the proliferation of weekly manga magazines such as *Weekly Shōnen Sunday* and *Weekly Shōnen Magazine* in 1959, peaking in exposure with *Weekly Shōnen Jump* in 1968.[19] This consumption was magnified through serial con-sumption of television episodes in anime through the debut of Osamu Tezuka's *Tetsuwan Atomu* (Astro Boy) in 1963.[20] However, beginning in the early 1980s with the spread of VHS video recorders, hobby maga-zines, and comics conventions, a generation of fans was birthed that began to collect and obsess over their favorite anime and manga cre-ations.[21] Anime and manga during this period became increasingly tied to a multiplicity of media formats, with serial television becoming but one avenue for consumption.

Various theorists, such as Otsuka Eiji and Ito Go, have used examples from anime and manga to discuss the nature of this fragmented sense of consumption.[22] Azuma Hiroki, however, is one of the few who uses video games as an entry point into understanding *otaku* consumption. Azuma, like Ito, argues that attractive character elements are what fuel strong fan attraction and consistent engagement, but he takes this idea to an even further degree. Azuma is particularly interested in the lack of distinction fans of anime or game subcultures tend to place on "originals" and "copies" of any given media property. Rather than the integrity or quality of a particular work, Azuma argues that fans of a given work are more interested in combinations of elements associated with "*moé*" or strong feelings of desire toward character.[23] He writes, "For [otaku], the distinction between the original and the spin-off products (as copies) does not exist; the only valid distinction for them is between the settings created anonymously (a database at the deep inner layer) and the individual works that each artist has concretized from the information (a simulacrum on the surface outer layer)."[24] Thus, a manga, an anime, and a coffee mug have no value distinction but are all equally legitimate entry points to what is truly valued by fans: the "database" of its *moé* elements or strongly affective character properties. Azuma calls this form of consumption *database consumption*, in reference to the prioritizing of attractive character elements from a collectively formed cultural database, rather than the narratives or worlds from which they derive.

Azuma calls database consumption "animalistic," since it means that fans no longer are interested in concepts that relate works to a larger social order, or as products of an "other," that is, an author.[25] Instead, any given work is hungrily consumed based on the affection that a fan has for the character designs and personalities. This sort of customizable interaction is on full display with *bishōjo* or "beautiful girl" games. Most of these games focus on their interactions with digital characters, with a large sub-genre on dating, so player agency is often relegated to responses to dialogue posed by the still character images. As players play through the game, the ways in which they answer questions or options affect the outcome. After finishing the game, players play through the game again and select different options for different outcomes, adopting "multiple personalities" in each replay in order to interact with a variety of characters. Azuma argues that this form of subjectivity is a "game-like realism" that stems from the many potential outcomes and directions players take on when playing through such games.[26] In the end, games are merely a means for accessing a multitude of different character types. Characters, then, can exist "outside narratives, in multiple narratives, and between narratives," as fan attraction to them is not based on anything directly connected to the narrative but instead is based on their various design and personality elements.[27] Database consumption is what fuels devotion to anime and anime-like games, where desire is a "drug addict"-like endless craving for new characters.[28]

I would like to focus on Azuma's contextualization of the character in his book (and its sequel) for the purposes of relating how Japanese fan consumption habits influence production and the role of the planner in F2P mobile games made in Japan. Azuma's description of character consumption patterns is borne out not only in the *bishōjo* anime games that he analyzes but also in various forms of mobile games. In some cases, database consumption is exhibited in games that combine "catching" and "role-playing games" where the objective is to collect hoards of characters for the purpose of assembling a great team of rare fighters, a genre whose most well-known representative is the global hit *Pokémon*.[29] In these games, the database has typically been a concrete table of monsters, quantifiable and classifiable like a taxonomical chart, but F2P mobile games allow for character churn with no discernable end. As players continue to play the game, new characters are constantly created as rewards for the players to acquire.

I borrow from Azuma to describe this system of revenue-motivated avatar creation as *database production*. In this system, developers are tasked with creating meaningful assets for players to acquire, largely through *shiyōsho* specification documents that use characters as collectible and obtainable assets to make the games as attractive as possible. Characters become a sort of product that players must spend a certain amount of time and money to acquire. Typically, these characters are represented in still images that resemble collectable cards within the game, and players must acquire them to field competitive units in order to progress in the game's world or against one another in battle. Such a system should ostensibly lend itself to easy customization and multiple media formats, markets, and audiences, as it has in the character-based media mix in Japan, but complications can emerge when databases from different production cultures and audiences mix.

In the following case study, I show how Japanese and global planners in a Tokyo-based mobile game studio engage in such database production on the near-simultaneous construction of a dark-fantasy mobile role-playing game produced in 2012–2013. The two working environments, and the responses by and toward players of the two games, reveal how game production teams attempt to face the needs and wants of their respective cultural audiences and their demands for attractive characters. This is especially the case with mobile games, however, as those who produce games and their subsequent events without regard to their respective audiences can face immediate responses in real time. In the following case study, these player responses to planner decisions comprise a contested arena for the assertion of agency, control, and the right to play a competitive but coercive video game.

DATABASE PRODUCTION IN THE CONTEXT OF TRANSNATIONAL GAME DEVELOPMENT

This case study will examine the design schemes of planners and the resulting player reactions through participant observation conducted from October 2012 to May 2013 at a mobile game studio called The Game Room. The project under observation is a F2P card-battle game called *Dragon Conquerors*.[30] *Dragon Conquerors*, or *DC*, is a useful case study, since it was initially developed by an international team of planners for a North American audience and subsequently reverse-localized for the Japanese market. The game gives us a perspective of two different production teams and play cultures of the same game at simultaneous junctures.

The case study employs a similar line of inquiry of that of "production studies" analyses from film and media studies, where observational fieldwork and participant observation are carried out in areas occupied by "below-the-line" workers in order to analyze the sense-making practices of cultural workers in media production.[31] This is particularly important in the case of F2P mobile game development, as the most relevant social activity for game developers is enacted not in boardrooms but "on set" in the perpetual operations work of the planners, programmers, and artists. The method used to analyze both the international and Japanese teams is that of "thick description," anthropologist Clifford Geertz's conception of describing participants' cultural context—in this case, that of the game's developers—in order to better understand their actions and behaviors.[32] While an array of developers collaborate and worked together to make *DC*, this case study will focus specifically on the behaviors and comments—through interviews and field notes—of planners, as they are central to the many different departments in the game studio and are in charge of the "live" operations of the game as outlined earlier in this chapter.

DC was modeled on similar card battlers popular at the time, such as Cygames' *Rage of Bahamut*, GREE's *Driland*, and KLab's *Sengoku Buster*, benefitting from the small exposure those games received with international players. Instead of those games' cute anime-inspired characters and aesthetics, *DC* aimed for the international market through a late medieval aesthetic that overtly mimicked dark-fantasy franchises such as the book and film franchise *The Lord of the Rings* and, more recently, the book and HBO television series *Game of Thrones*. This dark-fantasy theme was overlaid on a previously utilized, browser-based PHP game engine of a Japanese anime-inspired title set in the feudal period to create a version of the card battler that would hopefully appeal to a Western audience. An international team of planners set to work on transforming the former game's assets, replacing the "classes" of ninja, samurai, and feudal lords with "races" of humans, elves, and dwarves, and changing the backgrounds and interface from that of feudal-era Japan to a land of magic and dragons.

The objective of the game is straightforward. Players collect colorful character cards with attack and defense parameters called "warriors." These warriors are often obtained from slot games called *gacha*, where players pay to open a treasure box containing a warrior of varying rarity. The goal of the game is for players to form teams called guilds and attack other players in sets of one-on-one battles called guild wars. Each battle is waged against an opponent's avatar, and battles are won based on "attacks"—a tap on the screen to inflict damage to a player's "defense." Players with the strongest attack and defense parameters for their warriors typically win, as offensive warriors require making fewer attacks, while defensive warriors can withstand more opponent attacks, though determined players can persistently chip away at even strong players by replenishing their energy and attacking repeatedly. The participation in gacha and guild wars requires game currency that can be earned slowly over the course of the game or bought in bundles through in-game purchases. Gacha, for example, require "gems" in order to access them, while guild wars require "battle potions," which replenish the ability to attack, and "health potions," which replenish the ability to defend. Guilds and players who win these events obtain high ranks and rewards, as well as bragging rights on in-game message boards. If it is not clear at this point, players who repeatedly buy the best warriors from the gacha, or continually replenish energy in battle with bundles of health and battle potions, are typically the ones who spend the most money on the game to receive such upgrades.

Planners were responsible for conceiving all assets within the game, including its characters and the many colorful dragons, through *shiyōsho*. Each planner was tasked with an event and the construction of characters for that event, and these character concepts were then outsourced to graphic design companies specializing in hatching character and background art for games. How these characters were constructed often changed as development proceeded. For example, at the beginning of the game's construction, a single art director hatched most of the characters. But as the game went on, the pressure for the art director to produce more and more characters escalated to the point where the art director left work early one day in tears for "unfair treatment."[33] With the art director stretched to her breaking point, each planner became responsible for designing their own characters. Both the art director and planners used *shiyōsho* to direct how characters were designed by specifying character personalities, poses, faces, wardrobe, and other distinctive elements. This was done largely through cobbling together concept art from other databases of game art, film and animation stills, and fan-made illustrations on designer collation websites such as Pixiv and DeviantArt.

Thus, the planner's key conceptual toolkits were databases of character elements that comprised attractive character icons with which players already were familiar. Through collating or combining these elements, planners instructed designers and artists on what their desired assets should look like, what traits they should exhibit, or how they should behave. These characters were most often utilized in weekly in-game missions and events that featured different themes. In each event, players were encouraged to try to fight or pay for characters based on certain fantasy or genre themes familiar to players, and planners created these themed characters by drawing upon existing tropes, assembling various parts in a template, and then sending them to a designer to construct the finished product. An easy to understand example of this in *DC* was an event centered around dwarves, with specific dwarf characters composed of elements derived from well-known dark-fantasy franchise *Lord of the Rings*, the video game *Dragon Age: Origins*, and dwarf concepts from DeviantArt.

The system of database production had some important advantages for planners on *DC*. First, it created easily manageable assets. Planners created in-game rewards from collectible assets, so if characters were the primary assets, it reduced the need to think of new event ideas and allowed the planner to simply design attractive characters. Planners sent out instructions for character designs every week, so by drawing on familiar designs, they also reduced the need to create characters from scratch. Related to this, database production also mitigated risk in the form of completely new character designs that could prove to be unpopular with players unfamiliar with the whims of a planner's tastes. Planning events and characters through the database also was easily reproducible, as character designs could be customized and given alternate "skins" in order to allow them to be collected in multiple forms. These skins—usually in the form of different color combinations or content themes—could even be applied wholly to the game's engine. One planner told me that a single engine "could supply gameplay for three or four different templates."[34] Finally, database production could easily adapt to popular trends. With F2P mobile games often requiring less time to implement new events and assets, planners could design characters that responded to immediate consumer desires.

These advantages were also some of the drawbacks in game design. As planners merely chose from a database of options in order to create events, the originality of game events inevitably suffered. Planners were often pressured to come up with events on a constant basis, so a path of least resistance was often formed where new characters were constructed from preexisting templates or even recycled from previous events using alternate skins. This copy-and-paste ethos became standard procedure when planners were overtaxed with work. "I want to make better characters and better events," one planner told me. "But there isn't enough time. It would be ideal if I pass my other tasks to my co-workers when I'm handling my own event, but they also have their own tasks, so I just end up having to do my own tasks while making and operating an event."[35]

With a reliance on using characters as rewards, moreover, planners became less incentivized to implement new gameplay designs and events that took advantage of or provided upgrades to the existing game engine. Thus, events in *DC* frequently consisted of the exact same rules, goals, and outcomes, with the rewards simply exchanged to reflect the latest addition to the database. Planners hatched characters consistently with the idea that the more attractive they were—based on the concept art, character theme, and art budget—the better they would function as a reward. The game became more difficult and stressful to manage, since the most innovative characters were already implemented in the early stages of the game and planners frequently had less and less time to conceive of characters as anything other than event rewards.

These disadvantages were mitigated by the fact that *DC* catered to a wide swath of casual gamers, but both the plusses and minuses of database production were magnified when different teams of developers adopted it for multiple audiences. This is a rarity in production environments, where one development team will work on a game for a primary market and then employ or outsource a group to localize it—adopt the game to other countries' languages and cultural signifiers—for alternate markets. Games with large budgets can conduct simultaneous localization, where the game's assets are localized during its production, so that there is no delay between a game's release in multiple countries. In the case of *DC*, one development team of international planners worked on the English-language version of the game, while another development team of Japanese planners worked on a near-simultaneous localization of the same game. While this was not an ideal use of resources at the outset, the idea was that the game would eventually be released to Chinese, Korean, and European audiences once the Japanese and North American versions were successful. Database production in this context would seemingly work well for game design, as assets could be swapped out depending on the desires of each market, with modifications to certain areas where planners saw fit. Besides the story and language localization, there were five main differences in how the two games operated and were planned related to how the games integrated, monetized, or promoted its characters (Table 6.1).

While both versions of *DC* used the same database of character designs, the Japanese version altered certain designs to fit within expectations from Japanese players. The dark-fantasy elements were played down in some characters to make them more colorful and appear cuter, and the localization emphasized fantasy elements that were similar to Japanese RPGs. Witches, for example, were designed to reflect the aesthetic leanings of a group of young female characters from a popular anime series of witches,

Table 6.1 International vs. Japanese planning strategies		*International*	*Japanese*
	Characters	Based on genre	Based on need
	Events	Wide range of audiences	Culturally specific
	Promotion	Facebook, social media	Media mix, cross-promo
	Monetization	Whales and minnows	Whales
	Gameplay	Additions to narrative	Manipulation of engine

rather than their older and more brooding Western conception. In all, the database of "attractive" characters was deemed to be lacking in the international version of the game, which had based its characters and classes on the verisimilitude of the genre, rather than on characters that players would become attracted to base solely on their design as character icons.

Related to this, events were altered in several ways that pointed to how the planners viewed their audience. International planners, wanting to target as wide a base of potential players as possible, designed events with diverse genre themes. Even here, however, certain planners on the team exerted more influence based on their cultural upbringing in the target market. Events that American players would be more familiar with became dominant within the game world, and events based on American holidays—such as Thanksgiving, Christmas, and Independence Day—were universally green-lighted with characters hatched from turkeys and Santa's elves in order to ostensibly appease American players. The American planners became de facto experts on American culture, dispensing advice to design teams on what American player's desire and how they behave in game events. Japanese planners, similarly, hatched events and characters that appealed to the Japanese calendar of events—summer festivals, popular anime, and myths based on ancient folklore.

Promotional events exhibited tendencies that played up character seriality. The Japanese version of *DC*, for example, emphasized a media mix strategy to the game's characters, using "collaboration" events that incorporated characters from popular anime and video games into *DC* in order to provide incentives for players and to attempt to siphon off fans of those other media. The marketing department was especially creative with promotions, even having *DC* partner up with a fantasy-themed "maid café." For a limited time, players of the game would receive bonus codes that could be used in the game upon visiting the café and ordering special items. The international version had far fewer opportunities to exploit cross-media ties, largely since such partnerships would require planners to make business partnerships with media companies in Western territories. The planners for the international game used existing social media platforms, particularly Facebook, to create promotional events for the game that built on the personalities of existing characters and themes, though such events were limited to those who were predisposed to be fans of the game anyway—that is, those who liked the Facebook page.

Tension rose, however, when the two teams merged for scheduling purposes, and Japanese and international planners fought to prioritize their own cultural heritage within the game. With management requiring both teams to produce events and characters for both markets at the same time, the concept of localization became less important than simultaneous release. As the teams would be working on the same or similar assets, new events required that the two versions synch their event ideas. Planners pitched their event ideas to their respective directors, and both versions began to incorporate events from both teams of planners. Some planners objected to this concept, as they felt that their creative control was being compromised and the game was starting to "make little sense."[36] Budgets were being consolidated, however, and this meant that the number of characters—and events—that could be produced needed to be reduced. Both teams would have to work from a shared cultural database in order to produce characters and events for each version.

The resulting "multiculturalism" had some severe consequences for *DC*. Players of the international version wrote in to the studio, demanding that characters stop straying from its original creators' intent. According to the players, the resulting creations by the combined teams resulted in characters (and world) with little distinct flavor and that the developers were "drunk."[37] This came not as a result of international coproduction (the international team had representatives from over half a dozen different countries) but from the desire to simultaneously please two very different audiences, with pitches for events and new characters revolving around culturally significant landmarks rather than creative additions to the existing world. The dark-fantasy game soon became populated with Japanese samurai, Chinese folklore heroes, and cyberpunk robots. The Japanese director of the game—apparently reflecting the opinions of most Japanese players—did not view characters inconsistent to their world as an impediment to enjoying the game. Such characters merely reflected an alternate conception of that world, based on a temporary reality that such events allowed.

This sentiment reflects Azuma's assertion that characters can exist outside narratives or worlds as long as they harness attractive elements for their respective audiences. The Japanese team of producers, experienced as consumers themselves, understood this aspect of character consumption with regard to their version of the game, which creates character consumers out of players systematically, asking them to invest their time, money, and psychological well-being into collecting attractive characters. When the characters were not connected to their world, the international audience tended to openly rebel and question the authorial intent, even if expensive outsourcing firms designed the characters to be as attractive and as artistically spectacular as possible. In *DC*, international players expected, after a certain point, that characters conform to the established world largely formed by its existing database of characters, as well as the supplementary background images, music, and language of the game's interface.

Within teams, differences were also found between planners' designs for monetization and gameplay. Planners from Japan, with more knowledge of player psychology, were more open to finding ways to engage whales, whereas the international team had varying notions of engaging both whales and minnows. This difference in gaming philosophies created debates about the nature of play within teams, where the international and Japanese planners argued for different concepts of "fun" related to the value of characters. The Japanese team knew that whales were required to sustain the game's economy, so events and characters were tailored in a way to insure that a core few players competed/spent money for the best rewards. This often resulted in innovative ways of tweaking the game's engine to allow for different gameplay experiences and alternate conceptions of existing character assets. One Japanese planner organized an event that changed the icon for potions into "food" icons, telling players whoever was the "biggest glutton" would get a massive reward. Another Japanese planner tweaked the game's code to allow players to be able to attack without needing upgrades if they acquired a certain character. The international team, less focused on how it wanted to monetize its events, used characters to polish aspects of the game's interface and develop its narrative, and an incredible amount of time was spent making extensive lore. One planner spent two weeks creating stories for over 300 characters and a progressive narrative for the game's sixty-plus quest stages, while another planner created a world map based off of these stories, organizing the game's abstract movement across disparately connected screens into a logical movement through an imaginary fantasyscape.

A problem developed when the logic of the Japanese team of planners won out, and the international version of *DC* became tied to the Japanese version's emphasis on heavy whale monetization through tying characters to gameplay. The international version of *DC*, having developed its gameplay through tying characters to narrative and lore, was ill-equipped to develop innovative events that targeted non-Japanese players, a situation that was exacerbated by the fact that the international team of planners had less experience both making and playing such games in the first place. Rewards in the international version of *DC* simply became tougher to acquire without the necessary adjustment to a different group of players, and the hurdle for participation increased at a much more rapid pace when compared to the much more controlled coercive escalation of the Japanese version.

International and Japanese players had very different responses to planners' continuously changing design choices as they related to the game's characters. Both player audiences shared similar dissatisfaction with the game's coercive principles, with player retention rates skewing very similarly.[38] Moreover, players also paid for their experiences at roughly the same rates.[39] But player responses to game events, gameplay, and monetization were very different as judged by customer support inquiries, message board postings, Wiki comments, conversations in chat rooms, and, importantly, player activity in the game worlds. How characters in the games were used became the lynchpin to see how players responded; planners, meanwhile, were constantly on their toes reacting to player activity.

Japanese players, accustomed to the monetization methods of such games, voiced their displeasure through official channels such as Game Room's customer support email and in-game message boards. Emails and postings were pithy in their ire, complaining about the nature of such games in general and the greediness of corporations seeking to pad their pockets on the profits from addicted gamers. Players were keenly aware of the game's structure and showed a sophisticated understanding of how events were organized around characters and coercive game design principles, largely through playing the games or participating in massive online chat forums such as the Japanese textboard 2channel, where entire threads are dedicated to exposing games that are clearly targeted to high-spending players. While Japanese players were well versed in the game's design, they nevertheless urged planners to slow the game's progression into coercive events or begged planners for feature events that had more easily accessible rewards. On this note, players also wrote in suggesting ideas for future characters, hoping that if they could not control the game's funnel for participation, they could at least hope to influence its artistic direction and the production of attractive characters. Ultimately, there were not enough such responses to influence Japanese planners one way or another, suggesting that players assumed that such appeals would result in little meaningful change. The responses of players thus had little effect on the gameplay and character construction of the Japanese version of *DC*. Attractive characters went to a select few group of players, and players with less financial ability were only able to continue to acquire less attractive characters in events.

International players, on the other hand, had a range of responses that ultimately changed gameplay and character content. Similar to Japanese players, international players emailed customer support, though they also engaged through social media by hijacking Facebook promotions, using the comments section to sound off on bad game events and the evil of Game Room in general. Planners were pressured to monitor these pages, and some events attempted to softly integrate some player demands by using the Facebook page to poll players on what changes in the game they wanted to see most. Frustrated players also attempted to negotiate with Game Room and reason with developers. Some fans were enthusiastic, asking Game Room for sponsorships or name rights for a *DC* fan convention. Other players banded together, offering to buy the game from Game Room so they could, in theory, operate it the way they saw most fair to all players involved. Still others, whales from Western territories, covertly emailed customer support to speak to the planning team directly, stating how much money they've spent on the game as a negotiating tactic for seeing the changes they wanted in the game implemented to root out and ban cheaters, hackers, or other "immoral" players for "ruining the experience."[40] These players attempted to exert their socioeconomic status by attempting to buy a desired outcome through the planners themselves if they could not receive such outcomes in the game world. Eventually, planners caved to some of these demands under the threat of their highest-spending players jumping to another game. Finally, players took action and created separate, password-protected chat rooms to plan strategies that would speak to planners through in-game action. In one race event where rewards were set at high stages, players agreed to boycott racing past the 100th stage, and planners had to shell out top rewards to a large group of players despite having generated little in revenue for the week. In return, planners had to come up with ways for events to reward player individual efforts rather than their offline teamwork. Through the creative action of the players, future events ultimately had to take into account and attempt to discourage player resistance through either events that were friendlier to low-spenders or that upped the rewards to levels that high-spenders could no longer resist.

Ironically, for certain events, characters became less a symbol of status or power and more a means of visually articulating social unity and resistance. When all players began acquiring the same powerful and attractive characters, the means for competition was eliminated. Where characters were a form of currency and a means of corralling player behavior in the Japanese version, characters became co-opted as a form of player insurgency when faced with perceived or inconsistent game rules, design, and production. Planners were forced to make rare alternate versions of certain characters to encourage even further competition, until whales eventually asserted their financial position.

In contrast to the Japanese version of *DC*, where planners proceeded with their ideas with little interference from players, the international version of *DC* played out like a cat-and-mouse game of one-upmanship, where the game's ostensible creators were constantly reacting to the moves of organized, inexhaustible players. Planners actively attempted to squash player activity akin to how a large corporation might try to bust its working employees' labor union by infiltrating chat rooms or guilds and trying to anticipate the players' next move. Planners frequently stayed late after hours deliberating on the best method of "getting players to play the game the right way again."[41]

CONCLUSION

Database production resulted in two very different experiences of the same game due to the unexpected consequences of assuming characters and events would be handled in the same way by both groups of players. The players of the international game, in essence, rejected the planners' corrupting of the game's database. International players did not appreciate the changes in game direction and used characters in ways that were unintended from the developers' point of view. Japanese players were more accepting of these changes for several reasons that revealed their understanding of how the game's system worked, and that circumventing the rules would lead to an unplayable game.

In the end, both responses had little effect on the overall performance of the games, but quite a bit of difference in the experience. Whereas the Japanese version had future events and gameplay organized by planners through either maintaining or slightly improving the current system, the international version incorporated wild events and promotions that attempted to corral or respond to player behavior. Characters were the symbol of how players engaged with the game—as a form of admiration and acceptance or as a form of repulsion and resistance. The Japanese version of the game faced its own share of problems, but they were minimal as they related to character production and collection due to its audience's collective understanding of the game's design and, more importantly, its shared investment in the process of the game's cultural database of attractive characters. The international version of the game first encountered problems through the incorporation of characters incongruous to players' different cultural database, and players ended up using characters in unintended ways to assert their own control and participation in the game.

It is tempting to read this situation in nationally reflective terms, that is, Japanese players conformed while Western players asserted their individuality. But a closer analysis much more strongly suggests how established industrial practices influence player behavior. Japanese audiences, exposed to a decades-long history of mobile gaming and similar forms of entertainment, has dealt with media in a variety of formats that encourage fans to collect and admire characters. Players from this audience are more accustomed to the design and business models employed by these types of games and are understanding of the inherent limitations of the system. They tended to play and appreciate *DC* for the high-quality, realistic artwork of the characters that were very different from the typical anime-inspired designs of other card battlers, even if they were slightly modified to fit with the expectation of the domestic cultural database. Western players, however, feeling that their ideas of the cultural database had been subverted, fought for a semblance of control over the process of collection and placed an extreme priority on rankings and hierarchies in the game's world. Less content and trusting of planners in Japan to craft their gaming experience, and less familiar with the protocols of the card-battle genre itself, many players used familiar social media technologies to shape the gaming experience of their wishes.

I have used the case study of database production in the development and operations of *Dragon Conquerors* to show how moves by creators at the level of production can signal how work culture (and attitudes toward consumption) informs game spaces. More specifically, this case study in international game development illuminates the ways in which developers and players attempt to gain control of a product in which they have invested their time and money. Through both the changing roles of producers and the changing demographics of players in video games that are made for mobile platforms, creators are no longer something invisible in the process of consumption, inscribed into the text through the guiding hand of a video game "auteur" such as Will Wright or Shigeru Miyamoto. Because of this, if we want to understand how games or other forms of visual media work in companies, work in society, or work on us as individuals, then we must better understand the myriad ways in which production cultures organize, control, and reveal themselves to us and how our own cultures are influenced by and inscribed within those spaces of production.

Notes

1. According to the *Famitsu White Paper*, Japan's game industry grew by $9.4 billion in 2014, with nearly $6 billion of that growth attributed to the strength and spread of top-grossing "online games" delivered through smartphones, tablets, feature phones, and PCs. See *Famitsu White Paper 2015* (Tokyo: Kadokawa-Dwango, 2015).

2. Many such "virtual ethnographies" focus on the social communities birthed from online games and other more open-ended virtual worlds. For some examples of in-depth studies of discrete virtual communities, see Celia Pearce, *Communities of Play: Emergent Cultures in Multiplayer Games and Virtual Worlds* (Cambridge, MA: MIT Press, 2011); Tom Boellstorff, *Coming of Age in Second Life: An Anthropologist Explores the Virtually Human* (Princeton: Princeton University Press, 2010); and Dmitri Williams, Nic Ducheneaut, Li Xiong, Yuanyuan Zhang, Nick Yee, and Eric Nickell "From Treehouse to Barracks: The Social Life of Guilds in *World of Warcraft*," in *Games and Culture* 1, no.4 (October 2006), 338–361.

3. Here, Salen and Zimmerman discuss the role of the designer as "the individual game designer or the team of people that creates the game." Katie Salen and Eric Zimmerman, *Rules of Play: Game Design Fundamentals* (Cambridge, MA: MIT Press, 2004), 41.

4. The word "designer" in Japanese is typically used to describe designers of artistic and visual schemes, such as art, graphics, model, motion, effects, menus, or cut scene designers. See Fujihara Masahito, "Geemu kaihatsusha no kyaria keisei" in *Dejitaru geemu no kyōkasho* ("The Career Shape of Game Developers" in Textbook of Digital Games) (Tokyo: Digda Japan, 2010), 488–489.

5. Kay's book, *Japanmanship: The Ultimate Guide to Working in Videogame Development in Japan*, is one of the rare resources that instructs foreigners on how to find work in the video game industry in Japan. For a more broad overview of job titles and opportunities for new graduates in Japan, see Fujiwara Shoji, "Wagakuni no geemu kaihatsusha no maneejimento" (Our Country's Game Developers and Managements) in *Geemu sangyō ni okeru kaihatsusha jinzai ikusei jigyōhōkokusho* (Human Resource Management in Our Country's Video Games Industry) (CESA Japan, 2007), 45–80.

6. JC Barnett, "Working in Japanese Game Development: The Other Side of the Rainbow," *Gamasutra*, 20 August, 2007, http://www.gamasutra. com/view/feature/130043/working_in_japanese_game_.php.

7. See Chris Kohler, *Power-Up: How Japanese Video Games Gave the World an Extra Life* (Brady Games, 2005), 35–54 and Jennifer de Winter, *Shigeru Miyamoto: Super Mario Bros., Donkey Kong, The Legend of Zelda* (New York: Bloomsbury, 2015), 5–7, 31–34.

8. The relatively high price of 100 yen for each arcade machine in Japan is one reason for the arcade industry's sustained vibrancy compared to the empty or shuttered arcades of other countries. For an in-depth examination of the various types of games, game centers, game celebrities, and continued evolution of arcade gaming in Japan, see Brian Ashcraft, *Arcade Mania: The Turbo-Charged World of Japan's Game Centers* (Tokyo: Kodansha International, 2008).

9. For a list of the different metrics used by mobile game companies to track the performance of their games, see Shyamal Dave, "A Comprehensive List of Metrics for Free-to-Play Games," *Gamesbrief*, 27 May 2014, http://www.gamesbrief.com/2014/05/a-comprehensive-list-of-metrics-for-free-to-play-games/.

10. Collaborations provide the added value of allowing games to continually advertise their characters and designs to potentially different gaming audiences. For example, GungHo's hybrid puzzle-dungeon crawler, *Puzzle and Dragons*, has become well known for its various collaborations that feature limited-time characters from well-known games such as *Angry Birds* or *Super Mario*. For more examples of collaboration events between games, see Serkan Toto, "Examining a Unique Marketing Tool for Japanese Games: 'Collaborations,'" *Kantan Games Inc – Consulting and Advising on Japan's Mobile Gaming Industry*, 2013 May 2. http://www.serkantoto.com/2013/05/02/marketing-user-acquisition-japanese-mobile-games-collaborations/.

11. As planners are always being shifted in and out of game development teams based on the needs of the project, most F2P mobile games do not feature a staff credits list, another feature where mobile gaming harkens back to the early period of game development where designers were rarely given credit for their creations. *Final Fantasy Record Keeper*, however, includes a full staff credits page, with no fewer than three lead planners and nine other planners comprising the planning department.

12. Japanese game companies do not use these terms but refer to an equivalent by calling players *hai-kakin* and *mu-kakin* or "big spenders" and "non-spenders."

13. Ramin Shokrizade, "The Top F2P Monetization Tricks," *Gamasutra*, 26 June, 2013http://gamasutra.com/blogs/RaminShokrizade/20130626/194933/The_Top_F2P_Monetization_Tricks.php. Jennifer Whitson also analyzes the implications of such game monetization in the blurring of play and work in casual games. Calling this shift in developer focus from optimal play experiences to optimal monetization tactics, she calls this "instrumental play," a move toward corralling and controlling play into a set of rational and repetitive behaviors that are easier for developers to manage and regulate for the "new spirit of capitalism." See Jennifer Whitson, *Game Design by Numbers:*

Instrumental Play and the Quantitative Shift in the Digital Game Industry, Ph.D. dissertation (Carleton University, 2012).

14. Edward Castronova has chronicled the virtual world of *Everquest* in particular, concluding that the fictional planet of Norrath has its own economies of scale that rival global powerhouses. See Edward Castronova, "Virtual Worlds: A First-Hand Account of Market and Society on the Cyberian Frontier," *CESifo Working Paper Series*, no. 618, December 2001. Castronova has also chronicled the kinds of shadow economies of gold-mining and avatar-auctioning alluded to here in his paper, "The Price of 'Man' and 'Woman': A Hedonic Pricing Model of Avatar Attributes in a Synthetic World," *CESifo Working Paper Series*, no. 957, June 2003, which examines the relative lack of value attributed to female avatars in the virtual world.

15. The media mix actually has twin meanings in both as an advertising strategy and as a critical industrial concept to describe media synergy. The latter concept, pioneered in Japan under Kadokawa Haruki and his publishing company, is what is referred to here. For a description of this marketing strategy as it was developed in the 1970s and 1980s, see Kadokawa Haruki, *Wa ga tōsō: Furyō seinen wa sekai wo mezasu* (My Struggle: A Juvenile Delinquent Aims for the World) (Tokyo: East Press, 2005).

16. Henry Jenkins, *Convergence Culture: How Old and New Media Collide* (Cambridge: MIT Press, 2007), 97–98.

17. As Marc Steinberg notes, though the idea of the media mix was popularized in the 1980s under Kadokawa marketing strategies, it really emerged as a form of cross-media construction through the serial television adaptation of the popular comic *Tetsuwan Atomu* in the early 1960s. For a detailed description of this phenomenon, see Marc Steinberg, *Anime's Media Mix: Franchising Toys and Characters in Japan* (Minneapolis: University of Minnesota Press, 2012).

18. Marc Steinberg, "Condensing the Media Mix: *Tatami Galaxy's* Multiple Possible Worlds," in *Canadian Journal of Film Studies* 21, no.2 (2012), 88. Alex Zahlten also refers to the divergent possibilities inherent in Japanese media culture through examples in anime and manga, connecting textual strategies to industrial and economic practices to argue for a metaphorical concept of "liquidity" in world construction. See Alex Zahlten, "Media Mix and the Metaphoric Economy of World," in *The Oxford Handbook of Japanese Cinema* (Oxford: Oxford University Press, 2014), 438–456.

19. Oono Shigeru's account of the launch and success of *Weekly Shōnen Sunday* and *Weekly Shōnen Magazine* shows the influence of the manga magazine format on serial consumption. Oono states that the first issues of the magazines were hugely popular, selling 200,000 and 300,000 issues, respectively. See Oono Shigeru, *Sundei to Magajin: Sōkan to shitō no jūgonen* (Sunday and Magazine: The 15 Years from Launch to Mortal Combat) (Tokyo: Kobunsha, 2009), 66.

20. Yamaguchi Yasuo ed. *Nihon no anime zenshi* (Complete History of Japanese Animation) (Tokyo: Ten Books, 2004), 74–75.
21. Okada Toshio, *Otakugaku nyūmon* (Introduction to Otaku Studies) (Tokyo: Shincho Bunko, 1996), 8.
22. See, for example, Otsuka Eiji, *Teihon monogatari shōhiron* (A Theory of Narrative Consumption: Standard Edition) (Tokyo: Kadokawa, 1989) and Ito Go, *Tezuka izu deddo: hirakareta manga hyōgenron* (Tezuka is Dead: Postmodernist and Modernist Approaches to Japanese Manga) (Tokyo: NTT Shuppan, 2005). Based off of the postmodern theory of Jean-Francois Lyotard, Otsuka argues that otaku consume piecemeal narratives in order to become closer to its "grand narrative." Ito, on the other hand, draws upon semiotic theory to highlight the specific role of the *kyara*—or "character" icons—in manga as affective vehicles to which particular emotions and expectations are attached.
23. Azuma Hiroki, *Otaku: Japan's Database Animals,* trans. Jonathan E. Abel and Shion Kono (Tokyo: Kodansha, 2001), 42–47.
24. Ibid, 39.
25. Ibid, 86–88.
26. Azuma Hiroki, *Geemuteki riarizumu no tanjō: Dobutsukasuru posutomo-dan 2* (The Birth of Game-like Realism: The Animalizing Postmodern 2) (Tokyo: Kodansha, 2007), 142.
27. Patrick Galbraith, "Bishōjo Games: 'Techno-Intimacy' and the Virtually Human in Japan," in Game Studies 11, no.2 (May 2011).
28. Azuma, *Otaku*, 90.
29. I use the genre terms from Mark Wolf's interactive genre classification for video games. Mark Wolf, *The Medium of the Video Game* (Austin: University of Texas Press, 2001), 113–134.
30. While this case study is based on observational fieldwork in an actual game production environment, it will use fictional names for the video game studio and video game title to protect the anonymity of the developers and players.
31. John Caldwell and Vicky Mayer's studies on film and television production are two of the most useful examples for this method, as both combine ethnographic analysis of field sites with textual analysis of media texts and paratexts to come to conclusions about the individual agency of media workers and how this affects the production of media in society. See John Caldwell, *Production Culture: Industrial Reflexivity and Critical Practice in Film and Television* (Durham, NC: Duke University Press, 2007), and Vicki Mayer, *Below the Line: Producers and Production Studies in the New Television Economy* (Durham, NC: Duke University Press, 2011).
32. Clifford Geertz, "Thick Description: Toward an Interpretive Theory of Culture," in *The Interpretation of Cultures: Selected Essays* (New York: Basic Books, 1973), 5–6, 9–10.
33. Field notes, 29 November 2012.

34. Interview with planner, 26 January 2013.
35. Interview with planner, 6 May 2013.
36. Field notes, 15 March 2013.
37. Field notes, 19 March 2013.
38. About 60 % of players did not even finish the tutorial, a key measurement that tracks how players immediately engage with the game's mechanics.
39. Other key performance indicators, such as the number of daily active users (DAU) and the average revenue per paying user, were nearly the same for both games.
40. Field notes, 10 April 2013.
41. Field notes, 11 April 2013.

BIBLIOGRAPHY

Ashcraft, Brian. 2008. *Arcade mania: The turbo-charged world of Japan's game centers.* Tokyo: Kodansha International.
Azuma Hiroki. 2001. *Otaku: Japan's database animals,* trans. Jonathan E. Abel and Shion Kono. Tokyo: Kodansha.
———. 2007. *Geemuteki riarizumu no tanjō: Dobutsukasuru posutomodan 2* (The birth of game-like realism: The animalizing postmodern 2). Tokyo: Kodansha.
Barnett, J.C. "Working in Japanese game development: The other side of the rainbow," *Gamasutra,* 20 August 2007. http://www.gamasutra.com/view/feature/130043/working_in_japanese_game_.php (14 May 2015).
Caldwell, John. 2007. *Production culture: Industrial reflexivity and critical practice in film and television.* Durham: Duke University Press.
Castronova, Edward. 2001. Virtual Worlds: A First-Hand Account of Market and Society on the Cyberian Frontier. In CESifo Working Paper Series, no. 618.
———. 2003. The Price of 'Man' and 'Woman': A Hedonic Pricing Model of Avatar Attributes in a Synthetic World. In CESifo Working Paper Series, no. 957.
CESA Japan. 2007. *Geemu sangyō ni okeru kaihatsusha jinzai ikusei jigyōhōkokusho* (Human resource management in our country's video games industry). Tokyo: CESA.
Dave, Shyamal. "A comprehensive list of metrics for free-to-play games," *Gamesbrief,* 27 May 2014, http://www.gamesbrief.com/2014/05/a-comprehensive-list-of-metrics-for-free-to-play-games/ (22 March 2015).
de Winter, Jennifer. 2015. *Shigeru Miyamoto: Super Mario Bros., Donkey Kong, The Legend of Zelda.* New York: Bloomsbury.
Digda Japan. 2010. *Dejitaru geemu no kyōkasho* (Textbook of digital games). Tokyo: Digda Japan.
Galbraith, Patrick. 2011. Bishōjo games: 'Techno-Intimacy' and the virtually human in Japan. *Game Studies* 11(2). http://gamestudies.org/1102/articles/galbraith

Geertz, Clifford. 1973. Thick description: Toward an interpretive theory of culture. In *The interpretation of cultures: Selected essays*, 3–30. New York: Basic Books.

Ito Go. 2005. *Tezuka izu deddo: hirakareta manga hyōgenron* (Tezuka is dead: Postmodernist and modernist approaches to Japanese manga). Tokyo: NTT Shuppan.

Kadokawa-Dwango. 2015. *Famitsu white paper 2015*. Tokyo: Kadokawa-Dwango.

Kadokawa Haruki. 2005. *Wa ga tōsō: Furyō seinen wa sekai wo mezasu* (My struggle: A juvenile delinquent aims for the world). Tokyo: East Press.

Kay, James. 2012. *Japanmanship: The ultimate guide to working in videogame development in Japan*. Tokyo: Score Studios.

Kohler, Chris. 2005. *Power-Up: How Japanese video games gave the world an extra life*. London: Brady Games.

Mayer, Vicki. 2011. *Below the line: Producers and production studies in the new television economy*. Durham: Duke University Press.

Okada Toshio. 1996. *Otakugaku nyūmon* (Introduction to Otaku studies). Tokyo: Shincho Bunko.

Oono Shigeru. 2009. *Sundei to Magajin: Sōkan to shitō no jūgonen* (Sunday and magazine: The 15 years from launch to mortal combat). Tokyo: Kobunsha.

Otsuka Eiji. 1989. *Teihon monogatari shōhiron* (A theory of narrative consumption: Standard edition). Tokyo: Kadokawa.

Salen, Katie, and Eric Zimmerman. 2004. *Rules of play: Game design fundamentals*. Cambridge, MA: MIT Press.

Shokrizade, Ramin. "The top F2P monetization tricks," *Gamasutra*, 2013 June 26, http://gamasutra.com/blogs/RaminShokrizade/20130626/194933/The_Top_F2P_Monetization_Tricks.php (26 February 2015).

Steinberg, Marc. 2012a. *Anime's media mix: Franchising toys and characters in Japan*. Minneapolis: University of Minnesota Press.

———. 2012b. Condensing the media mix: *Tatami galaxy's* multiple possible worlds. *Canadian Journal of Film Studies* 21(2): 71–92.

Toto, Serkan. "Examining a Unique Marketing Tool for Japanese Games: 'Collaborations,'" *Kantan Games Inc – Consulting and Advising on Japan's Mobile Gaming Industry*, 2013 May 2. http://www.serkantoto.com/2013/05/02/marketing-user-acquisition-japanese-mobile-games-collaborations/ (24 March 2015).

Whitson, Jennifer. 2012. "Game Design by Numbers: Instrumental Play and the Quantitative Shift in the Digital Game Industry," Ph.D. diss, Carleton University.

Wolf, Mark. 2001. *The medium of the video game*. Austin: University of Texas Press.

Yamaguchi Yasuo (ed). 2004. *Nihon no anime zenshi* (Complete history of Japanese animation). Tokyo: Ten Books.

Zahlten, Alex. 2014. Media Mix and the Metaphoric Economy of World. In The Oxford Handbook of Japanese Cinema, edited by Daisuke Miyao. Oxford: Oxford University Press, 438–456.

PART III

Social Impacts

CHAPTER 7

Hong Kong Net-Bar Youth Gaming: A Labeling Perspective

Sara Liao

This chapter explores how Hong Kong youth perceive their collective gaming experience in net-bars and how they negotiate their images and identities in such a cultural setting. Net-bar is also called Internet café, net café, cybercafé, or Internet bar in gaming literature.[1,2] However, unlike other similar names referring to a place providing public Internet access, net-bar specifies two important cultural implications. On one hand, the word "bar" is an imported term from the English language, firstly describing pubs or night clubs. Its Chinese translation (吧) in general connotes undesirability of a place, where social interactions often involve moral delinquency and excessive behaviors such as binge drinking. Net-bar is a term that represents negative designations in the public's imagination. On the other hand, the term reflects the boom of net-bar business and multiplayer gaming in East Asian countries

I highly appreciate the editor Austin Lee's critical insights for this chapter, which helped me sharpen my analytical focus. I also thank him for generating the idea of charting out the coping strategies for the youth to react to social labels.

S. Liao (✉)
Department of Radio-Television-Film, University of Texas at Austin,
Austin, TX, USA

© The Author(s) 2016
S.A. Lee, A. Pulos (eds.), *Transnational Contexts of Development History, Sociality, and Society of Play*, East Asian Popular Culture,
DOI 10.1007/978-3-319-43820-7_7

including Japan, South Korea, and Taiwan, where net-bars or Internet cafés are essentially LAN gaming centers, especially for the youth.[3] These two socio-cultural meanings jointly create the public perceptions of net-bars. The social discourse of net-bar gaming is generally pejorative in Hong Kong: in media outlets and daily conversations, the net-bar is constructed as a place where the youth gather and engage in delinquent behaviors. Therefore, the government, social workers, media, and other interest groups demand that net-bars should be monitored and controlled, for the purpose of protecting the youth.

Discussions on the social designations of net-bar gaming rarely focus on the voices of the majority of net-bar goers, the youth. Through this a socio-cultural backdrop, and largely informed by scholarship on deviance and societal reaction, I investigate Hong Kong net-bar youth's perceptions on gaming and their strategies to manage their images and identity in their reaction to social designations. Specifically, this chapter asks: *how do the net-bar youth perceive social designations, and what do they do to deal with the labels?* I conduct this study by analyzing qualitative data drawn from focus group interviews of 20 Hong Kong students aged from 15 to 20. Some designations of net-bar goers recurring in the youth's narratives include: Dokuo, a reference to Hong Kong young men who are poisonously obsessed with anime and video games; MK boys, a term referring to young provocative punks and hipsters haunting Mong Kok area; sex-seeking; and excessive vulgarity. Interestingly, these labels are terms of not only how the youth perceive what other people think of themselves, but also how they stereotype other net-bar goers. They actively distance themselves from and resist such designations by identity negotiation strategies including avoiding, normalizing, neutralizing, professionalizing, and quitting. Through the youth's interpretations and negotiation of the labels applied to them, the collective experience of net-bar gaming is articulated.

In the following, I first review the literature on labeling perspective to formulate the theoretical framework of this study. Then I provide my research method. Next, I discuss the Hong Kong context of gaming culture and net-bar going. Within this context, I analyze some social labels attached to net-bar goers and how the youth interpret and negotiate with these labels. A discussion is provided at the end, with a note on the limitations of this study.

Labeling Perspective

Labeling perspective, also known as societal reaction theory, takes the social reaction of others toward a certain behavior or a group of people as the fundamental parameter when defining deviance and social problems. Deviance is not regarded as an etiological terminology but as a social construct that is created and identified through social interactions. It is a designation or a label attached to someone. Many sociologists in the 1960s and 1970s loosely formed a "labeling school," a new sociology of deviance.[4] Frank Tannenbaum, Edwin Lemert, John Kitsuse, Howard Becker, Erving Goffman, Kai Erikson, and Thomas Scheff, to name a few, were pioneers that have studied deviance from an interactionist perspective.

Existing literature has identified two propositions of labeling theory. First, because deviance is not an inherent quality, some social elements such as race, gender, class, sexuality, ethnicity can influence the labeling process, when the labeler and the labeled contest within a certain socio-cultural context.[5] This proposition highlights power dynamics in a specific social context where the label is born. The second core of the labeling perspective relates to a self-fulfilling prophecy.[6] This proposition puts forth that deviance labels generate stereotypical views toward the norm violators, while other members of the society/group manifest an exclusionary reaction to deal with deviant behavior.[7] The biased and/or hostile attitude to those being labeled, and their limited participation in conformity, in turn alternates self-perception that internalizes a deviant identity, and deviant ascription ultimately becomes a "master status."[8]

These two propositions lead us to think about the dynamics and complexity of social life. The further deviance is not inevitable when taking social elements into consideration. In different socio-cultural settings, individuals may react to the labels differently. They acquire information about other's perceptions on them and subsequently and subjectively adjust self-image in response to how they understand the label. Because the label of deviance is unstable and constantly in relationship with social actors, it becomes a routine for those being labeled to negotiate the identity to adjust to social life.

Here, Erving Goffman's work provides insights into the process of labeling and identity management. He defined stigma as a situation of the individual who is disqualified from full social acceptance, an attribute that is deeply discrediting.[9] Using autobiographies and case studies, Goffman examined how people manage impressions of themselves when they are away from social norms. His study revealed that people who are stigmatized may not be sure how others really think about them, and that they do not choose between two options—acceptance or resistance—in their response to the social designation. Rather, they adopt various strategies to adjust their images and negotiate their identity in relation to other "normal" people.

Though the early definition and theoretical foundation of stigma emphasized labeling as a process and a relationship between the labeler and the labeled, the bulk of scholarship on societal reaction theories largely overlooks the perspective of the labeled; most studies came from an "outsider perspective."[10] That is, research on societal reaction concerned mostly with how and why the labeler express social stigmas and what strategies can be used to reduce such prejudices. It must be noted that, roughly starting in the 1960s, the popularity of labeling theory, with its interactionist components, can be seen as a direct reaction to the dominance of structural functionalist views on deviance. Scholars in previous decades believed that deviance and social problems could be revealed in a causal relationship as a result of psychological determinacy and/or structural conditions. It shifted the sociological tradition to societal reaction and its relation to the deviance in particular contexts.

These studies of social reactions to stigmas had their heyday during the 1970s while ebbing thereafter, even to the extent of being pronounced dead. Not until the 1990s, scholarship of societal reaction surged to emphasize the importance of studying the stigmatized group/individual, which has brought new insights into previous theoretical and empirical work. In a review of the historical development of labeling perspective, Plummer pointed out that it is a generational theory, which, in its widest sense, continues questioning social phenomena yet for another generation of sociologists.[11] This position is more apt, as many recent works on deviance and social controls have refashioned the core themes of labeling perspective.[12] In a recent issue dedicated to studies of social stigma, Barreto and Ellemers identify five major themes standing out in this area of research: (1) contextual factors influencing social prejudice; (2) interactive nature of stigma—interaction between the labeler and the labeled;

(3) disparate findings of how social stigma affects the self; (4) the function of group identification; and (5) how social stigma affects task performance.[13]

In this chapter, I put forth the role of the net-bar youth to understand how they perceive the social labels of their net-bar going and gaming behaviors as well as what their strategies are to manage their images and identity related to the stigma, both as a group and an individual. Moving beyond the labeling literature, three implications are derived from my point of view.

First, instead of focusing on the internal factors of individual elements causing social labeling, I emphasize the social context which induces undesirable social designation to the people who belong to certain groups. Past research usually associated the term deviance with certain types of rule violation, including crime and delinquency, mental illness and other psychological problems, drug use and addiction, and sexual activities. The introduction of the societal reaction approach expands the scope of study to myriad forms of deviance, as it is being created, defined, and labeled through context-specific social processes. As mentioned above, net-bars are essentially multiplayer gaming centers in Hong Kong. The social discourse of gaming has influence on perception of the specific place of the net-bar as well as the net-bar goers. Exploring the contextual factors contributes to the understanding of net-bar youth's perceptions and negotiation of their identities.

Second, studying the stigmatized group/individual, the net-bar youth in this case can enrich the scholarship of both societal reactions and game studies. Most of the previous research emphasized the psychological and behavioral effects of gaming, such as video game addiction.[14] Few have taken the individual perceptions of social designations into consideration.[15] Because of the interactive nature of social labels, it is necessary to understand how the net-bar goers perceive the social prejudice toward their behaviors and how they interpret the meanings that the society attributes to their actions.

Third, this study explores both individual and collective images and identity of the net-bar youth. As gaming centers, net-bars often serve as a base for the youth groups to play video games together. Group identity developed in this process may influence individual members of the group. How will this group identity affect the youth's perception of the labels? How will it affect their interpretation of their individual identity in relation to social stigma? These are the aspects that I seek to explore in this chapter, through the youth's articulation and narrative as group members.

METHOD

To investigate the youth's perceptions of social ideas toward net-bar gaming, I conducted focus group interviews as a qualitative research method. The purpose of the interviews was to invite conversations among groups of net-bar goers who had similarities in cultural experience while differences in personal expressions and perhaps also in their interpretations of social interaction. Thus, three groups of informants, 20 people total, were recruited from personal contacts with a snowballing process to conduct peer group interviews. All participants were students aged from 15 to early 20s. One group was comprised of high school students and the other two were made up of college students. Informants in each group were acquaintances and net-bar friends with each other. The peer group interviews were designed to create a familiar environment for the net-bar youth to articulate their personal as well as collective experience. The interviews were conducted in February to early March, 2013. Each interview was recorded and coded afterwards. To ensure confidentiality, a pseudonym was used for each participant.

The participants came from different districts in Hong Kong Island, Kowloon, and New Territories: one in Eastern, two in Southern, two in Kowloon City, one in Yau Tsim Mong, two in Wong Tai Sin, two in Tuen Mun, three in Tsuen Wan, two in Yuen Long, one in Tai Po, and four in Sha Tin. The average number of their family members was four, and only one in twenty was single parenting. The participants' average monthly family income was between HK$20,000–29,999 (approx. US$2,580–3,871). Although participants came from diverse geographical backgrounds, they were identical in their gender (male) and occupation (student). It is understandable that all participants were male students because net-bar goers are overwhelmingly men and that students are the major customers of net-bars. These characteristics are consistent with findings of a local net-bar survey.[16]

THE NET-BAR AND THE YOUTH IN HONG KONG

Before getting into the analysis, in order to better situate this study, it is necessary to provide some information about youth and net-bars in Hong Kong. Hong Kong is a media-, Internet-, and technology-saturated metropolis. Up to 2014, Hong Kong had the fastest Internet access in the world and the overall high-speed Internet penetration rate of 73%.[17] The game sector is part of the creative industry in Hong Kong, contributing to its digital economy. Hong Kong gaming culture is largely influenced by Japanese and Korean popular cultures of games, manga, and comics.[18] Net-bars contribute to the game industry through the specific position they established in society: instead of being a mere access point to the Internet, net-bars are places for multiplayer gaming as a collective activity. This is a unique feature of gaming culture in Hong Kong, as well as in many East Asian countries. Although no specific number of net-bars in Hong Kong is available, an increasing number of franchise locations have established in recent years, largely monopolized by three big enterprises: i-One, Msystem, and G-Force.

In Hong Kong, gaming culture has flourished since the 1980s. Since the first introduction of console games, such as *Dragon Quest*, *Final Fantasy*, and *Super Mario*, a variety of game magazines have entered the market. At the turn of the century, arcade/game centers and net-bars became highly popular. It was trendy for the youth to play in net-bars and show off their gaming skills.[19] Yet, the vogue of gameplay in game centers and net-bars has become a large concern in the eyes of moral entrepreneurs, such as the government, social advocacy organizations, and the media, which regarded net-bars as a "dangerous space" for the youth[20] and argued that they should be kept away from such a place.[21] These social entities played a crucial role in defining deviance by strategically projecting moral judgment. The net-bar youth were often treated as game addicts and social problems that need to be regulated and controlled.

These ideas of youth deviance are in line with how people expect a norm-conforming youth should be. In other words, the net-bar youth are acting out a way of life that does not meet the social imagination and cultural construction of the youth. In Hong Kong, for example, it is common to expect young people between 15 and 19 years of age to study hard and get into college. This expectation enabled the flourishing business of cram schools, where students are intensively tutored to pass the entrance exams for high schools or universities.[22] Such an expectation is deeply rooted in the historical construction and social imagination of the youth. Though the traditional saying goes "young people are the key to the future," the youth are frequently depicted as social problems. As Dick Hebdige noted, "in our society, youth is present only when its presence is a problem, or is regarded as a problem."[23] Concerning young people, society is immersed in pejorative narratives, such as high unemployment rates, increasing number of young drug abusers, deviant youth culture, and bullying in school, to name a few, which makes it easy to blame young people and places them in a disadvantaged position.[24,25]

The mid-1960s witnessed the rise of Hong Kong youth's own culture of "Ah Feis" (literally as Teddy boys). Since then, young people have frequently been constructed as antisocial and dangerous, especially after the riots in 1966 and 1967. In the 1970s, the drastic upsurge of reported juvenile crime rates further alarmed society.[26,27,28] Moving onto the 1980s–1990s, the new generation was accused of losing the drive and dedication their parents had possessed to make Hong Kong prosperous.[29] Then, at the turn of the twenty-first century, an increasing number of youth were involved in the public discourses of substance abuse, gangsters, sex trades, delinquency, and other forms of subcultures. Since the "youth" is constructed as a social category, society predominantly perceives young people as being "anti-social, marginal and pathological in society," who act against norms and should "be controlled and regulated on the plea of their abnormality."[30] As Gray suggests, Hong Kong youth are frequently presented as social problems, which require government interventions.[31] Recreational places of the youth, such as game centers, KTV rooms, and net-bars became the primary targets of monitoring and control.

The youth, however, are not passively accepting the social expectations imposed on them. Having virtually unlimited access to the media and information, the youth are able to create and participate in various forms of subculture, such as indie bands and otaku culture.[32,33] The rapidly changing society provides them with opportunities to experience more freedom, to experiment with different lifestyles and social relationships, and to create their ways of expression and culture. With the advancing information and communication technology, the voice of the youth can be spread out through many channels, allowing them greater social presence. A recent example is the significant role that students/young people took in the protests of MNE (moral and national education).[34] Despite its increasing importance, there is a dearth of research examining Hong Kong youth from a cultural perspective, which might be attributable to other factors that characterized (late) modernity such as the emergence of diasporic cultures, as well as the temporal and spatial changes in the creation and sustainability of youth cultures.[35]

Setting against such a background, this study focuses on how the youth perceive and interpret social labels associated with their collective gaming activities in net-bars. Based on the data collected from focus group discussions, below I will focus on two parts. In the first part, I articulate the social labels of the net-bar youth, analyzing the tags that people put on the youth. These labels include Dokuos, MK boys, sex-seeking, and excessive vulgarity. The second part examines how the youth develop their strategies to deal with these labels, through which they manage conflicts of identity, that is, who they are and who others think they are. The strategies of avoiding, normalizing, neutralizing, professionalizing, and quitting are primary concerns in this part. A discussion of these findings follows.

Social Labels on Net-Bar Youth

In all the discussions around the topic of net-bar gaming, the informants expressed their feelings about how others consider what the net-bar is and who they are; they articulated that people who do not go to net-bars and play games would think the net-bar goers are different groups of people. A recurring pattern through their narratives is that, in addition to how their perception of what the social stigma of net-bar is, they also label other net-bar goers with similar prejudice. In other words, while the net-bar goers think people see them as Dokuos, MK boys, sex-seeking, and vulgar teens, they distance themselves from these labels but use the same labels to stereotype other net-bar goers. They are both the labeled and the labeler, stigmatized and the stigmatizer. Before discussing this irony, I will elucidate several frequently occurred labels of net-bar youth: Dokuos, MK boys, sex-seeking, and excessive vulgarity.

Dokuo (毒男)

The idea of Dokuo originated from a Japanese TV drama broadcasted in 2004, *Densha Otoko*. The name referred to single men who lack confidence in dealing with the outside world and interacting with women. Later, the HK Golden Forum borrowed this term to refer to Hong Kong young men who were poisonously obsessed with anime and video games. The meaning thus changed significantly and became more pejorative. Dokuo as a subcultural term has prevailed in Hong Kong in recent years, used both as a noun and an adjective to both indicate a person and describe the quality of a certain behavior. In many spats in online forums and social networks, the meaning of Dokuo has been largely extended, referring to who have never dated a girl, who are introvert, who have average look, who are in the lower social class, who are poor, and who criticize "Hong

Kong girls."[36] An incidence that this term gained greater social attention happened in 2007, when a user from Golden Forum posted a Dokuo checklist, listing 23 criteria to represent a Dokuo's physical appearance and daily behaviors. An online news portal named *NextMedia*, an affiliate to *AppleDaily*, has reproduced this checklist, accelerating the spread of the word.

MK Boys

MK boys refer to young people who wander around the Mong Kok area, dressed up in a pompous way. They are seen as punks, hipsters, Ah Feis, and so forth. They usually have their hair dyed gold and are claimed to have some connections with gangs. My informants talked a lot about how people would think they are MK boys if people knew that they go to net-bars and have some physical traits, such as gold hair and hippie outfits. While describing the general public impression of net-bar goers as MK boys, the youth also expressed their own opinion of what a MK boy really is.

Spencer stated that, "Sometimes you'll see girls accompanying boys to net-bars, and those (boys) are MK boys," because few girls will go to net-bars. According to the informants, MK boys usually come out very lateat night and play in the net-bar; thus the informants were only aware of MK boys' existence but had no interaction with them directly. The MK boys were seen to be extremely rude and fierce, and were accused to have bonds with gangs. Steve argued that there were many MK boys with a gangster background and they frequently caused troubles in net-bars; he said, "Almost every net-bar has hired a bouncer, who is a member of a gang, to which the net-bar manager will pay periodically. And he will help to keep away those who are troublesome."

These statements were based on what the informants heard, rather than what saw by themselves. The youth rejected the label of MK boys on themselves, while applying the same label to other net-bar goers.

Sex-Seeking

When net-bars first became popular in Hong Kong, some girls in the net-bars provided one-to-one instruction on Internet surfing ostensibly while actually offering companionship and possibly sex services, primarily for middle-class men.[37] This phenomenon has widely seen in Hong Kong society, where net-bars are one of possible places where the service provider and the customer to "hook up."[38] It is similar to compensated dating originated in Japanese popular culture, where old men give money as a compensation for young girls' companionship and/or for sexual favors. Since early 2000, Hong Kong government has made efforts to ban the sex business in net-bars. In 2003, Hong Kong police arrested 82 underage girls between 14 and 17 years of age for providing sex services in net-bars. From 2004 onwards, the police has been cracking down sex business particularly in entertainment places to eradicate underage prostitution; such a business in net-bars has ebbed as a result.[39,40]

My informants in general have seldom experienced sex-related issues in net-bars. Most of them believed that this kind of net-bars operated not in Hong Kong but in Mainland China; or, they exist only in certain areas where sex business prospers. For example, Quentin claimed, "I've really never heard of this kind of stuff. It's so crazy. I bet it must be the net-bars in Temple Street.[41] It must be." The youth also acknowledged that some special private net-bars would operate this kind of business back in time. Frederick said that they knew about girls who touted sex services in net-bar as "Internet instructors," providing instruction on how to surf the Internet as a guise. Isle further explained this phenomenon by referring to "fish ball stalls" and that "the Internet instructor is an updated version of a fish ball girl."[42] Interestingly, many youth argued that people would search for pornography in net-bars, most of whom were middle-aged men, and they suspected they would look for sex services in net-bars as well. Sometime those people would behave improperly and disturb others. Steve shared a story, "So many people watch porn in net-bars! One day I went to a net-bar early in the morning. A guy watched pornography there, and then slept on the sofa. He would not leave so the manager had to call the police. When the police arrived, he was still reluctant to stand up. And after he stood up, we found a nasty thing on the sofa!"[43]

Excessive Vulgarity
My informants mentioned about three images that they considered other people would perceive net-bar goers as: smokers, drug dealers/users, and those who use foul language.

According to the youth, smokers were less likely to be seen in net-bars, though not completely disappeared. This is because Hong Kong has amended the Smoking (Public Health) Ordinance in October 19, 2006, and enacted it in January 1, 2007. This enactment aimed to create friendly places for the youth to go to after school. However, my informants stated that some net-bars still allowed smoking, which made them suffer from second-hand smoking and smell unpleasantly after playing in net-bars. They would not be surprised if people still hold the perceptions of net-bar goers as smokers, not only because smoking still exists in net-bars, but also because the mass media reproduces this stereotype.

In addition, they claimed that drug dealing and use would occur to people's mind when talking about net-bars.[44] Most of the time, the informants accused the media to broadcast hearsays about net-bar drug dealing. "They (the media) like to exaggerate things," said Zach. They articulated on this issue in three ways. Firstly, they denied using drugs in net-bars. Secondly, they believed that MK boys would probably trade and take drugs, although they claimed that people dealing drugs in net-bars were none of their business. Max put it in this way, "There were always bad people doing bad things. And you cannot blame the place and everybody in it."

Thirdly, the youth I interviewed reported the excessive use of foul language in net-bars. They recognized that the vulgar expressions and dirty words would spread out easily when playing games. They themselves frequently spoke out profanity when they played games in net-bars while not in other places. They also gave an example that elementary school students seemed to be easily influenced by foul language in net-bars.[45] Zack illustrated, "Once I went to play *Nobunaga's Ambition* and beat the avatar of an elementary school student who was sitting next to me. He cried out 'Fuck!' really loud… they say fuck anytime anywhere. When they win the game, they say fuck; when they lose, they say fuck; when they kill someone (in game), they say fuck; and when they are chased away, they also say fuck. For them, it is so easy to say fuck."

Negotiating Image and Identity: Strategies to Deal with Labels

As I mentioned previously, the youth played the roles between the stigmatized and the stigmatizer; when they realized social prejudice and labels toward them, they strategically distanced themselves from those negative designations, and even used the stigma to label other net-bar goers. In order to do so, they practiced different strategies to manage their own images and negotiate their identities as students, sons, good citizens, and ultimately ordinary people, for presenting themselves in front of others. These young people admitted that the stereotypical view toward net-bar

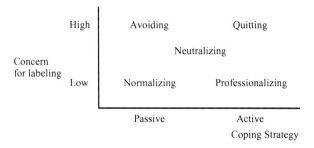

Fig. 7.1 Negotiating image and identity through coping with labels

goers is valid to some point as there are potential threats in net-bars that might lure teenagers to engage in deviant behaviors. Interestingly, on one hand, the youth tended to reject negative tags and downplay the effects of being labeled. On the other hand, they tried to adjust themselves through managing their images and identity in order to cope with negative designations, even though they claimed the designations were not based on real conditions. Being both the labeled and the labeler, they knew not only exactly what was happening in net-bars from their gaming experience but also how not to follow a deviant path.

Based on the degree of their concerns for labeling, their coping strategies also have different degree of action. By providing different scenarios of coping with social labels, I categorize the five types of negotiation strategies in the chart below (Fig. 7.1).

Avoiding

When the net-bar youth are highly concerned with the labels, they would avoid having conversations about net-bar gaming. This is an instinctive response to social labels. Avoidance works effectively for secret deviants, whose "improper act is committed, yet no one notices it or reacts to it as a violation of the rules."[46]

For example, many of the youth had experience of going to net-bars after school without telling their parents and their schoolmates, because of the fear of being punished by parents and being ostracized by their peers. Yana confessed that he never told his schoolmates about playing in net-bars when he was in middle school, until he met other students who shared his gaming interests in net-bars. During the discussion, Dominic recollected his experience 10 years ago, when he was in elementary school and smoking was not banned in net-bars. He complained that the air in net-bars was messed up along with people "boiling tobacco" and his school uniform was always smelly.[47] "I had a trick," said Dominic, "Usually when I went home after playing in net-bars, around 6 pm, my mom was not back from work and the house was empty. I quickly threw the uniform into the washing machine before anyone noticed that I went to net-bars and got smelly." In doing so, people could not find out their identity as net-bar goers, assuming them as ordinary students who conformed rules and norms in school and at home.

Normalizing

In many sociological studies of identity management, such as organization studies, criminology, and medical sociology, normalizing is a process as well as strategy to manage social stigma and deviance (Kramer 2010).[48,49] In the case of net-bar gaming, normalizing is understood as a strategy that the youth utilized to either favor or proactively be against social stigma. My informants underscored how the changing social environment and new ways of thinking would incorporate the deviant identity into everyday life, making net-bar gaming as a "normal" activity and net-bar goers as "normal" people in the public's eyes. This is vividly demonstrated in how the net-bar youth reacted when confronting the designation of Dokuo.

The net-bar youth expressed their concerns about being labeled as Dokuo or in Dokuo-style. Most of them seemed neither favor nor disfavor this label. From their physical appearance, they were hardly categorized as Dokuo. Yet, sometimes they would claim that, as Honda said, "we are all good boys, though also Dokuos." This acknowledgement was "self-mockery," according to his peers who broke out of laughter during the interview. Once other people learned that they were game fans and frequent net-bars goers, they would tag the net-bar youth as Dokuos to interpret their behavior. Expressions like "girls think those boys who go to net-bar everyday are very Dokuo" (Carl) and "those who don't go to the net-bar would say we are so Dokuo" (Zach) were common. As the conversation revealed, Dokuo as a negative label is not applicable to every net-bar youth but limited to those who do not conform to social expectations. For example, if the youth behaved as good students with good grades, they would rarely be accused as Dokuo.

By contrast, academically struggling students were more likely to be tagged as Dokuos. However, rather than arguing against being labeled as Dokuos, the youth, on one hand, emphasized the value of collective activities in net-bar gaming. For them, collective gaming was an important aspect that strengthened social ties and bonds within in the group, which contradicts the loner stereotype attached to Dokuo. On the other hand, they juxtaposed net-bar gaming and other leisure activities such as jogging, justifying their behaviors as non-rule-breaking. In their understanding, being labeled as Dokuo may have multiple meanings; playing games in net-bars did not necessarily lead to the deviant identity associated with a Dokuo.

Neutralizing

Another strategy employed by the youth to manage their images is to add socially desirable elements into their identities. This strategy aims to neutralize people's perceptions toward the labels on the net-bar youth.

One of the elements that the society desires is education. The high school teens group were concerned significantly more with being labeled as Dokuos, compared to the college groups. The high school youth talked about being watched by teachers and parents and were afraid of being ostracized by their schoolmates once they were labeled as Dokuo. In discussion with the high school teens, Zach put it, "If you enter college, people just assume you are good students, and they care less about whether you are Dokuo or not." Quentin added, "True, you perform really well then people will compliment you even though you are playing in net-bars." They suggested that college students, especially those in top universities such as Hong Kong University (HKU), Chinese University of Hong Kong (CUHK), and Hong Kong University of Science and Technology (HKUST), were less likely to be perceived as deviants by others.

This line of narrative was in concert with what the informants in the college groups claimed. Honda recollected that his parents once told him, "after you getting into college, you can do whatever you want," implying that they will not forbid him from going to net-bars and playing games with friends. Indeed, he did not need his parents' permission after going to college. The college youth were less confused and struck with being called Dokuo or other social stigma attached to net-bar gaming, largely because their identity as college students offset the negative labels associated with net-bar goers. Fredrick also stated that college life would help develop their social networks and acquire more independence from parents. He added, "people assume you know what to do with your life."

Nevertheless, even though the "normal" good-student identity overshadows the deviant identity, it does not substantially affect the image of a whole group of net-bar goers. Although the informants acknowledged that adding the socially desirable elements into their identity can help reduce stigma, not every one of them actually made efforts to neutralize people's perception toward them.

Professionalizing

Although not common, some of the youth expressed their interests in developing gaming into a career that could make a living. A prominent example can be found from one of my informants' profession: gold farming.

Max was in his final year of high school. Usually students at that time would feel great pressure from the Hong Kong Certificate of Education Examination (HKCEE). However, his peers said that his main business was playing video games, not studying. He was stepping into the world of gold farming, where hardcore players dig into the game to acquire in-game currency and exchange real-world money with other players. He opened many accounts in different online games, spent lots of time to gather rare items and high-level avatars, which he sold to other players with a hefty price tag.

Max: Some trades are really crazy! A trick for thousands of dollars! I surely do it everyday!
Lester: The parents spoil the chick-chicks.[50] They give them so much money.
Steve: That's what Max can take advantage of.
Max: I'm just fine with the situation. Sometimes I buy a piece with $200 dollars (approx. US$26) but can sell it up to $700 (approx. US$90).
Lester: How much time do you spend to work on the items?
Max: Two weeks, more or less.
Lester: So you get your job! Playing games!

Max: Well, I can earn around $4–5000 dollars (approx. US$516–645) per month now. And it's true, that's my main business. But I think those who spend huge money on exchanging virtual goods are really stupid. Many people spend over $1000 (approx. US$129) to buy virtual goods per week! Can you believe it? Aren't they crazy?

Max now plays less frequently in net-bars for security reasons but more frequently at home. No one knows how long this job will last for him; it could be a temporary excursion, considering that there are many more competitive gold farmers in Mainland China.[51] Yet through their conversation, Max and his peers seemed less inclined to continue their education into college. To professionalize their gaming, the youth try to negotiate their identity and justify their positions. Such efforts are precarious, without any guaranteed outcome.

Quitting

For the net-bar youth, another way to negotiate other people's perception toward them might be simply quitting. Quitting the net-bar gaming allows them to detach themselves from the social designations of net-bar goers. The informants revealed that their gaming groups were becoming smaller as members left. This happened more frequently among college informants than high schoolers.

Ben: One of our old friends is very disciplined.
Xander: He behaved quite rational. When somebody suggested we should play another hour, we all, except him, immediately agreed.
Ben: He's not a friend, anyway.
Lance: He didn't treat us as a friend! Always leaves early.
Honda: You know? That's why he's working at i-Bank and we are still sitting in i-One.
Xander: He went to HKU. He's quite successful now.
Spencer: Every time after playing nightlong, we all regret not leaving with him.
Honda: He is successful.

Xander: He's leaving.
Spencer: He's no longer your research object.
Lance: Perhaps he is the object of another research, ha!
Frank: He's no longer one of us.

In this case, exiting the peer group and quitting games in net-bars is a personal choice mostly due to changing environments. College informants agreed that getting into college granted them more autonomy and opportunities to choose their lifestyle, which would make some people turn to activities other than net-bar gaming. From the conversation among the informants, their friend who left their gaming group cared more about conventional views of success: academic excellence, well-paying job, and quality of life. Once a person achieves a higher social status through education and work, he would probably follow the social conventions of viewing the net-bar as an undesirable place for his image.

For some other people who still remain in collective gaming activities, their gaming groups are facing declining membership. As revealed, some of the informants' conversation came up with a feeling of nostalgia. Immediately after graduating from high school, the college youth usually gathered once a month. Participation gradually declined over time; their appointments would be canceled for various reasons. Jack put forth, "We did not have much time to play together at net-bars unless we are in the same colleges, or even in the same departments." Dominic added, "We seldom go (to net-bars) alone. I have a friend who always had a time conflict with our gatherings because he took a course which we did not. Sometime later he just quit and no longer played with us." In this case, members quit net-bar going not because of social stigma but because of changing situations.

DISCUSSION

By analyzing how Hong Kong youth perceive social stigma toward them as they play games in net-bars, as well as how they negotiated their images and identity to cope with negative designations, this study offers two implications.

First, the net-bar youth are both the labeled and the labeler. They not only think they are negatively perceived by others but also use those stereotypes to label other net-bar goers. The social stigma does not only affect how the youth react to social labels but also affect how they perceive other stigmatized people. Though it is unclear how this mechanism works for the teens, it is safe to say that the youth constantly refuse being labeled as unconventional, partially by allying with social standards to stereotype other net-bar goers. They are playing around the roles of "insiders" and "outsiders": when being accused deviant, they defend themselves with both insiders' view by arguing that the public is ignorant of what net-bars really are and outsiders' view by distancing themselves from the accused deviant identity of net-bar goers. The different positioning and the changing social context complicate the understanding of the labeling process, where the line between the labeled and the labeler blurs.

Second, when the youth perceive the stigma on them, they try to manage their images and identity to cope with the labels. The process is important in that the youth try to make sense of the social labels while at the same time redefine and reinterpret the social meanings attached to their identity. Here, a reconciliation of individual identity and collective identity can possibly occur, when individual behaviors and reactions are connected to groups of net-bar goers who create and participate in the formation of a subculture. Through the youth's expression, interpretation, and negotiation of the labels, what they articulate is not only gaming or friendship but also a significant part of their identity, lifestyle, and culture.

Third, the collectivist aspect of gaming is important in the net-bar youth's negotiation of social stigma. Despite the social prejudice toward net-bar goers, many of them still prefer playing in net-bars over playing individually at home, largely because of sociality, companionship, and friendship. Such group identification may or may not alleviate the pejorative labels attached to net-bar goers. Yet it is a significant part of cultural identification of the net-bar youth, which may also explain why some of the college student informants were nostalgic about their gaming experience in the past. The collective gaming also reflects the collectivistic cultural practice in East Asian countries at large.[52]

Limitations

This study examined the social labels attached to net-bars from the perspectives of Hong Kong youth. However, the study might have overlooked the opinions of various groups, which might be different from those of the youth. Thus, a follow-up study on different groups, such as the government, school, media, parents, who often designate net-bar youth as deviants, would be helpful to understand the labeling process.

Another weakness of this study is the non-representative sample. The gender composition in this study makes it difficult to depict a comprehensive picture of net-bar youth culture. Although it would be difficult to recruit net-bar girls due to their low numbers, investigating this population may yield some interesting results. For example, as social expectations toward men and women are different, net-bar girls would be perceived to be in a more dangerous situation compared to their male counterparts. In addition, the labels may have more negative effects on girls. Nevertheless, my informants reported that the number of girls visiting net-bars was growing, though slightly, during the past several years. What the girls' presence in the net-bar means, how their experience constructs their identity, how they perceive the labels attached to them, and whether they feel the same pressure and use the same strategies as their male counterparts are some of the questions to be investigated.

NOTES

1. Mehmet Gürol and Tuncay Sevindik, "Profile of Internet Café Users in Turkey," *Telematics and Informatics* (2007): 59.
2. Huhh Jun-So, "Culture and Business of PC Bangs in Korea," *Games and Culture* 3(2008): 26.
3. Holin Lin, "Gendered Gaming Experience in Social Space: From Home to Internet Café," Paper presented at the DiGRA 2005 Conference, Vancouver, British Columbia, Canada, June 16–20, 2005.
4. James A. Holstein, "Defining Deviance: John Kitsuse's Modest Agenda," *The American Sociologist* 40 (2009): 54.
5. Raymond Paternoster and Leeann Iovanni, "The Labeling Perspective and Delinquency: An Elaboration of the Theory and an Assessment of the Evidence," *Justice Quarterly* 6 (1989): 364.
6. Ibid, 362–363.
7. James D. Orcutt, "Societal Reaction and the Response to Deviation in Small Groups," *Social Forces* 52(1973): 263.
8. Howard S. Becker, *Outsiders: Studies in the Sociology of Deviance* (London: Free Press of Glencoe, 1963), 33.
9. Erving Goffman, *Stigma: Notes on the Management of Spoiled Identity* (New York: Simon & Schuster, 1963), 3–4.

10. Daphna Oyserman and Janet K. Swim, "Stigma: An Insider's View," *Journal of Social Issues* 57(2002): 2.
11. Ken Plummer, "Labeling Theory Revisited: Forth Years on," 2011, accessed April 20, 2013, http://www.chicagomanualofstyle.org/tools_citationguide.html.
12. Ryken Grattet, "Labeling Theory," in *The Routledge Handbook of Deviant Behavior*, ed. Clifton D. Bryant (London and New York: Routledge, 2011), 127–28.
13. Manuela Barreto and Naomi Ellemers, "Current Issues in the Study of Social Stigma: Some Controversies and Unresolved Issues," *Journal of Social Issues* 66 (2010): 432–433.
14. Chong-Wen Wang et al., "Prevalence and Correlates of Video and Internet Game Addiction among Hong Kong Adolescents: A Pilot Study," *The Scientific World Journal* 2014(2014): 5.
15. Anne Brus, "A Young People's Perspective on Computer Game Addiction," *Addiction Research & Theory* 21(2013): 367.
16. Anthony YH. Fung, "Hong Kong Gamers Study Report 2011 (project Code 4001-SPPR-09)," *Creative Industries*, March 8, 2012, accessed November 4, 2012, http://creativeindustries.com.cuhk.edu.hk/wp-content/uploads/2012/03/Hong-Kong-Gamer-Study-Report-2011-English.pdf.
17. "Internet Usage in Hong Kong—Statistics and Trends," *Go-Global*, August 6, 2014, accessed December 5, 2015, http://www.go-globe.hk/blog/internet-usage-hong-kong/.
18. Benjamin W. Ng, "Consuming and Localizing Japanese Combat Games in Hong Kong," in *Gaming Cultures and Place in Asia-Pacific*, ed. Larissa Hjoth and Dean Chan (New York and London: Routledge, 2009), 89–93.
19. Tin, "The Evolution of Local Game Culture," *East Touch, Culture Club*, May 22, 2012, A183–187.
20. Lin, "Gendered Gaming."
21. Other regions of Asia have similar social discourse on the negative effects of net-bars. For example, Brian Ashcraft in 2010 has reported that Japanese net cafés are refugee camps of scum and villainy. In Mainland China, Taiwan, and South Korea, there were reports of people gaming to death, in a literal sense. Brian Ashcraft, "Japanese Net Cafes Are a Wretched Hive Of Scum And Villainy," Kotaku, December 9, 2010. Accessed May 9, 2013, http://kotaku.com/5709983/japanese-net-cafes-are-a-wretched-hive-ofscum-and-villainy.
22. Ng Shun-Wing, "Cram Schools: Students are Paying for Dependence on Private Tutors," *Hong Kong Economic Times*, June 20, 2011, Commentary sec.
23. Dick Hebdige, *Hiding in the Light: On Images and Things* (New York: Comedia, 1988), 17.

24. Sammy Wai-sang Chiu, "Rethinking Youth Problems in a Risk Society: Some Reflections on Working with 'Youth-at-Risk' in Hong Kong," in *Working with Youth-at-Risk in Hong Kong*, ed. Francis Wing-lin Lee (Hong Kong: Hong Kong University Press, 2005), 105.

25. Cherry Sze Man Ho and Emy Yee Ming Law, "Life Education on Working with Youth in Hong Kong Social Context: Critical Perspective" (Paper presented at the International Conference on Working with Youth in a Rapidly Changing World, Hong Kong, November, 2003).

26. Hong Kong Government, *White Paper on "Aims and Policy for Social Welfare in Hong Kong"* (Hong Kong, 1965).

27. Hau-lin Tam, "'Delinquent Behaviour as a Kind of Body Politics' Against Adult Regulation—Young People's Discourses in Hong Kong." *Children and Youth Services* 33(2011): 878.

28. Agnes Mung-Chan Ng, *Social Causes of Violent Crimes among Young Offenders in Hong Kong* (Hong Kong: Social Research Centre, The Chinese University of Hong Kong, 1975).

29. Kam C. Wong, *Policing in Hong Kong: Research and Practice* (UK: Palgrave Macmillan, 2015).

30. Tam, "Delinquent Behaviour," 878.

31. Patricia Gray, "The Struggle for Juvenile Justice in Hong Kong 1932-1995," *Hong Kong Law Journal* 26 (1996), 303–04.

32. Eric Ma, "Emotional Energy and Sub-cultural Politics: Alternative Bands in Post-1997 Hong Kong." *Inter-Asia Cultural Studies* 3(2002): 189.

33. Lin Wan-Ying and Zhang Xinzhi, "Exploring Online-Offline Social Capital Construction of the "Otaku" Youth in Hong Kong," *Mass Communication Research* 112(2012): 233.

34. Te-Ping Chen, "Protest over 'Brainwashing' Schools," *Wall Street Journal*, September 2, 2012, accessed December 1, 2015, http://blogs.wsj.com/chinarealtime/2012/09/02/thousands-protest-hong-kongs-moral-and-national-education-push/.

35. Mark Cieslik and Gary Pollock, *Young People in Risk Society: The Restructuring of Youth Identities and Transitions in Late Modernity* (Aldershot: Ashgate), 10.

36. The term "Hong Kong girl" is another subcultural term referring to material girls.

37. Lo Man-Li, "Net-bar Sexy Girls with 70K/m Income," *AppleDaily*, July 6, 2002.

38. Pauline Chiou, "Girls Sell Sex in Hong Kong to Earn Shopping Money," *CNN*, October 13, 2009, accessed December 2, 2015, http://www.cnn.com/2009/WORLD/asiapcf/09/24/hongkong.teenage.prostitution/index.html?eref=rss_topstories.

39. Huangfu Pingli, "Hong Kong Police Cleanup Pornographic Net-bar, Caught up Owners of Prostitution Rings," *Xinhua News Agency*, March 31, 2004.

40. Yip, Tse, and Tang, "The Police Are Strictly Monitoring Pornographic Net-bars." *WeeklyLaw*, accessed February 24, 2013, http://www.weeklylaw.com/2012/07/警方嚴厲打擊色情網吧.html.

41. It is an area notorious for prostitution and sex business.

42. The fish ball stall here is not a street-side food stall that sells fish balls, typical Hong Kong snack. It is a place that sex business takes place. It was very popular in the 1980s–1990s in Hong Kong. Girls who provided sex services were mostly adolescents. Clients gave a nickname to such place by comparing the girls' growing breasts to fish balls. These girls were called fish ball girls.

43. The guy was masturbating while watching pornographic videos.

44. Central District Council, *Regulation on Net-bars*, 97/2009 (Hong Kong, 2009), http://www.districtcouncils.gov.hk/archive/central_d/pdf/2009/CW_2009_097_TC.pdf.

45. In Hong Kong, elementary school students are allowed to visit net-bars.

46. Becker, *Outsiders*, 20.

47. In Cantonese, boiling tobacco (煲烟) means smoking. It is the lively analogy to describe the scene when people smoke and the smokes wind around.

48. Judith A. Clair, Joy E. Beatty, and Tammy L. Maclean, "Out of Sight but not out of Mind: Managing Invisible Social Identities in the Workplace," *Academy of Management Review* 30 (2005): 83.

49. Ronald C. Kramer, "Vaughan, Diane: The Normalization of Deviance," in *Encyclopedia of Criminological Theory*, ed. by Francis T. Cullen, and Pamela Wilcox (Sage Publications, 2010), 977–979.

50. My informants called the childish elementary school students as "elementary school chicks." This word stems from a Cantonese slang, originally referring to elementary school kids without irony. In recent year, it is popularized through the Internet, negatively designating those who think and act in a childish way and often ask for trouble. When talking about the younger generation in net-bars, the informants showed depreciative manners toward them. From their point of view, the elementary school kids in the net-bar were spoiled children, who probably came from middle-class families. Their parents gave them too much pocket money and they spent it lavishly.

51. Julian Dibbell, "The Life of the Chinese Gold Farmer," *The New York Times*, June 17, 2007, accessed December 1, 2015, http://www.nytimes.com/2007/06/17/magazine/17lootfarmers-t.html?_r=0.

52. Larissa Hjorth, "The Game of Being Mobile: One Media History of Gaming and Mobile Technologies in Asia-Pacific," *Convergence: The International Journal of Research into New Media Technologies* 13(2007): 378.

BIBLIOGRAPHY

Ashcraft, Brian. 2010. Japanese net cafes are a wretched hive of Scum and Villainy. *Kotaku.* Accessed 9 May 2013. http://kotaku.com/5709983/japanese-net-cafes-are-a-wretched-hive-of-scum-and-villainy.

Barreto, Manuela, and Naomi Ellemers. 2010. Current issues in the study of social stigma: Some controversies and unresolved issues. *Journal of Social Issues* 66: 431–445.

Becker, Howard S. 1963. *Outsiders: Studies in the sociology of deviance.* London: Free Press of Glencoe.

Brus, Anne. 2013. A young people's perspective on computer game addiction. *Addiction Research & Theory* 21: 365–375.

Central District Council. 2009. *Regulation on Net-bars*, 97/2009. Hong Kong. http://www.districtcouncils.gov.hk/archive/central_d/pdf/2009/CW_2009_097_TC.pdf

Chen, Te-Ping. 2012. Protest over 'Brainwashing' schools. *Wall Street Journal.* http://blogs.wsj.com/chinarealtime/2012/09/02/thousands-protest-hong-kongs-moral-and-national-education-push/. Accessed 1 Dec 2015.

Chiou, Pauline. 2009. Girls sell sex in Hong Kong to earn shopping money. *CNN.* http://www.cnn.com/2009/WORLD/asiapcf/09/24/hongkong.teenage.prostitution/index.html?eref=rss_topstories. Accessed 2 Dec 2015.

Chiu, Sammy Wai-sang. 2005. "Rethinking youth problems in a risk society: Some reflections on working with 'Youth-at-Risk' in Hong Kong." In *Working with youth-at-risk in Hong Kong*, edited Francis Wing-lin Lee. Hong Kong: Hong Kong University Press.

Cieslik, Mark, and Gary Pollock. 2002. *Young people in risk society: The restructuring of youth identities and transitions in late modernity.* Aldershot: Ashgate.

Clair, Judith A., Joy E. Beatty, and Tammy L. Maclean. 2005. Out of sight but not out of mind: Managing invisible social identities in the workplace. *Academy of Management Review* 30: 78–95.

Dibbell, Julian. 2007. The life of the Chinese gold farmer, *The New York Times.* http://www.nytimes.com/2007/06/17/magazine/17lootfarmers-t.html?_r=0. Accessed 1 Dec 2015.

Fung, Anthony YH. 2012. Hong Kong gamers study report 2011 (project Code 4001-SPPR-09). *Creative Industries*, March 8. http://creativeindustries.com.cuhk.edu.hk/wp-content/uploads/2012/03/Hong-Kong-Gamer-Study-Report-2011-English.pdf. Accessed 4 Nov 2012.

Goffman, Erving. 1963. *Stigma: Notes on the management of spoiled identity.* New York: Simon & Schuster.

Grattet, Ryken. 2011. Labeling theory. In *The Routledge handbook of deviant behavior,* ed. Clifton D. Bryant, 121–128. London/New York: Routledge.

Gray, Patricia. 1996. The struggle for juvenile justice in Hong Kong 1932–1995. *Hong Kong Law Journal* 26: 301–319.

Gürol, Mehmet, and Tuncay Sevindik. 2007. Profile of internet café users in Turkey. *Telematics and Informatics* 24: 59–68.

Hebdige, Dick. 1988. *Hiding in the light: On images and things.* New York: Comedia.

Hjorth, Larissa. 2007. The game of being mobile: One media history of gaming and mobile technologies in asia-pacific. *Convergence: The International Journal of Research into New Media Technologies* 13: 369–381.

Ho, Cherry Sze Ma, and Law, Emy Yee Ming. 2003. Life education on working with youth in Hong Kong social context: Critical perspective. Paper presented at the International Conference on Working with Youth in a Rapidly Changing World, Hong Kong.

Holstein, James A. 2009. Defining deviance: John Kitsuse's modest agenda. *The American Sociologist* 40: 51–60.

Hong Kong Government. 1965. *White Paper on "Aims and policy for social welfare in Hong Kong."* Hong Kong.

Huangfu, Pingli. 2004. Hong Kong police cleanup pornographic net-bar, caught up owners of prostitution rings. *Xinhua News Agency.* http://big5.xinhuanet. com/gate/big5/news.xinhuanet.com/legal/2004-03/31/content_1394671.htm. Accessed 18 Apr 2013.

Huhh, Jun-Sok. 2008. Culture and business of PC bangs in Korea. *Games and Culture* 3: 26–37.

"Internet Usage in Hong Kong—Statistics and Trends." *Go-Global,* August 6, 2014. Accessed 5 December 2015. http://www.go-globe.hk/blog/internet-usage-hong-kong/

Kitsuse, John I. 1962. Societal reaction to deviant behavior: Problems of theory and method. *Social Problems* 9: 247–256.

———. 1975. The 'new conception of deviance' and its critics. In *The labelling of deviance: Evaluating a perspective,* ed. Walter R. Gove, 273–284. Beverly Hills: Sage.

Kramer, Ronald C. 2010. Vaughan, Diane: The normalization of deviance. In *Encyclopedia of criminological theory,* ed. Francis T. Cullen, and Pamela Wilcox, 977–979. Beverly Hills: Sage.

Lemert, Edwin McCarthy. 1951. *Social pathology: A systematic approach to the theory of sociopathic behavior.* New York: McGraw-Hill.

———. 1967. *Human deviance, social problems, and social control.* Englewook Cliffs: Prentice Hall.

Lin, Holin. 2005. Gendered gaming experience in social space: From home to internet café. Paper presented at the DiGRA 2005 Conference, Vancouver, British Columbia, Canada.

Lin, Wan-Ying, and Xinzhi Zhang. 2012. Exploring online-offline social capital construction of the "Otaku" youth in Hong Kong. *Mass Communication Research* 112: 233–270.

Lo, Man-Li. 2002. Net-bar sexy girls with 70K/m income. *AppleDaily*. http://hk.apple.nextmedia.com/news/art/20020706/2699218. Accessed 18 Apr 2013.

Ma, Eric. 2002. Emotional energy and sub-cultural politics: Alternative bands in post-1997 Hong Kong. *Inter-Asia Cultural Studies* 3: 187–200.

Ng, Agnes Mung-Chan. 1975. *Social causes of violent crimes among young offenders in Hong Kong*. Hong Kong: Social Research Centre, The Chinese University of Hong Kong.

Ng, Benjamin W. 2009. Consuming and localizing Japanese combat games in Hong Kong. In *Gaming cultures and place in Asia-pacific*, ed. Larissa Hjoth, and Dean Chan, 83–101. New York/London: Routledge.

Ng, Shun-Wing. 2011. Cram schools: Students are paying for dependence on private tutors. *Hong Kong Economic Times*, Commentary sec. http://www.hket.com/eti/article/bb197f8b-534e-41e3-baf0-e153eccc4194--195116?sectionId=007. Accessed 2 May 2013.

Orcutt, James D. 1973. Societal reaction and the response to deviation in small groups. *Social Forces* 52: 259–267.

Oyserman, Daphna, and Janet K. Swim. 2002. Stigma: an insider's view. *Journal of Social Issues* 57: 1–14.

Paternoster, Raymond, and Leeann Iovanni. 1989. The labeling perspective and delinquency: An elaboration of the theory and an assessment of the evidence. *Justice Quarterly* 6: 359–394.

Pfohl, Stephen. 1994. *Images of deviance and social control: A sociological history*, 2nd edn. New York: McGraw-Hill.

Plummer, Ken. 2011. Labeling theory revisited: Forth years on. http://www.chicagomanualofstyle.org/tools_citationguide.html. Accessed 20 Apr 2013.

Tam, Hau-lin. 2011. 'Delinquent behaviour as a kind of body politics' against adult regulation—Young people's discourses in Hong Kong. *Children and Youth Services* 33: 878–887.

Tin. 2012. The evolution of local game culture." *East Touch, Culture Club*, A183–187.

Wang, Chong-Wen, Cecilia L.W. Chan, Kwok-Kei Mak, Sai-Yin Ho, Paul W.C. Wong, and Rainbow T.H. Ho. 2014. Prevalence and correlates of video and internet gaming addiction among Hong Kong adolescents: A pilot study. *The Scientific World Journal* 2014: 1–9.

Wong, Kam C. 2015. *Policing in Hong Kong: Research and practice.* New York: Palgrave Macmillan.

Yip, Tse, and Tang. 2013. The Police Are Strictly Monitoring Pornographic Net-bars. *WeeklyLaw.* http://www.weeklylaw.com/2012/07/警方嚴厲打擊色情網吧.html. Accessed 24 Feb 2013.

CHAPTER 8

Development of an Internet Gaming Addiction Scale Based on the DSM-5's Nine Diagnostic Criteria with South Korean Gamer Samples

Hongsik Yu

INTERNET GAMING ADDICTION ISSUES IN SOUTH KOREA

Along with the phenomenal growth in the popularity of Internet gaming over the last decade, Internet gaming addiction has emerged as one of the fastest growing forms of addiction worldwide. Previous studies have provided game addiction rates across countries. For example, 9.4% of Dutch adolescent online game players aged between 12 and 18 years (Lemmens et al. 2009, 88), 3.4% of Hungarian gamers (Demetrovics et al. 2012, e36417), 11.9% of German active gamers (Grüsser et al. 2007, 290), and 8.7% of Singaporean children and adolescents (Choo et al. 2010, 826) were classified as Internet game addicts.

South Korea is a nation considered to have the most intense Internet gaming culture with high prevalence rates of addiction (Block 2008, 306; Seok and DaCosta 2012, 2145). Korea is known not only as the

H. Yu (✉)
School of Media & Communication, Chung-Ang University,
Seoul, South Korea

© The Author(s) 2016
S.A. Lee, A. Pulos (eds.), *Transnational Contexts of Development History, Sociality, and Society of Play*, East Asian Popular Culture,
DOI 10.1007/978-3-319-43820-7_8

211

country with the highest penetration of high-speed Internet broadband with relatively less expensive cost but also to have one of the most rapidly growing Internet game industries. There was, however, the dark side of the advanced infrastructure and the flourishing industry. According to national surveys (NIA 2010; 2014), prevalence rates of Internet addiction were 9.2% in 2006, 8.5% in 2009, and 7.0% in 2013. The prevalence rates in 2013 were equivalent to 2.3 million South Koreans. More specifically, the rate of adolescent Internet addiction was 11.7% in 2013. The overall Internet addiction rates in South Korea are decreasing, but the Internet addiction rates of South Korean adolescents seem to be higher than the aforementioned Internet gaming rates of Dutch adolescents. The rates of adolescent Internet addiction were equivalent to 0.73 million South Korean adolescents. Among these adolescents, the prevalence rates of middle schoolers (12.5%) and college students (12.4%) were slightly higher than those of elementary students (11.0%) and high schoolers (10.8%). Most of the adolescent Internet addicts were presumed to be Internet gaming addicts as the main purpose of Internet use was Internet games.

Some tragic incidents of excessive Internet gaming have attracted public attention and raised social concerns about excessive Internet gaming in South Korea from the early 2000s. For example, in 2005 a male adult died due to 90 hours of consecutive playing of an Internet game without taking proper meals and getting sleep (BBC News 2005). In 2009, a 3-month baby starved to death because the baby's parents were gaming addicts who played 10 hours per day and did not provide proper meals for the baby. In 2010, a middle-school student killed his mother who scolded him for excessive Internet game play and then committed suicide (Choi 2013). These stories and others have made Internet gaming addiction of adolescents and young adults an important social issue in South Korea.

Harsh criticism has concentrated on a specific type of Internet game known as massively multiplayer online role playing game (MMORPG). This type of game genre allows a very large number of gamers to play together, taking the roles of characters in a virtual world and cooperating with other gamers to achieve goals. MMORPGs are also well known for the non-fixed, persistent game story and structure in which game publishers regularly introduce and update new content. In this specific genre of Internet games, gamers are required to continue playing to obtain game items such as weapons and armor. The aforementioned death incidents occurred during the play of this type of Internet games.

Parents, civil right advocates, psychiatrists, police makers, and South Korea's Ministry of Gender Equality & Family have expressed their concerns regarding excessive Internet game play of adolescents. They have publicly pursued regulations that limit accessibility to and excessive playing of Internet games to ensure sufficient sleep and healthy growth of adolescents. In reaction to this regulation, the Internet game industry and the Ministry of Culture, Sports & Tourism have opposed the introduction of any kind of regulations on Internet games. They have refuted such criticism and do not acknowledge the existence of Internet gaming addiction. They also argue that Internet games are cultural creative products, which are beneficial to the overall Korean economy and job creation. The arguments between the two opposing sides have continued for several years.

In April 2011, both sides finally reached an agreement to introduce a specific regulation on Internet games in the Juvenile Protection Act. The regulation is known as the Shutdown System. According to the law, it prohibits adolescent gamers under the age of 16 from accessing Internet game servers between midnight and 6 a.m. by requiring that Internet game providers block access to servers. The regulation immediately stirred up controversy, and a civic group filed a petition to the Korean Constitutional Court. In April 2014, the Court ruled the Internet game Shutdown System constitutional. The Court explained that the Shutdown System neither infringes the fundamental, constitutional rights of adolescents and their parents nor the Internet game industry.

Although the Shutdown System regulation has been in effect for several years, debates about its effectiveness have continued between various interest groups. After a long period of discussion, the Korean government decided to ease the regulation in September 2014. According to the amendment to the Shutdown System, the ban can be lifted upon parental request. That is, if parents decide to allow their children to play Internet games between midnight and 6 a.m., the children will be permitted to do so. The amendment was aimed to allow adolescents to control excessive gaming hours with parental guidance and responsibility. The amendment came after President Park Geun-hye requested regulatory reform in order to secure future growth engine businesses of South Korea and revitalize economy with a deregulation approach.

INTERNET GAMING ADDICTION AND ITS EXPLICIT DIAGNOSTIC CRITERIA

The primary concern in this chapter is with Internet gaming addiction and the criteria that can be developed and applied to diagnose it. It is necessary to address some issues related to the way in which diagnostic criteria influence Internet gaming addiction decisions. First of all, we need to understand the definition of addiction. Although we frequently use Internet gaming addiction, the term addiction requires a pathological diagnosis with acceptable and agreeable criteria. In this regard, Internet gaming addiction is not accepted as a pathological behavioral addiction. The only pathological behavioral addiction is gambling addiction. Thus, there has been considerable debate as to whether Internet gaming addiction really exists.

Some previous studies have explored which diagnostic criteria constituted the Internet gaming addiction (Charlton and Danforth 2007, 1542–1543; Choo et al. 2010, 826; Demetrovics et al. 2012, e36417; Grüsser et al. 2007, 291; Kim and Kim 2010, 392–393; Lemmens et al. 2009, 79–80; Seok and DaCosta 2012, 2143–2144). Previous studies with screening instruments, mostly adapting the pathological gaming criteria, have identified the six core diagnostic criteria of Internet gaming addiction: salience, mood modification, tolerance, withdrawal symptoms, conflict, and relapse. These are similar to the six common components of behavioral addictions postulated by Brown (1993) and Griffiths (1996, 1998, 2005b).

Several additional criteria have been identified. For instance, Demetrovics et al. (2012) identified a six-factor structure of game addiction: preoccupation, interpersonal conflicts, withdrawal symptoms, overuse, immersion, and social isolation. Lemmens et al. (2009, 79–80) additionally found the criterion problems on their game addiction scale for adolescents. In their research, the criterion problems referred to intrapsychic conflicts or conflicts with other activities such as school work and socializing, while the criterion conflict was limited to the interpersonal conflicts. Kim and Kim (2010) identified the following five criteria: euphoria, health problems, conflict, failure of self-control, and preference for virtual relationship over face-to-face interaction.

The findings of these previous studies suggested some useful diagnostic criteria but reached no global consensus on principle criteria for identifying an Internet gaming disorder. One reason of failure in reaching a consensus was that previous studies assessed Internet gaming addiction with only slight modifications of the diagnostic criteria which have been used to identify substance use disorders and pathological gambling. Previous studies have overlooked that Internet gaming disorder is different from substance-related and gambling disorders. Another reason for disagreement is that previous studies have utilized statistical methods such as exploratory factor analysis on different age samples and game genres. This statistical approach could result in differential diagnostic criteria and measurement items that were suitable only for target age gamers (e.g., children, adolescents, young adults, or active gamers) or specific game genres (e.g., massive multiplayer online role playing games).

Responding to the addictive potential of Internet games and the growing concerns of Internet game-related public health problems in many countries, the American Psychiatric Association (APA) has begun to consider whether Internet gaming addiction could be added as a pathological disorder in the fifth edition of *Diagnostic Statistical Manual of Mental Disorders* (DSM-5). The APA, however, decided not to add Internet gaming addiction as a formal disorder but to include it in Section III of the DSM-5, where uncertain mental illnesses that require more research to be considered formal disorders are introduced (APA 2013a, 795–798). In the process of reaching the decision, the APA recommended further studies on Internet gaming addiction with nine specified diagnostic criteria (Table 8.1) in order for approval as a formal disorder in the next edition, DSM-6 (APA 2013b, 795).

The APA's nine criteria provide significant guidance for further exploring what components comprise Internet gaming addiction. Previous studies

Table 8.1 Definitions of Internet gaming addiction criteria on DSM-5

Proposed criterion	Definition
Salience	Preoccupation with Internet games. (the individual thinks about previous gaming activity or anticipates playing the next game; Internet gaming becomes the dominant activity in daily life)
Tolerance	The need to spend increasing amounts of time engaged in Internet games
Relapse	Unsuccessful attempts to control the participation in Internet games
Withdrawal symptoms	Withdrawal symptoms when Internet gaming is taken away (e.g., irritability, anxiety, or sadness; nonphysical signs of pharmacological withdrawal)
Mood modification	Use of Internet games to escape or relieve a negative mood (e.g., feelings of helplessness, guilty, anxiety)
Conflict	Has jeopardized or lost a significant relationship, job, or educational or career opportunity because of participation in Internet games
Deception	Has deceived family members, therapists, or others regarding the amount of Internet gaming
Continued excessive use	Continued excessive use of Internet games despite knowledge of psychosocial problems
Loss of interests	Loss of interests in previous hobbies and entertainment as a result of, and with the exception of, Internet games

on gaming addiction have concentrated on the adaption of the DSM-IV's ten diagnostic criteria for pathological gambling (Choo et al. 2010, 824; Lemmens et al. 2009, 79–80), as both addictions, gaming and gambling, were evaluated to share similar elements for behavior addictions (Griffiths 2005a). This approach was initiated by a psychologist named Kimberly Young within the realm of Internet addiction. Applying this approach, Young (1996) developed an eight-item questionnaire for diagnosing Internet addiction. Some studies developed measurement scales for assessing Internet gaming addiction with a modification of diagnostic criteria for pathological gambling and substance dependence in the *International Classification of Diseases* (ICD-10, WHO 1993) or DSM-IV criteria for substance dependence (Grüsser et al. 2007, 291; Tejeiro Salguero and Bersabé Morán 2002, 1602). These previous studies identified important diagnostic criteria for Internet gaming addiction; yet, there is still incongruity on which diagnostic criteria comprise the addiction.

The Present Study

The present study develops a reliable and valid scale to measure Internet gaming addiction based on the nine diagnosis criteria proposed by the APA in May 2012 and confirmed in Section III of the DSM-5. As reviewed earlier, diverse diagnostic criteria for Internet gaming addiction have been suggested by many previous studies. While there are similar or common criteria among the aforementioned studies, no standardized diagnosis criteria were proposed. The recent publication of nine diagnostic criteria in Section III of the DSM-5 plays an important role in reaching consistent diagnostic criteria for Internet gaming addiction. In many countries, diagnostic criteria in various versions of the DSM have been utilized to diagnose mental disorders.

The APA's nine criteria are important, as the framework provides an opportunity for resolving the diverse views on what constitutes gaming addiction. The APA asserted that future studies need to provide evidence with the proposed nine diagnostic criteria in order to qualify for a formal disorder. Thus, the current study responds to the need for further research on the proposed diagnostic criteria for Internet gaming addiction by focusing on a broader range of age groups from middle-school students to young adults. This study specifically focused on Internet games because they are considered more addictive than console and mobile games and they require a considerable or excessive amount of playing time to keep up with the games (Charlton and Danforth 2007, 1534; Seok and DaCosta 2012, 2143).

Another aim of the present study was to classify Internet game addicts and to examine the prevalence rates with the proposed nine diagnostic criteria. In order to attain such goals, this study was carried out among adolescent and young adult gamers in South Korea. While South Korea is considered to have an intense Internet gaming culture, there is no systematic investigation about the prevalence rates of Internet gaming addiction. Thus, this current study provides empirical information about the prevalence rates on a broader range of age groups in South Korea while investigating the addictive characteristics of gaming addiction that occur in an intense Internet gaming culture.

In order to develop and validate an Internet gaming addiction scale with the above nine criteria, this study adopted the second-order factor model of gaming addiction scales presented by Lemmens et al. (2009) and Kim and Kim (2010). Lemmens et al. (2010, 84–85) developed the second-order factor model of game addiction scale for adolescents. The scale consisted of seven criteria modified from the DSM-IV's pathological gambling, and those criteria were explained by one higher-order factor named online game addiction. Kim and Kim (2010) also created a similar second-order factor model of Problematic Online Game Use Scale. This scale was composed of five diagnostic criteria, which were then explained by one higher-order factor named problematic online game use. These previous studies explained that the underlying diagnostic criteria for Internet gaming addiction could be accounted for by one higher-order factor. This present study adopted the second-order factor structure model of Internet gaming addiction, incorporating the nine diagnostic criteria into the model.

Procedure and Samples

A survey was conducted in October 2012 among middle- and high-school students and young adults (ages 20–34) in seven major metropolitan cities and all eight regional provinces in South Korea. In the surveying of middle- and high-school respondents, a paper-and-pencil questionnaire was distributed during school hours after gaining permissions from school principals and class teachers. Middle- and high-school student respondents were assured that their answers would not be shown to their teachers or parents. The survey for young adults was administered in the form of face-to-face interview with the same questionnaire. After the informed legal guarantee of confidentiality and privacy protection was provided through both a verbal explanation and a written form, respondents were asked to sign a consent form if they agreed to continue. Most respondents signed and completed the survey within 20–25 minutes.

After completing the data-gathering process, the responses of survey respondents were screened. Respondents who had not played Internet games in the last three months from the survey time point were excluded from further statistical analyses. In addition, the respondent cases which had incomplete answers were also exempt. After this procedure, 620 cases of middle-school students, 329 cases of high-school sample, and 187 cases of young adults were excluded.

The sample of middle-school students was composed of 2473 respondents and was randomly split into two non-overlapping groups in order to cross-validate the structure of the Internet gaming addiction scale across the same population. Thus, Sample 1 ($N = 1237$) consisted of 737 males (59.6%) and 500 females (40.4%) with a mean age of 14.96 years (SD = 0.81). Sample 2 ($N = 1236$) consisted of 737 (59.65%) males and 499 (40.4%) females with mean age of 14.98 years (SD = 0.82).

In order to cross-validate the dimensional structure identified in the above two samples, two additional samples of different age groups were used. Sample 3 ($N = 571$) of South Korean high-school students was composed of 376 males (65.8%) and 195 females (34.2%). The mean age of respondents was 16.14 years (SD = 0.73). Sample 4 ($N = 376$) consisted of participants of ages in through their 20s and early 30s. Among the respondents, the early 20s group, aged from 20 to 24 years, was 33.8% of the sample, the late 20s from 25 to 29 years was 29.0%, and the early 30s from 30 to 34 years was 37.2%. The age of respondents varied between 20 and 34 years with a mean age of 27.11 years (SD = 4.38).

Measures

Measurement Items for Internet Gaming Addiction Initially, 59 measurement items, representing the nine underlying diagnostic criteria of Internet gaming addiction, were created by means of (i) a comprehensive review of previous studies on game addiction and (ii) three separate focus group interviews with 21 undergraduate and graduate students who had experienced excessive Internet game use. Subsequently, the 59 items were subjected to a content validity procedure with 20 experts, such as psychiatrists, media effects researchers, and addiction counselors.

With this procedure, 36 measurement items were selected, and four items for each of the nine criteria were evenly included (see Table 8.1). The wordings of these items were slightly modified with the help of a middle-school teacher to enhance the understanding of middle- and high-school respondents. The items were randomized in the survey questionnaire, and a semiannual criterion was adopted from Young (1998) and Lemmens et al. (2009, 83). According to these studies, Internet users or gamers can be classified as addicts when they meet specified diagnostic criteria for 6 continuous months. Therefore, the 36 items were preceded by the statement: "During the last six months ..." The respondents rated the items on a 5-point scale, and response categories ranged from 1 (*never*) to 5 (*very often*). All respondents answered the 36 items, and these responses were used to develop a 27-item scale in which each of the nine criteria was composed of three items.

The 27-item Internet gaming addiction scale was checked for its construct validity by analyzing the correlation between scores on the scale and the variables that have empirically established interrelationships with game addiction. The variables were time spent on Internet games, maladaptive cognition, physical aggression, and life satisfaction. To check the concurrent validity of the scale, the shortened version of the game addiction scale for adolescents developed by Lemmens et al. (2009, 86–87) was employed. Only the respondents in Samples 3 and 4 were asked to answer the questions, exempting middle-school students in the Samples 1 and 2 in order to reduce the response burden (Table 8.2).

Time Spent on Internet Games It has been identified as an indicator of gaming addiction (Choo et al. 2010, 827; Grüsser et al. 2007, 291; Lemmens et al. 2009, 83). Game addicts spent significantly more time on games than those who were not addicted. Therefore, this present study used the same variable to check the construct validity of a new Internet gaming addiction scale. If the scale had a strong correlation with time spent on Internet games, it would be evidence for its construct validity. Two separate questions were used: "On average, how many hours do you spend on Internet games per day during the week days?" and "On average, how many hours do you spend on Internet games per day during the weekends?" To calculate the average daily usage of Internet game, the following processes were employed. First, to obtain the total weekday amount of usage, the average weekday usage was multiplied by the

Table 8.2 The 27 items and nine diagnostic criteria of the Internet gaming addiction scale

Factor	Measurement items
Salience (.74)	1. I am preoccupied with Internet games until late night 2. I think about playing Internet games most of the day* 3. I play Internet games almost every day – *Without paying attention to other things, I get absorbed in Internet games*
Tolerance (.86)	4. I am contented when I spend increasing amounts of time on Internet games 5. I play longer Internet games than before for getting the same level of satisfaction that I felt before 6. I can get satisfaction more and more from increased amount of time on Internet games* – *The time for playing games extends by day*
Relapse (.87)	7. I play Internet games much longer than originally intended 8. Even though I decided not to play Internet games, I still play again and again* 9. I have made unsuccessful attempts to reduce Internet game use – *I have failed several times to stop Internet game.*
Withdrawal (.79)	10. I get restless or anxious when I am unable to play Internet games or suddenly reduce amount of time 11. I get nervous or mad when Internet games are taken away 12. I get irritated or upset when I cannot play Internet games as much as I want* – *I feel depressed when unable to play Internet games*
Mood modification (.80)	13. I play Internet games to release stress* 14. I play Internet games to make me feel better 15. I play Internet games to relieve the negative mood in real life – *I play Internet games to escape from stressful real life*
Conflict (.71)	16. Gaming causes serious problems on my family relationships* 17. I neglect my important duties (e.g., homework, appointment, work) because of Internet gaming 18. Playing games have risked my relationships with friends – *My performances at school or work have declined due to game playing*
Deception (.82)	19. I have lied to family members about time spent on Internet games* 20. I have been told to reduce the amount of time on Internet games 21. I secretly played games as much as I want, trying not to let my family members or other significant ones notice – *I have tried to conceal my game playing*

(*continued*)

Table 8.2 (continued)

Factor	Measurement items
Continuous excessive use (.79)	22. I have continued excessive Internet game use despite knowledge of physical health problems (e.g., shoulder pain, eye sight) 23. Despite conflicts with family members, I have continued to play Internet games excessively * 24. Despite lack of sleeping and fatigue due to Internet games, I have still played games – *I have continued to play Internet games, despite hindrance to my study or work*
Loss of interests (.75)	25. After playing Internet games, I have not continued to pursue other previous hobbies that I enjoyed 26. Playing Internet games is the most exciting entertainment, as compared to other activities 27. After playing games, I have lost interests in other types of entertainment (e.g., movies, dramas) * – *I have lost interest in other activities, except games*

Note. The numbers in the parentheses indicate Cronbach's alpha (Cronbach's alpha is a widely used measure of reliability. It is a tool that is intended to measure the internal consistency of measurement items that are supposed to measure the same phenomenon. Although there are different opinions about the acceptable values of Cronbach's alpha, an appropriate or acceptable alpha value of .70 or better has been recommended (Nunnally and Bernstein 1994). The items with italics indicate the removed ones from the Internet gaming addiction scale.

* included in the 9-item shortened version of the 27-item Internet gaming addiction scale

number of weekdays (5 days). Second, to obtain the total weekend amount of usage, the average weekend usage was multiplied by the number of days on the weekend (2 days). Third, the total weekly amount of usage was calculated by summing both the total weekday and weekend amount of usage. Fourth and lastly, the average daily usage of Internet game was obtained by dividing the total weekly amount of usage by 7 days.

Physical Aggression In previous research, gamers who played for longer period times or were addicted to Internet games showed higher scores on aggression (Grüsser et al. 2007, 291; Kim et al. 2008; Lemmens et al. 2009, 87; Mehroof and Griffiths 2010). Therefore, this study expected a high correlation between the game addiction scale and aggression. Aggression was measured by the Physical Aggression Subscale from Buss and Perry's (1992) Aggression Questionnaire. Eight out of the nine items were selected. Several of these items were: "If somebody hits me, I hit back", "I get into fights a little more than the average person", and "I have become so mad that I have broken things". The respondents in Samples 3 and 4 were asked to rate each items on a scale of 1 (*totally disagree*) to 5 (*totally agree*). Cronbach's alpha on this scale was .81 in Sample 3 (M = 2.11, SD = 1.10) and .84 in Sample 4 (M = 2.08, SD = 1.06). The items were averaged to produce the physical aggression scale.

Life Satisfaction It was measured using four items modified from the five-item Satisfaction with Life Scale (Diener et al. 1985). According to previous studies, Internet game addicts or heavy gamers display lower satisfactions with their daily lives (Kim and Kim 2010, 394–395; Lemmens et al. 2009, 86–87). Therefore, this study adopted the life satisfaction scale to examine the construct validity of the Internet gaming addiction scale. The respondents in Samples 3 and 4 were asked to evaluate the degree of satisfaction with their life as a whole. The items were: "I am satisfied with my life", "My life is joyful", "My life is miserable", and "In general, my life is filled with happiness". The response option ranged from 1 *(totally disagree)* to 5 *(totally agree)*. After reversing the responses on the third item, Cronbach's alpha on the items was .95 in Sample 3 (M = 3.48, SD = 1.17) and .93 in Sample 4 (M = 3.37, SD = 0.95). The items were averaged to create the life satisfaction scale.

Game Addiction Scale for Adolescents The shortened version of Lemmens et al.'s (2009, 86) game addiction scale for adolescents was employed to check concurrent validity[1] of the gaming addiction scale. It was composed of seven items, and examples of the items are "Did you think about playing a game all day long?", "Did you spend increasing amounts of time on games?", and "Did you play games to forget about real life?" Every item in the game addiction scale was preceded by the following statement: "How often during the last six months …?" Respondents in Samples 3 and 4 answered the items on a 5-point scale (1 "never" – 5 "very often"). Cronbach's alpha of the items was .87 in Sample 3 of high schoolers (M = 1.42, SD = 0.81) and .90 in Sample 4 of young adults (M = 1.62, SD = 0.92). The items were averaged to create the scale.

FINDINGS

Descriptive Results

In order to identify the equivalence between Samples 1 and 2, the average daily usage of Internet games on the two samples was compared. As seen in Table 8.3, the middle schoolers in Samples 1 and 2 spent 1.68 and 1.67 hours per day playing Internet games, respectively, indicating no differences on the average time spent on games. More specifically, the two samples showed no differences on the average weekday usage of games, $t(2471) = 0.40$, $p = .69$. The results also indicated that two samples showed no differences on the average weekends' usage of games, $t(2471) = 0.42$, $p = .68$. The high schoolers in Sample 3 played Internet games 1.66 hours per day, and the young adults in Sample 4 spent 2.77 hours per day playing Internet games. In all four samples, the usage of Internet games during weekends was greater than that of week days, and male players spent more time than female players on Internet games.

An analysis of variance with the Student-Newman-Keuls (S-N-K)' post hoc test was performed on the merged data of four samples to compare daily average usage of Internet games. The results showed that the usage of Internet games was significantly different among the four samples on weekdays ($F_{3, 3426} = 90.49$, $p < .001$) and weekends ($F_{3, 3426} = 29.95$, $p < .001$). Young adults spent more time playing Internet games than middle schoolers and high schoolers during week days and weekends. Middle schoolers spent more time playing games than high schoolers during week days, while high schoolers played games more than middle schoolers during the weekends.

DEVELOPMENT OF THE INTERNET GAMING ADDICTION SCALE

To examine the presumed second-order factor structure of the Internet gaming addiction scale, the present study assumed that each of the nine criteria was composed of three measurement items and that the nine criteria could be accounted for by a higher-order factor titled Internet gaming addiction. Therefore, analysis of structural equation modeling (SEM) using AMOS 20.0 was carried out.

Table 8.3 Descriptive results of time spent on Internet games per day among the samples

Sample	Week days	Weekends	t-value	Combined			t-value
				Total	Males	Females	
Sample 1	1.16^{Ba}	2.20^{Ab}	22.35***	1.68^A	2.09^b	1.07^a	12.69***
(n = 1237)	(2.02)	(2.02)		(1.48)	(1.58)	(1.58)	
Sample 2	1.18^{Ba}	2.17^{Ab}	22.08***	1.67^A	2.08^b	1.07^a	12.78***
(n = 1236)	(1.32)	(1.93)		(1.45)	(1.55)	(1.03)	
Sample 3	.88^{Aa}	2.44^{Bb}	20.23***	1.66^A	1.90^b	1.18^a	5.96***
(n = 571)	(1.14)	(2.09)		(1.41)	(1.52)	(1.00)	
Sample 4	2.31^{Ca}	3.24^{Cb}	11.29***	2.77^B	3.00^b	2.43^a	2.63**
(n = 376)	(2.05)	(2.35)		(2.04)	(2.05)	(1.97)	
F	90.49***	29.95***	–	57.91***	24.35***	58.03***	–

Note. The numbers in the parentheses indicate standard deviations. Comparisons between means indicated by lowercase superscripts are within rows only (*horizontal*) by *t* test and means not sharing a lowercase superscript differ significantly at $p < .05$ by *t* test. Comparisons among means indicated by uppercase superscripts are within columns only (*vertical*) by *F* test, and means not sharing an uppercase superscript differ significantly at $p < .05$ by S-N-K test. ** $p < .01$, *** $p < .001$

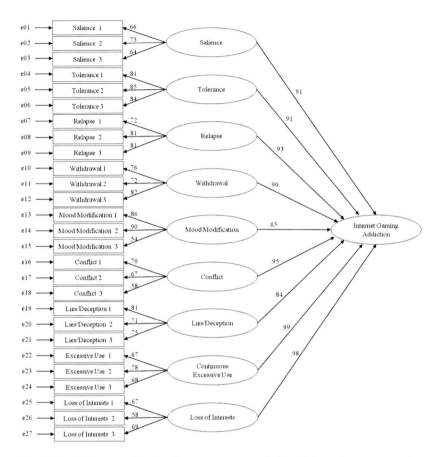

Fig. 8.1 The second-order factor structure of the 27-item Internet gaming addiction scale on the combined sample (N = 3420) (*Note*: Factor loadings are standardized coefficients)

Figure 8.1 depicts the dimensional structure of this study's hypothesized second-order factor model. As indicated in the Appendix, 9 out of the preselected 36 items were excluded as the items showed the lowest factor loading among 4 items or a decreased adequate goodness of fit index of the nine-factor model. The goodness of fit of the model was evaluated using three indices: the Tucker-Lewis fit index (TLI), the comparative fit index (CFI), and the root-mean-square error of approximation (RMSEA) and its 90% confidence level (90% CI). These indices are considered useful indices for evaluating model fit with a large size of samples. Acceptable values for TLI and CFI are greater than .90, and RMSEA values less than .08 are considered as a reasonable fit (Byrne 2001; Hu and Bentler 1995; Ullman 1996). This study also reports χ^2 values and the χ^2/df ratio only for reference because these indices are sensitive to sample size, particularly when the sample size is large (Schumacker and Lomax 1996).

An initial analysis of SEM on Sample 1 showed that the 27-item nine-factor model resulted in an acceptable level of model fit, χ^2 (315, N = 1237) = 2134.8, $p < .001$, TLI = .895, CFI = .905, RMSEA = . 068 (90 % CI: .066; .071), χ^2/df ratio = 6.78. All factor loadings of the 27 items on the nine first-order factors were above .57 in standardized scores. All factor loadings of the nine first-order factors on the second-order factor (Internet gaming addiction) were above .69. Another SEM analysis on Sample 2 was completed to cross-validate the nine-factor model. The model with Sample 2 provided an acceptable fit to the data, χ^2 (315, N = 1236) = 2082.0, $p < .001$; TLI = .894, CFI = .905, RMSEA = .067 (90% CI: .066; .070), χ^2/df ratio = 6.61.

To examine whether the nine-factor model provided an optimal fit to the data of different age groups, a multi-sample analysis was carried out with the three samples (Sample 3, Sample 4, and the merged sample of Sample 1 and Sample 2). The unconstrained model yielded an acceptable model fit, χ^2 (945, N = 3420) = 5638.04, $p < .001$, TLI = .901, CFI = .911, RMSEA = .038 (90% CI: .037; .039), χ^2/df ratio = 5.97. To check whether all measurement and structural loadings were the same across the three samples, the unconstrained model was compared to the constrained model where measurement and structural loadings were equal across the different age samples. The constrained model showed a significant change of chi-square, $\Delta\chi^2$ (52, N = 3420) = 517.46, $p < .001$. This indicates that, although the nine-factor model was not significantly different across the three samples, some measurement and structural loadings were slightly different.

Overall, although some model fit values on the three samples did not reach the conventional minimum value, the results indicated that the nine-factor model was acceptable. The 27-item game addiction scale of this study had a Cronbach's alpha of .95 in Sample 1 (M = 1.47, SD = 0.84), .96 in Sample 2 (M = 1.43, SD = 0.82), .95 in Sample 3 (M = 1.51, SD = 0.86) and .96 in Sample 4 (M = 1.85, SD = 0.97).

A Shortened Version of the Internet Gaming Addiction Scale

This study also examined a shortened version of the 27-item Internet gaming addiction scale with the highest measurement loadings from each of the nine first-order factors. If the 9-item shortened version can provide validity as the 27-item scale, data collection would be more economical and the burden on respondents reduced (Lemmens et al. 2009, 86).

In order to select nine items from each of the nine factors, a SEM analysis was carried out on the merged sample. As presented in the appendix, the analysis showed that the 9-item second-order factor model resulted in an acceptable level of model fit, χ^2 (27, N = 3420) = 420.61, p < .001, TLI = .962, CFI = .971, RMSEA = .065 (90% CI: .060, .071), χ^2/df ratio = 15.58. Cronbach's alpha was .89 in the merged sample (M = 1.57, SD = 0.91). A multiple-sample analysis on the three samples was performed to check whether the 9-item nine-factor model provided an optimal fit to the data of the different age groups. The unconstrained model yielded an acceptable model fit, χ^2 (81, N = 3420) = 539.78, p < .001, TLI = .955, CFI = .967, RMSEA = .041 (90% CI: .037; .044), χ^2/df ratio = 6.66. Compared to the unconstrained model, the constrained model on measurement and structural loadings produced a significant chi-square change, $\Delta\chi^2$ (16, N = 3420) = 112.87, p < .001. Overall, the results indicate that the short version of the nine-factor model is acceptable; however, some measurement and structural loadings were significantly different across different age samples. Cronbach's alpha on the nine items was .89 in all three samples (the merged sample of Samples 1 and 2, M = 1.51, SD = 0.88; Sample 3, M = 1.59, SD = 0.91; Sample 4, M = 1.88, SD = 0.98, respectively).

Establishing the Validity of the Internet Gaming Addiction Scale

Two analyses were undertaken to determine whether the Internet gaming addiction scale is a valid measure. First, the present study tested the construct validity of the scale. Construct validity can be checked by examining relationships between a measurement scale and concepts that are logically related to the phenomenon being measured. Thus, mean scores on both versions of the Internet gaming addiction scale were subjected to correlation analyses with time spent on Internet games, physical aggression, and life satisfaction. As seen in Table 8.4, both 9-item and 27-item versions showed moderate correlations with time spent on Internet games

Table 8.4 Correlations between the Internet gaming addiction scales and psychosocial variables

	Sample 3 (N = 571)		Sample 4 (N = 376)	
	27-item scale	9-item scale	27-item scale	9-item scale
Time spent on Internet games	.393**	.386**	.298**	.332**
Physical aggression	.193**	.161**	.358**	.352**
Life satisfaction	−.096*	−.075	−.159**	−.121**
Game addiction scale for adolescents	.813**	.800**	.862**	.838**

* $p < .05$, ** $p < .01$

and physical aggression. The two versions indicated the expected direction of correlation with the life satisfaction variable; however, the degree of negative correlation was low. In addition, the correlations of the 9-item version did not significantly differ from those of the 27-item version. The correlations were also highly comparable across both samples, except for the physical aggression variable. With regard to the physical aggression variable, young adults in Sample 4 seemed to show higher correlation coefficients compared to high schoolers in Sample 3.

Second, the present study assessed the concurrent validity of the Internet gaming addiction scale. Thus, mean scores on both versions of the scale were correlated with the seven-item version of game addiction scale for adolescents (Lemmens et al. 2009, 87). As seen in Table 8.4, the two versions of the scale had very strong correlations with the 7-item game addiction scale. The correlations of the versions of the Internet gaming scale with the Lemmens et al.'s scale did not significantly differ between both samples. Thus, these results are suggestive of the validity of the 9-item and 27-item Internet gaming addiction scales, and the 9-item version was just as valid as the 27-item scale.

Determining Addiction with Latent Class Analysis

A latent class analysis (LCA) was performed in Mplus 6.2 to identify the group and proportions of Internet gaming addicts and subtypes of gamers. LCA enables the respondents to identify the distinctive latent groups of Internet game users, offering a continuum from an addicted group to a nonaddicted one (Wang and Wang 2012). Thus, this study carried out

LCA on the nine diagnostic criteria and with two- to five-class models on the combined sample (N = 3420). Multiple model fit statistics and indices were considered together to determine the optimal number of classes: the Akaike's information criterion (AIC), the Bayesian information criteria parsimony index (BIC), the sample-size adjusted Bayesian information criteria parsimony index (ABIC), entropy, the Lo-Mendell-Rubin likelihood-ratio test (LMR LR test), and the Adjusted Lo-Mendell-Rubin likelihood-ratio test (ALMR LR test). Smaller values of AIC, BIC, and ABIC indicate better model fits. In cases of the LMA LR test and the ALMR LR test, the significant p-value (<.05) indicates that the adding of an additional class improves model fit, as compared to one less class model. Entropy indicates better classification when an entropy value approaches closer to 1.0 (Wang and Wang 2012).

The results of the LCA indicated that a four-class solution was adequate for this study. As Table 8.5 shows, the values of the AIC, BIC, and ABIC gradually decreased as the number of latent classes was added each time. However, the adding of a class into the four-class model did not decrease those values greatly in the five-class model. The level of entropy was adequate for all models, showing that the two-class model had the highest level of entropy. Except for the five-class model, the p-values of the LMR LR and ALMR LR tests in the first three models were significant. Therefore, the five-class model could be rejected. Based on these results of model fit statistics and indices, the four-class model was accepted as the optimal one for this study.

As presented in Fig. 8.2, the first class (65.5% of the total sample) represented regular gamers who have no risk of Internet gaming addiction

Table 8.5 Fit indices of LCA models on the nine criteria of the Internet gaming addiction scale (N = 3420)

Number of classes	AIC	BIC	ABIC	Entropy	LMR LR test p-value	ALMR LR test p-value
Two class	48758	48930	48841	.976	<.0001	<.0001
Three class	43461	43694	43573	.962	<.0001	<.0001
Four class	41405	41699	41547	.939	.0014	.0016
Five class	40507	40863	40678	.920	.5747	.5770

Note: *AIC* Akaike's information criterion, *BIC* Bayesian information criteria parsimony index, *ABCI* sample-size adjusted Bayesian information criteria parsimony index, *LMR LR test* Lo-Mendell-Rubin likelihood-ratio test, Adjusted Lo-Mendell-Rubin likelihood-ratio test

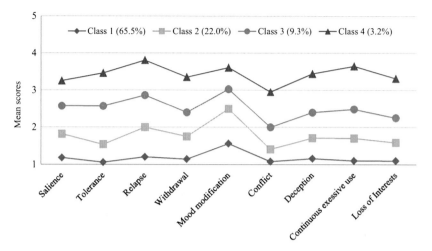

Fig. 8.2 Latent class analysis on the nine factors was found in four classes. The first to third classes represent no risk, low/medium risk, and at-risk gamer groups for Internet gaming addiction, respectively. The fourth class represents the addicted Internet gamer group.

and showed the lowest estimated mean scores on the nine factors. The second class (22.0%) represented gamers who have a low or medium risk of Internet gaming addiction. The third class (9.3%) can be defined as gamers who are at risk of Internet gaming addiction. The fourth class (3.2%) represented addicted gamers who showed the highest scores on all nine factors. Specifically, those addicted gamers in the fourth class conveyed somewhat elevated scores on the "relapse", "mood modification", and "continuous excessive use" criteria. On the contrary, they showed the lowest scores on the "conflict" criterion. The score on the factor was below the middle point of the 5-point scale. The addicted group was 2.3% in the merged sample of Samples 1 and 2, 4.9% in Sample 3, and 6.9% in Sample 4.

Based on these results, a cut-off score of 3 on each of the nine diagnostic criteria is adequate for identifying individual symptoms and for classifying addicted gamers with the polythetic system. The system was applied by the DSM-IV for diagnosing other pathological disorders such as gambling disorder. In the DSM-5, the APA also proposed this system for diagnosing Internet gaming disorder in the future, requiring endorsement of at least half of the proposed nine criteria. Thus, a cut-off score of 3 on the nine diagnostic criteria for Internet gaming addiction is applicable for a positive diagnosis with the polythetic system.

DISCUSSION

This study developed a new 27-item measurement scale. Compared to previous gaming scales that modified the diagnostic criteria for pathological gambling or substance dependence, the present study's gaming scale was based on the nine criteria for Internet gaming addiction specified by the APA. The 27-item Internet gaming addiction scale was composed of the nine criteria, and each criterion was measured with three items. The present study adapted the second-order factor structure of the Internet gaming addiction scale as presented in previous studies (Kim and Kim 2010, 393; Lemmens et al. 2009, 84–85). The 27-item scale of this study was valid across the separate samples of middle-school students, high-school students, and young adults. Its shortened 9-item version also showed adequate model fits to the data. That is, the 27- and 9-item nine-factor measurement structure of the scale was valid across different age groups.

The present study also examined the construct and concurrent validities of the new scale. In the samples of high-school students and young adults, the 27- and 9-item versions of the scale showed moderate correlations with time spent on games and physical aggression, as well as strong correlations with another game addiction scale developed by Lemmens et al. (2009, 86–87). As expected, both versions showed negative correlations with life satisfaction, although the strength of correlations was somewhat weak. Therefore, both construct validity and concurrent validity of the scale were satisfactory. In addition, compared to other scales, the new scale of the present study can have merit in identifying Internet gaming disorder as an independent disorder. As reviewed earlier, the existing scales proposed by previous studies have applied the criteria for diagnosing pathological gambling. The new scale included the specified diagnostic criteria for Internet gaming disorder and can be used as a diagnostic tool for practitioners, parents, and gamers confronted with the undesirable consequences of excessive or compulsive gaming. Applying the new scale can provide clear prevalence estimates of Internet gaming disorder and empirical evidence to qualify for an independent disorder in the upcoming DSM-6.

The result of the present study with LCA indicated that 3.2% of South Korean adolescent and young adult gamers were classified as addicted gamers. Even though there was a limitation to the interpretation due to sample size differences, the addiction rate increases as age increases on a linear trend. The addiction rate of 2.3% in middle schoolers doubled to 4.9% in high schoolers and tripled up to 6.9% in the young adult group.

The present study identified the three criteria (relapse, mood modification, and continuous excessive use) which were prominent among game addicts, while the criterion conflict showed the lowest scores among those addicted gamers. Previous studies have shown that some criteria might be more prominent in diagnosing Internet gaming addicts. For example, Demetrovics et al. (2012) found that social isolation and withdrawal symptoms were significant indicators of gaming addiction, while "preoccupation" and "overuse" were less significant indicators. Beard and Wolf (2001, 379–381) argued that three criteria (conflict, lies/deception, and mood modification) were more important than the others for diagnosing Internet addiction. Also, Choo et al. (2010, 826) found that the mood modification criterion was most prominent. Charlton and Danforth (2007, 1539) and Seok and DaCosta (2012, 2146–2147) identified the four criteria (conflict, withdrawal, relapse, and behavioral salience) for diagnosing gaming addiction were the core factors.

It is likely that the aforementioned three criteria can be more applicable in diagnosing gaming addiction of adolescent and young adult gamers captivated to the specific type of Internet game known as MMORPG. The present study was based on Internet gamers in South Korea. In the Korean gaming context, console games are not popular. Gamers prefer to play the well-known MMORPG genre, and Internet game addiction of Korean gamers was highly associated with this game genre. Therefore, the scale validated in this study may not be applicable in console game contexts. Practitioners need to keep in mind that the scale can be more applicable to detect a specific subtype of Internet gaming addiction. That is, gaming addicts to MMORPG may easily endorse the three core components on this scale. It is also reasonable to suggest that other subtypes of Internet game addiction may endorse other diagnostic components on this scale. Thus, this study recommends that professional practitioners should look towards at least three criteria with the time spent on MMORPG and its preference when diagnosing Internet game addiction with this scale. In addition, professional practitioners need to consider both potential problems of relationships with friends and family members in environmental contexts as well as other symptoms such as depression, physical aggression, and anxiety in individual contexts.

Based on this study's results, it is logical to suggest that researchers and practitioners need to be aware of both the positive and negative impacts on individual and social lives as a result of Internet gaming, especially in South Korean game culture. That is, this study does not identify Internet gaming addiction by neglecting the vibrant gaming culture that can be considered as part of living in the twenty-first century. Gaming is a part of South Korean popular culture, and playing Internet games provides entertainment while increasing opportunities for socializing with others, especially with peer groups. Gaming is also important from industrial to economic perspective. Amid an economic slowdown in recent years, the Internet game industry has provided many job opportunities by exporting Internet games to other countries. However, it is also true that Internet games have caused physical health problems on adolescents and young adults and have led to tragic incidents related to excessive usage. In this vein, we need to understand Internet gaming addiction in order to introduce social medical services and relevant policies for helping addicted gamers in society.

Future studies need to place additional attention on mobile games and social network games (SNGs). SNGs are a new type of Internet game and run on social network sites. They are designed to interact with gamers' existing personal social networks and have become popular in recent years with proliferation of smartphones and tablet PCs. In contrast to the fact that previous Internet games are attractive for children, adolescents, and young adults, especially males, SNGs are popular to a more general audience, including adults aged 40 or above and/or females. This explosive growth SNGs play on broad segments of the Internet gaming population has its own important implications for research. Future studies should examine the addictive potential of SNGs and the negative consequences experienced by the players, especially older generations and females.

One limitation of the present study is that it adopted a semiannual criterion for assessing Internet gaming addiction, using the statement "during the last six months" in the measurement items. This criterion was adopted from Young (1998) and Lemmens et al. (2009, 83). However, after collecting and analyzing the data, the APA decided to recommend a 12-month period criterion in the Section III of DSM-5. Therefore, future studies should adopt the 12-month period criterion for assessing gaming addicts within a polythetic system, requiring the endorsement of five or more on the nine specified criteria for Internet gaming addiction.

An additional limitation of the present study is that it was carried out among South Korean gamers. Thus, the results cannot be easily generalized to other countries that have different game cultures and languages. Future studies need to compare the results of this study with samples from other countries' gaming populations, thus improving the scale to be more suitable for other countries and their gamers. Future studies in different cultural contexts also need to consider preferred game genres or game types. If gaming addiction in other cultural contexts involves other game genres, studies of various game genres can be beneficial for understanding and clarifying potential subtypes of Internet gaming addiction.

In conclusion, the present research is an initial step towards developing a new scale to measure addictive Internet gaming by responding to the APA's diagnostic criteria for screening Internet gaming disorder. The new diagnostic criteria were initially proposed in May 2012, and the final version was included in the DSM-5's Section III in May 2013. This study with the criteria provides a scientific evidence of Internet gaming disorder among South Korean adolescents and young adults. The results also support the APA's efforts to classify Internet gaming addiction as official pathological disorder in the sixth edition of the DSM. The author of this study hopes that further studies provide more scientific and clinical field trial evidence of Internet gaming addiction with the new nine criteria.

Note

1. Concurrent validity is closely related to predictive validity, which assesses certain degree of accuracy of a measurement instrument in predicting some future outcome. Concurrent validity can be assessed by checking whether a new measurement instrument correlates well with an established measurement instrument.

Acknowledgment I would like to thank the Ministry of Gender Equality & Family, South Korea, for allowing me to participate in the project as a researcher and for granting me permission to study the data for my own research purposes.

References

———. 2013a. Internet gaming disorder.. http://www.dsm5.org/. Accessed 06 Jan 2013.

———. 2013b. *Diagnostic and statistical manual of mental disorders, (DSM-5®)*. American Psychiatric Pub.

BBC (British Broadcasting Corporation). 2005. "S Korean dies after games session." *BBC News*, August 10. http://news.bbc.co.uk/2/hi/technology/4137782.stm. Accessed 18 May 2015.

Beard, Keith W., and Eve M. Wolf. 2001. Modification in the proposed diagnostic criteria for internet addiction. *CyberPsychology and Behavior* 4(3): 377–383.

Block, Jerald J. 2008. Issues for DSM-V: Internet addiction. *The American Journal of Psychiatry* 165(3): 306–307.

Brown, R.I.F. 1993. Some contributions of the study of gambling to the study of other addictions. In *Gambling behavior and problem gambling*, ed. William R. Eadington, and Judy A. Cornelius, 241–272. Reno: University of Nevada Press.

Buss, Arnold H., and Mark Perry. 1992. The aggression questionnaire. *Journal of Personality and Social Psychology* 63(3): 452–459.

Byrne, Barbara M. 2001. *Structural equation modeling with AMOS: Basic concepts, applications and programming.* Mahwah: Erlbaum.

Charlton, John P., and Ian D.W. Danforth. 2007. Distinguishing addiction and high engagement in the context of online game playing. *Computers in Human Behavior* 23(3): 1531–1548.

Choi, He-suk. 2013. "Game addiction bill touches off national debate." *Korean Herald*, November 13. http://www.koreaherald.com/view.php?ud=20131113001080. Accessed 18 May 2015.

Choo, Hyekyung, Douglas A. Gentile, Timothy Sim, Dongdong Li, Angeline Khoo, and Albert K. Liau. 2010. Pathological video-gaming among singaporean youth. *Annals of Academic Medicine Singapore* 39(11): 822–829.

Demetrovics, Zsolt, Róbert Urbán, Katalin Nagygyörgy, Judit Farks, Mark D. Griffiths, Orsolya Pápay, Gyöngyi Kökönyei, Katlin Felvinczi, and Attila Oláh. 2012. "The development of the problematic online gaming questionnaire (POGQ)." *PloS one* 7(5): e36417. doi:10.1371/journal.pone.0036417. Accessed 15 July 2012.

Diener, E.D., Robert A. Emmons, Randy J. Larsen, and Sharon Griffin. 1985. The satisfaction with life scale. *Journal of Personality Assessment* 49(1): 71–75.

Griffiths, Mark D. 1996. Behavioural addictions: An issue for everybody? *Journal of Workplace Learning* 8(3): 19–25.

———. 1998. Internet addiction: Does it really exist? In *Psychology and the internet: Intrapersonal, interpersonal, and transpersonal implications*, ed. Gackenbach Jayne, 61–75. San Diego: Academic Press.

———. 2005a. The relationship between gambling and videogame playing: A response to Johansson and Gotestam. *Psychological Reports* 96(3): 644–646.

———. 2005b. Components model of addiction within a biopsychosocial framework. *Journal of Substance Use* 10(4): 191–197.

Grüsser, Sabine M., Ralf Tahlemann, and Mark D. Griffiths. 2007. Excessive computer game playing: Evidence for addiction and aggression? *CyberPsychology and Behavior* 10(2): 290–292.

Hu, Li-tze, and Peter M. Bentler. 1995. Evaluation model fit. In *Structural equation modeling: Issues, concepts, and applications*, ed. Hoyle H. Rick, 76–99. Newbury Park: Sage.

Kim, Min G., and Joohan Kim. 2010. Cross-validation of reliability, convergent and discriminant validity for the problematic online game use scale. *Computers in Human Behavior* 26(3): 389–398.

Kim, Eun J., Kee Namkoong, Taeyun Ku, and Se J. Kim. 2008. The relationship between online game addiction and aggression, self-control and narcissistic personality traits. *European Psychiatry* 23(3): 212–218.

Lemmens, Jeroen S., Patti M. Valkenburg, and Jochen Peter. 2009. "Development and Validation of a Game Addiction Scale for Adolescents." *Media Psychology* 12(1): 77–95. doi: 10.1080/15213260802669458

Mehroof, Mehwash, and Mark D. Griffiths. 2010. Online gaming addiction: The role of sensation seeking, self-control, neuroticism, aggression, state anxiety, and trait anxiety. *CyberPsychology, Behavior, and Social Networking* 12(3): 313–316.

NIA (National Information Society Agency of Korea). 2010. *2010 Survey on the Internet Addiction.* http://www.nia.or.kr. Accessed 17 June 2013.

———. 2014. *2013 Survey on the Internet Addiction.* http://www.nia.or.kr. Accessed 14 Apr 2015.

Nunnally, Jum C., and Ira H. Bernstein. 1994. *Psychometric theory*, 3rd edn. New York: McGraw-Hill.

Schumacker, Randall E., and Richard G. Lomax. 1996. *A beginners guide to structural equation modeling.* Mahwah: Erlbaum.

Seok, Soonhwa, and Boavenura DaCosta. 2012. The world's most intense online gaming culture: Addiction and high-engagement prevalence rates among South Korean adolescents and young adults. *Computers in Human Behavior* 28(6): 2143–2151.

Tejeiro Salguero, Ricardo A., and Rosa M. Bersabé Morán. 2002. Measuring problem video game playing in adolescents. *Addiction* 97(12): 1601–1606.

Ullman, Jodie B. 1996. Structural equation modeling. In *Using multivariate statistics*, ed. Barbara G. Tabachnick, and Linda S. Fidell, 709–811. New York: Harper Collins.

Wang, Jichuan, and Xiaoqian Wang. 2012. *Structural equation modeling: Applications using Mplus.* New York: Wiley.

WHO (World Health Organization). 1993. *The ICD-10 classification of mental and behavioural disorders: Clinical descriptions and diagnostic guidelines.* Geneva: WHO.

Young, Kimberly S. 1996. "Internet addiction: The emergence of a new clinical disorder." Paper presented at the annual meeting for the American Psychological Association, Toronto, Canada, August 15.

———. 1998. *Caught in the net: How to recognize internet addiction and a winning strategy for recovery.* New York: Wiley.

Index[1]

[1] Note: Page numbers with "n" denote endnotes.